Fishing Saskatchewan

— Other books in the Discover Saskatchewan Series —

Discover Saskatchewan: A Guide to Historic Sites

Discover Saskatchewan: A User's Guide to Regional Parks

Canoeing the Churchill: A Practical Guide to the Historic Voyageur Highway

Fishing Saskatchewan

AN ANGLER'S GUIDE TO PROVINCIAL WATERS

by **Michael Snook**

Discover Saskatchewan Series Editor
Ralph Nilson

Canadian Plains Research Center, 2004

UNIVERSITY OF
REGINA

Sage Communications Inc.
Box 503
Lumsden, Saskatchewan, Canada S0G 3C0
sagecommunications@sasktel.net
www.saskangler.com

National Library of Canada Cataloguing in Publication

Snook, Michael, 1948-
    Fishing Saskatchewan : an angler's guide to provincial waters / Michael Snook.

(Discover Saskatchewan series ; 4)
Includes bibliographical references and index.
ISBN 0-88977-166-9

1. Fishing—Saskatchewan—Guidebooks. I. University of Regina. Canadian Plains Research Center. II. Title. III. Series.

SH572.S25S56 2004   799.1'1'097124   C2003-907049-2

Published by
Canadian Plains Research Center, University of Regina
Regina, Saskatchewan, Canada S4S 0A2
Tel: (306) 585-4758 • Fax: (306) 585-4699
e-mail: canadian.plains@uregina.ca • http://www.cprc.uregina.ca

Cover Photograph: Michael Snook
Cover Design: Donna Achtzehner, Canadian Plains Research Center
Index prepared by AM Indexing

Printed and bound in Canada
Printed on acid-free paper

We acknowledge the financial support of the Government of Canada through the Book Publishing Industry Development Program (BPIDP) for our publishing activities.

This book is dedicated to the memory of Ed and Edith Snook.

TABLE OF CONTENTS

Foreword viii

Preface..ix

Acknowledgements..xi

Introduction xiii

Chapter One: The Fish of Saskatchewan...1

Chapter Two: Fish Stocking in Saskatchewan..17

Chapter Three: Commercial Fishing in Saskatchewan...........................27

Chapter Four: Fishing in Saskatchewan...35

Chapter Five: Fly-fishing in Saskatchewan 67

Chapter Six: Ice Fishing in Saskatchewan 91

Chapter Seven: Competitive Fishing in Saskatchewan 105

Chapter Eight: Caring for your Catch 113

Chapter Nine: Guided Fishing Trips..123

Chapter Ten: Where to Fish in Southern Saskatchewan 133

Chapter Eleven: Where to Fish in Central Saskatchewan 159

Chapter Twelve: Where to Fish in Northern Saskatchewan 187

Chapter Thirteen: Fisheries Management and Conservation................199

Chapter Fourteen: Parting Words 211

Appendices
    A. Travel Contacts...215
    B. Clubs, Associations, Tournaments 216
    C. Northern Fly-in Fishing Gear...218
    D. Gear Lists..221
    E. Tackle Shops and Other Sources..225
    F. Further Reading and References..227

Glossary of Terms 230
Index 237

FOREWORD

Welcome to this new edition in the "Discover Saskatchewan Series." We are so fortunate to have such excellent sport-fishing opportunities in Saskatchewan. People who like to fish can put their hooks in the water and pull fish out of most bodies of water in the province. Many of these waters produce trophy quality fish.

Fishing experiences have provided many lasting memories for me. When I was a child, we visited my mother's childhood home on the bank of the South Saskatchewan river near Macrorie, where we would catch chub and goldeye on long strings of hooks set out in the river. These lines would be tied to a stake in the sand on the riverbank; an old heavy bolt would be tied to the end to weigh down the line against the river current and then thrown as far out into the river as the line would allow. This main line would have several smaller perpendicular lines with eagle hooks baited with grasshoppers. We'd play on the beach as the chub and goldeye ate the feast we offered them— and then we would feast on them.

My father, a Lutheran pastor, was also an avid fisherman. He inherited his enthusiasm for fishing from *his* father, who, as a young Norwegian lad, began his fishing in the North Sea. When my grandfather emigrated to Canada, he landed on the prairie but took sojourns north to La Ronge (a challenge in the early days of the province) to fish with friends from around his homestead near Parkbeg. My dad followed in this behaviour and was successful enough in 1954 to be featured on the front page of the *Prince Albert Herald* with a large lake trout he had taken out of La Ronge. So, as might be expected, I caught the fishing "bug" from my parents and have passed it on to my family, too. In the mid-1990s Suzie (my spouse) landed a huge northern pike in Tobin Lake; our daughter Anna had caught a very large walleye in the same lake a couple of years earlier. Trips to many other locations around the province always yielded great family stories about wonderful times on the boat together and enjoying shore lunches. These experiences and successes found us planning numerous family trips across North America that involved fishing in salt and fresh water. Suzie's parents even chartered a boat for us to fish bluefish off Nantucket. Bethany, our eldest daughter, has fished while on her travels to different continents; she spent last summer in a fishing resort on the Kenai Peninsula just out of Seward, Alaska. When we visited her at "Millerslanding" she was a deckhand on a halibut boat and was becoming very adept at cleaning the significant catch. She was certainly putting the love of fishing she developed in Saskatchewan to work for her summer job. I have brought many friends to fish our northern waters and they have always left elated at the experience of hooking a big northern.

Michael Snook has done a wonderful job of highlighting the excellent fishing opportunities and possibilities in this great province. I was thrilled when he agreed to put pen to paper and work on this manuscript. Enjoy all the information and stories he has managed to craft into this volume of *Discover Saskatchewan* and take the time to appreciate what exceptional experiences can be had fishing and enjoying the great natural beauty in Saskatchewan. I hope that reading this book will inspire you to plan a trip of your own.

—*Ralph Nilson, Series Editor*

PREFACE

When I first arrived in Saskatchewan in 1984 to take on a new position with CBC Radio, the last thing on my mind was fishing. Like many who are unfamiliar with the province, I did not think of Saskatchewan as an ideal destination for an avid angler. And for a time, the place did nothing to change my mind. In 1984, southern Saskatchewan was experiencing a major and extended drought. The temperature in early August approached 40°C (104°F). There were almost as many grasshoppers in our yard as there were surviving blades of grass.

That winter, the drought broke with a heavy snowfall in the south. If I had known where to ice-fish, it would have been a tough winter to get to the fish. By spring, my wife, myself, and our daughters had begun to explore the province. We discovered the Qu'Appelle Valley, Last Mountain Lake, and the Cypress Hills that summer, and I got in a little shore fishing at Valeport Marsh, and some fly-fishing in Loch Leven. That second winter was a time to find out where the local tackle shops were, and to really get down to doing some research—maps, magazines, tourism publications—and a whole new picture began to emerge. I had just moved from the Ottawa valley, and the Quebec–Ontario border is a land of water, water, and more water. A short drive from home in one direction—walleye. A short drive in another direction—bass. And in a third direction—channel cats. The Ottawa itself held all these species and more—northern pike, the occasional muskie and sturgeon. And not too far off the beaten track lay some of the best brook trout waters anywhere. It seemed like angling paradise, and a hard act to follow—until I got to know Saskatchewan better.

During the past eighteen years or so, I've fished in a lot of places in this province, and barely scratched the surface. A partial list would include the four Qu'Appelle lakes adjacent to the town of Fort Qu'Appelle; Last Mountain Lake, Lake Diefenbaker, the South Saskatchewan and North Saskatchewan rivers, Tobin Lake, Codette Lake, ponds and streams in the Cypress Hills, the Narrow Hills, the Duck Mountain area, parts of the Churchill River, a few fly-in lakes in the far north, a raft of small southern ponds, and more. These lakes and rivers alone could provide a lifetime of fishing adventures, but there's a lot more territory on my list yet.

I've learned more about fishing from Saskatchewan's waters, and more important, from Saskatchewan's anglers, than anywhere else in Canada that I've wet a line. All of that experience, good advice, and exposure to some of the best fishing in the world served as good preparation for the phone call I got from Ralph Nilson suggesting I consider writing this book.

It has been a couple of years in the making and has changed its character more than a few times. With the encouragement of Ralph and more than a little help from the Canadian Plains Research Center, it has now settled down to be the little book you hold in your hands. This is a guide book. It is not a technical manual (though it does contain, as any fishing book must, a little "how-to"). It is not a complete set of instructions for the uninitiated to take up one of the world's finest recreational activities. And it isn't another collection of fishing yarns.

Rather, it is an attempt to provide the reader, whatever his or her level of experience and interest in recreational angling, with a sense of the wonderful range of fishing experiences that awaits him or her in Saskatchewan. It offers to both residents and visitors alike the opportunity to explore one of the most diverse fisheries in Canada, set in a variety of physical settings that range from bald prairie to dense northern forest, from tiny spring creek to the immense Churchill River watershed, from stocked ponds of a few acres to the massive Lake Diefenbaker Reservoir.

From six-inch perch to thirty-pound lake trout, Saskatchewan offers up the treasures of the natural world to any angler who ventures forth to find them. Some of the fishing places in this book are as close as your own back yard, if you are lucky enough to live here; some require a journey into distant northern wilderness.

Either way, if you're "gone fishin'" in Saskatchewan, you are fishing some of the best waters anywhere. I hope this book helps you enjoy them just a little bit more.

See you on the water.

—Michael Snook

A NOTE FOR THE READER: Every effort has been made to provide accurate information. However, there is always a lag between research and publication, and the angling world is ever changing. Our knowledge of fishing techniques, and fish biology and behaviour advances each year; government regulations change; outfitters retire. By the time this book gets into the hands of readers, some of the information will likely be out of date. For this reason, all anglers, whether resident or visiting, are encouraged to make use of sources listed in the appendices (and referred to in a number of chapters) to obtain the most up-to-date, accurate information.

A NOTE ABOUT WEIGHTS AND MEASURES: Readers will find both metric and American weights and measures in *Fishing Saskatchewan*. While the metric system is the Canadian standard, American measures are included for two major reasons: first, many visiting anglers to the province are from the United States and are therefore unfamiliar with metric measures; second, the fishing world has traditionally operated with feet, inches, pounds, and ounces and, in fact, fishing rods, reels, line, and tackle are still sold using traditional weights and measures. We have favoured readability over rigid consistency and, to that end, have followed these guidelines:

Fish Weight and Length: In Chapter 1, the weight and length of record fish as documented by Saskatchewan Environment are expressed in metric, with American equivalents in parentheses.

Water depth: since most depth finders can be set for either the metric or American system, we have expressed depths in both systems.

Fishing equipment: Rod length, lure weights, and line test weights are expressed in American measures, since this is how they are sold.

Distances: Distances posted on Saskatchewan's highway signs are all in metric measure; here we also include the conversion to miles in parentheses, rounded off to the nearest full mile.

Temperatures: Again, temperatures in Saskatchewan are recorded in Celsius. Any references to temperatures also provide the Fahrenheit equivalent in parentheses.

Other: in all other cases, conversions are included when these do not detract from the readability of the text.

ACKNOWLEDGEMENTS

This book would not have been possible without the assistance of many people. My apologies to anyone inadvertently left out—whether mentioned here or not, your help has been much appreciated.

Everything starts somewhere, and in my case, I caught the fishing bug early from three men: my father, Ed Snook, who taught me how to stillfish for "pickerel" in Lake Nipissing; his fishing buddy, Bev Stroud, whose enthusiasm for speckled trout was hugely infectious; and my grandfather, Harry Paynter, who introduced me to the smallmouth bass, and whose old bamboo fly rod I still have.

Along the way, I've shared boats and shorelines with a lot of excellent anglers, all of whom have taught me something about the sport. My thanks to Gary Folk (a great ice fisherman); to tournament fishing partners Bob Kirkpatrick, Phil Lopinski, John Phipps, Michael Coupland, and Dick Van Der Velden; to T.J. Schwanky, writer and television producer/host ("The Outdoor Quest") and Don Lamont, host of *The Complete Angler* television series, who introduced me to the world of professional angling.

Tackle shop operators are an essential part of the fishing scene everywhere, and in Saskatchewan, three of them have been particularly helpful over the years: Greg and Gord Prokopetz (Pokey's Tackle Shop in Regina); Bill Graham (Great Northern Rod and Reel in Regina), and Brian Dygdala (The Fishin' Hole in Saskatoon).

Outfitters and guides take us to some of the world's very special fishing spots. Thanks to outfitter David McIlmoyl and guides John and Tony Charles of Churchill River Voyageur Lodge for showing me some of the best fishing on the Churchill River. Thanks also to Rob Schulz, operator of G & S Marina Outfitters, who introduced me to carp fishing on Last Mountain Lake.

Those individuals who work in the field of fisheries and habitat management contribute to the health and sustainability of recreational angling in ways that often go unrecognized. Special thanks to Bruce Howard, formerly of Saskatchewan Environment, now with Fisheries and Oceans Canada; to Jerry Banks, Kevin Calelle, Harvey Janke, Murray Koob, Tom Maher, and Ryan Mulligan, all with Saskatchewan Environment Fish and Wildlife Branch; and to Bob Herbison and Mary-Anne Wihak of the Parks and Special Places department, all of whom have helped in various ways with the research and development that led to the writing of this book

A number of newspaper and magazine editors have given me a chance to write over the years. Without them, outdoor writers across Canada would have no readers for their work, no chance to practise their craft. My thanks to Brian Bowman, George Gruenefeld and Tracey Ellis of *Western Sportsman/Canada's Outdoor Sportsman* magazine; to Teddi Brown, former editor of *Outdoor Canada*, and to Foster Barnsley, Pat Carlson, and Rob Vanstone of the Regina *Leader Post*.

As an outdoor writer and tournament angler, I've enjoyed the co-operation and support of several fishing tackle and equipment companies. Thanks to Brent Tarr, John Booth, Art Stein, and Heather Page of Pure Fishing Canada; to John Peterson and John Crane at Northland Fishing Tackle; and to Conrad Maurice, Bob Clark, and Steve Rae of Eagle/Lowrance Canada for their support over the years, and for their assistance with some of the material in this book.

The colour illustrations of Saskatchewan's fish species by Tim Halstrom were generously provided by Saskatchewan Environment. The historical photographs reproduced in the book are from the Saskatchewan Archives Board. Thanks to David McLennan, Canadian Plains Research Center, who obtained and digitally scanned the images. Many of these charming photographs came to the Saskatchewan Archives Board from Saskatchewan Government Photographic Services (now defunct). While the individual photographers are not recorded and therefore cannot be acknowledged, the historical record their images provide of fishing in the province over the past century is invaluable. The photographs on pages 102 and 159 are from the Melville-Ness Collection of the Saskatchewan Archives Board and are reproduced with the permission of Moira Remmen.

Special thanks to Gail Snook, who reads every word I write and through more than three decades of marriage has encouraged both my incurable addiction to fishing and my desire to write about it.

Three individuals at the University of Regina made this book possible: Dr. Ralph Nilson, the series editor, who asked me to write the book; Brian Mlazgar, publications coordinator of the Canadian Plains Research Center; and Donna Achtzehner, editorial assistant, Canadian Plains Research Center, whose patience and attention to detail improved every aspect of it.

—*Michael Snook*

INTRODUCTION: THE BEST KEPT SECRET

Saskatchewan, like the coyotes who live in her open lands, is a trickster who plays a tremendous practical joke on travellers driving across her major east–west highways. Drive the Trans-Canada in spring or early summer and, more likely than not, what you'll see is a dull brown land, fields tilled and seeded, barely sprouting, and the yellow-green of rolling grasslands. Catch a windy day and the dull haze of brown dust may obscure the horizon, a ghostly echo of the dust bowl.

Drive through this land during the peak of summer, and a patchwork of blue flax, yellow canola, gold wheat, and pale green grass covers the land as far as the eye can see below a sky of unbelievable blue. It is an agricultural spectacle matched nowhere else in the world. Travel along the same road after harvest, and the short brown stubble of dried grasses suggests a poorly kept suburban lawn, left unwatered during the family vacation. You'll pass by shallow sloughs, rich with birdlife, shrinking in the heat of the summer sun, glistening blue amid the rusts of autumn. But there's nothing here to call out to the heart of an angler, nothing to holler: "Stop the car, get your gear out, launch your boat. This is a place to fish!"

It is a grand illusion, a trick played by the landscape and the path taken by the highway. The reality is something else entirely—dotted with tens of thousands of lakes, streams, ponds, reservoirs, and rivers, Saskatchewan is a world-class fishery, home to trophy walleye, pike, lake trout, rainbow trout, carp, and a host of other sport fish.

For anyone who takes the time to get off the main roads, to check the maps and follow his nose to water, the rewards are considerable. The fishery is not only rich and varied, it is unpressured. Even in the accessible south, where some of the best fishing holes lie within an hour's drive of major population centres, angling pressure is only moderate. Saskatchewan is sparsely populated, with fewer than a million people in its entire geography. Its two largest cities are Regina, with a population under 200,000, and Saskatoon, at just over that number. While a few favourite spots receive more than their share of interested anglers, most waters see fewer visitors in a year than a Toronto freeway sees during a single rush hour.

Across the southern third of the province, fishing opportunities include shore fishing stocked ponds for rainbow trout, fly-fishing streams for brookies and browns, and trolling or drifting big reservoirs for walleye and pike. All of this fishing is accessible by automobile, with modern conveniences, accommodations, and restaurants not far away. This is fishing that the whole family can enjoy on a warm summer day; at the same time, it's fishing that can challenge the veteran trophy hunter.

The central third of Saskatchewan, as far north as the Churchill River watershed, is still accessible by road, much of it paved, all of it driveable without four-wheel drive. This central part of the province puts a wilderness fishing experience within reach of the average angler who can't afford a fly-in trip, but still longs for quality angling far from the bustle and noise of southern cities and farms.

In the centre of the province, Highway 2, running north from Prince Albert to La Ronge, and Highway 102 from La Ronge north through the Churchill rivershed and onward to Southend on Reindeer Lake, provide access to some of the best angling in Saskatchewan.

On the west side of the province, paved Highway 155 takes you north from Green Lake to waters like Lac La Plonge, Canoe Lake, the headwaters of the Churchill River, and ultimately to Lac la Loche. The village of La Loche is a jumping-off point for float plane flights even further north.

The northern third of Saskatachewan calls out to the more adventurous. But even here, remote fisheries like Wollaston and Reindeer lakes can be reached by driving on gravel roads into the northern bush. Two hundred kilometres from the end of the pavement at La Ronge lies the village of Southend, and access to Reindeer Lake. Nearly 350 more kilometres of gravel road takes you to Wollaston Lake Landing. Another 85 kilometres or so and you arrive at Points North Landing, where an airstrip provides access to some of the finest remote fishing in all of northern Saskatchewan. While these roads shouldn't be attempted by the faint of heart, they are practical to travel in a light truck or sport-utility vehicle, and the first stretch, from La Ronge to Missinipe, is regularly travelled by ordinary passenger cars.

For those who prefer to keep their wheels on paved roads, dozens of northern fishing lodges are accessible by float plane from La Ronge and other northern towns. Some wilderness lodges arrange for direct flights, either from Saskatoon, which is serviced by national and international carriers, or from Winnipeg in neighbouring Manitoba. Few places in the world offer such ready access to the kind of extraordinary wilderness angling experiences found north of the fifty-fifth parallel.

At the very northern edge of Saskatchewan, tucked up against the border with the Northwest Territories, are a few very special lakes, with names like Selwyn, Tazin, Ena, Scott, and Misaw. These lakes host lodges that specialize in big fish—trophy lake trout, northern pike, and grayling. Most of the outfitters here have implemented strict catch-and-release rules for all mature fish, keeping only a few smaller ones each day for shore lunch or supper. The result is spectacular trophy angling.

Anglers fishing these lakes, along with the waters of Lake Athabaska, Wollaston Lake, and Reindeer Lake, have a chance to catch the fish of a lifetime—pike over 14 kilograms (30 pounds) and lakers over 18 kilograms (40 pounds). The same watersheds are home to one of the most beautiful of northern freshwater fish—the Arctic grayling.

From the far north to the farthest reaches of the south, Saskatchewan is full of angling surprises.

Tucked into the valley of the Souris River is Boundary Dam Reservoir, created to hold cooling water for the Shand power-generating station. The return of warm water to this reservoir creates a unique habitat, home to the most northerly population of largemouth bass in North America. Two brand new reservoirs in the same region of the province, Rafferty and Alameda, have started to produce extraordinary walleye fishing, with anglers reporting one-hundred-fish days.

Between the far northern reaches of the provinces and the U.S. border, anglers will find a wide variety of superior angling. The Saskatchewan River system, Lake Diefenbaker, and Last Mountain Lake hold great populations of perch, walleye, and pike. In these waters, walleye over 4.5 kilograms (10 pounds), pike over 8 kilograms (20 pounds), and jumbo perch are caught every year, in all seasons.

The Churchill River is home to some of the best river walleye fishing anywhere. Go to the right part of this river, and you can catch and release one hundred walleye or more in a single day of fishing.

European anglers travel all the way to Last Mountain Lake and the Qu'Appelle River system to chase world-class carp—fish in excess of 14 kilograms (30 pounds). And fly fishers flock to southwestern Saskatchewan's Cypress Hills, as well as to the Cub Hills in the central part of the province to pursue rainbows, brookies, browns, and splake, all present as a result of extensive stocking and fisheries management extending back to the beginnings of the twentieth century.

According to a major survey of sport fishing conducted in Saskatchewan in 1995, there were 184,226 licensed anglers in the province at the time. There were 43,950 non-resident anglers fishing in the province that year, more than half of those from the United States. Saskatchewan resident anglers like the fishing in their home province so well that they hardly ever leave to fish elsewhere. In the 1995 survey, only 12 percent of licensed adult anglers reported fishing outside the province. Anglers spent about twelve and a half days each fishing during the year. A remarkable total of 365,252 days was spent by anglers ice fishing.

Most visiting anglers fished in northern Saskatchewan, while most residents spent their time in the south. Anglers reported catching 10.1 million fish that year, with 3.9 million of them kept for a total weight of 2.9 million kilograms (6.38 million pounds). Sixty-eight percent of anglers reported practising catch-and-release fishing in that year, a percentage that has been steadily and gradually increasing over the years. Anglers spent more than $95 million on fishing-related activities in 1995, about 75 percent of it spent on food, lodging, and complete fishing "packages." Resident and non-resident anglers invested more than $27 million in their boats alone in 1995.

Counting activities indirectly related to fishing and allowing for a "spin-off" factor determined by economists, the total value to the Saskatchewan economy of recreational fishing in 1995 was well over $400 million, making it a very important contributor to the provincial economy.

As every angler knows, fishing isn't just about catching fish. It's about spending time in the outdoors, getting away from the daily routine, enjoying the beauty of nature, and visiting with friends who share our love for fishing. Most anglers choose their fishing destination based on the quality of the experience they will have—considering everything from lack of pollution, to absence of noise, crowds, and traffic. We go fishing at spots that we think are beautiful, spots that are likely to hold our favourite species in reasonable numbers, spots where we can just relax. We enjoy the challenge of outwitting our fishy adversaries, and we like eating the fish we catch.

All of these factors combine to make up what might be called the "fishing experience," but no list of factors can possibly convey the quality of life that simply being there brings. Brian Knoll of McTaggart, Saskatchewan, sent me this story about what fishing means to him:

> In 1986, two of my sons—Shane, age 6, and Michael, age 8—and I went ice-fishing at Nickle Lake just outside of Weyburn, where the Wildlife Federation was holding a Fish Derby that day. I registered myself and we went to the ice shack for a day of fishing. After about a half-hour of setting up and digging the ice holes,

Shane said, "Dad, I think I got a big one!" I turned around in disbelief, but there was the line just sizzling through his mitts. Mike, the older brother, said, "He does have a big one!" and went over to help his little brother. Both boys were pulling up line hand over hand until they got him out of the hole and onto the floor of the shack. It was big, so off we went to weigh it. Since Shane wasn't registered for the Derby, we knew he couldn't win anything, but wanted to know the weight. Larry Olfert from the Wildlife Federation said it might be the biggest pike of the year caught by a junior angler and, sure enough, that spring at the Wildlife Banquet, Shane won the trophy for the biggest pike—8 pounds, 11½ ounces.

Both boys have been hooked on fishing ever since! Now every time I go ice-fishing, it brings a smile to my face remembering those two youngsters bringing up a fish that was, in their eyes anyway, 'the Monster.'

I've been a conservationist all my life when it comes to both the fish I pursue and the waters they inhabit. I learned, literally at my father's knee, the importance of protecting the resource. He spoke often about his concerns that high possession limits and pollution were harming our home waters in northern Ontario. It turns out he was right.

As a long time proponent of both catch-and-release and selective harvest fishing practices, I'm an advocate of the use of barbless hooks. They are not required by regulation in Saskatchewan except on waters that are designated catch-and-release. Any angler who plans to release fish in any waters should fish barbless. However, as is evidenced by the tackle photos in this book, very few hooks and lures (with the exception of a few fly-tying hooks) come out of the box barbless. Carry needle-nose pliers and flatten down the barbs on your lures—the fish will thank you for it by surviving release much better.

Many of the archival photos in this book depict large catches of fish, or large fish that are kept. Some of them show practices that, by today's standards, would be totally inappropriate and, in some cases, illegal. These are photographs of the past, of a fishing legacy that reaches back centuries. They reflect a time when our appreciation and understanding of the resource was different than it is now. These photos serve as both a documentation of our fishing culture and heritage and a reminder of how things might be if we take much better care of the fishery in the present, and future, than we have in the past.

Like all populated regions of the planet, Saskatchewan suffers from the effects of human pollution. While many of our lakes and rivers are relatively pristine, a number are not. Agricultural run-off, sewage effluent, mining, and industrial outflows all contribute to the problem. The individual angler can contribute to the solution by using modern, high-efficiency outboards, avoiding spills of gasoline and oil into our waters, leaving no trashy traces of their presence on lakes or streambanks, and speaking out against the abuse of our waters wherever and whenever they see them.

This book is intended to enhance the experiences that fishing brings to all of us, to give the resident and visiting angler alike a few additional resources to help them explore the breadth and depth of fishing opportunities in Saskatchewan. From locations to techniques, from tackle to tips on using it, from sources to outfitters, we hope this book will provide the reader with a thorough guide to fishing in Saskatchewan that will prove useful for many years to come.

CHAPTER ONE
THE FISH OF SASKATCHEWAN

ARCTIC GRAYLING • *(Thymallus arcticus)*

The grayling wins the prize for most beautiful fish found in Saskatchewan, or almost anywhere else. Its stream-lined body is a subtle blend of blues, blacks, and purples, highlighted with a touch of pink. Its head is an irides-cent pink and olive colour, with green and gold eyes. But it's the

TIM HALSTROM/SASKATCHEWAN ENVIRONMENT

astonishing dorsal fin that first captures the angler's attention. It rides like a sail above the back of the fish, shades of black and grey, speckled with purple and green spots, and band-ed along the very top with red. Once you've seen one, you'll know why mere words can never accurately describe the Arctic grayling.

Grayling prefer the clear, icy-cold water of northern Saskatchewan's Canadian Shield country, the southern boundary of which is the Churchill River. They favour the flowing water of rivers and creeks, but are also found close to shore in northern lakes, particularly near inflowing or outflowing streams.

Grayling spawn in spring, about the time the ice breaks up, in small, fast-flowing streams. Spawning habitat is rocky or gravelly bottom, and the female simply lays her eggs in the current.

Grayling eat bugs—beetles, larvae, hoppers—so your tackle box should include some very small jigs (1/16 ounce) and small plastic tails in various colours, particularly black, white, yellow, and brown. Fly fishers, take note: grayling feed actively on the surface, trying out almost everything that floats by. They also inhabit pocket water on small streams. Grayling have soft, delicate mouths, so a gentle touch is needed once you've hooked up to this feisty sport fish.

The Arctic version of this fish is one of five grayling found around the world, distrib-uted around the north polar regions, and is the only one found in Canada.

The average size of grayling caught by anglers is between .5 and 1 kilogram (between 1 and 2 pounds). The current Saskatchewan record for a kept fish is 1.96 kilograms (4 pounds, 5 ounces), caught on the Fond du Lac River in 1966. The largest live-release grayling in Saskatchewan was caught in 1990 on Highrock Lake; it measured 53 centimetres (21 inches).

While grayling can be good table fare, they should be cooked quickly after they are caught, as the quality of the flesh deteriorates rather quickly. Grayling are a bland, white-fleshed fish, more fun to catch and release than to eat.

BROOK TROUT • *(Salvelinus fontinalis)*

The brookie, or speckled trout, is an introduced species in Saskatchewan. It is native to eastern Canada and, depending on where you run across it, you may also hear this fish called a square-tail, a sea trout (where they have access to salt water), a speckled char, and even a mud trout. A great eating fish and a terrific sport fish, it has been stocked widely across the country.

TIM HALSTROM/SASKATCHEWAN ENVIRONMENT

Properly classified as a char rather than as a trout, its body ranges from almost black to a light golden green, depending on the water colour in its home habitat. The brookie gets the nickname "speckled" because of the many spots on its sides—white, and red ringed with blue. The front edges of the fins on the lower side of their body are distinguished by a thin white line, bordered by a black line.

The brookie is most often associated with small waters—streams, beaver ponds, small lakes–and it prefers cool to cold water. Prairie spring creeks and creek-fed ponds are typical habitat for brook trout in Saskatchewan, where they have been stocked in the south, central and northern regions, wherever suitable habitat can be found.

Brook trout are fall spawners and will reproduce naturally in some Saskatchewan habitat. They feed on aquatic insects and their larvae and on terrestrial insects such as hoppers, ants, bees, and beetles. They'll also feed on small minnows, crayfish, worms, and even frogs. This makes them a favourite for fly anglers who use light tackle to fool nervous brookies in small clear waters. Spinning tackle should be small (the tiniest spinners and jigs and very small spoons), and light monofilament lines on ultralight tackle make for great sport.

Brook trout caught by anglers are typically a half-kilogram in size or less. They do, however, grow much larger given the right habitat. Fish weighing 1 to 4 kilograms (2 to 8 pounds) are taken in more remote places where fishing pressure is light, and one of the biggest brookies ever, at just under 7 kilograms (15 pounds, 7 ounces), was caught just after the turn of the twentieth century in the Nipigon River in Ontario. The largest brookie ever taken in Saskatchewan weighed in at 2.78 kilograms (6 pounds, 2 ounces) and was taken on Lake Amyot in 1973.

The brookie is an excellent eating fish. Since most fish caught by anglers are smaller in size, they are usually gutted and pan-fried whole. Flesh of brook trout can range from a pale pink to a dark orange, depending on diet, habitat, and time of year. Like all fish, brookies should be kept cold if they are not going to be eaten right away, and cleaned and washed out as soon as possible.

BROWN TROUT • *(Salmo trutta)*

The brown trout, another European import, lives up to its name, with a light brown body covered with black and irregular red spots. Also called Loch Leven trout, Von Behr's trout, English brown trout, German brown trout, European brown trout (everyone lays claim to this guy), or simply brownie, the brown trout was first introduced in Canada before the turn of the century. The brown is in fact found throughout Europe and the British Isles.

The brown stocks well, thrives in every setting from quiet small streams to large lakes, and is sometimes said to provide unfair competition for the native brook trout—not an issue in Saskatchewan where both species are "exotic." Browns can stand warmer, lower quality water than brookies.

TIM HALSTROM/SASKATCHEWAN ENVIRONMENT

Brown trout spawn in streams with gravelly bottoms or near rock reefs near shore in lakes. Eggs are laid in the fall in a depression that the female scoops out of the bottom, where they are fertilized by the male.

Brown trout eat insects, crustaceans, smaller fish, and minnows. They are very wary, commonly feed at night, and can be tough to catch. Because of their varied diet, they can be caught with fly gear or spinning tackle. When found in large lakes, trolling with spinning gear is a more effective angling technique. But casting flies on small streams to big brown trout is a treat for any fly fisher.

Brown trout taken from larger lakes, or sea-run varieties, tend to be silvery in colour and quite large—one of the largest on record is a 10-kilogram (22-pound) brown caught in Newfoundland. The average size is 3 to 6 kilograms (6 to 13 pounds). The average-sized brown trout found in Saskatchewan is 1 to 2.5 kilograms (2½ to 5½ pounds). Saskatchewan's biggest kept brown trout tipped the scales at 8.06 kilograms (17 pounds, 11 ounces) and came from Piprell Lake in 1987. The largest released brown measured 74.3 centimetres (just over 25 inches), caught in Shannon Lake in 2001.

Like all trout, browns are tasty table fare.

BULLHEAD • BROWN (*Ictalurus nebulosis*) and BLACK (*Ictalurus melas*)

Both brown and black bullhead are found in Saskatchewan, primarily in the Souris Basin in the far southern reaches of the province and in the Qu'Appelle River system.

The brown bullhead is the most common member of the North American catfish clan found in Canada, though its range is very limited in Saskatchewan. One of the hardiest of fishes, it is also called the bullpout, horned pout, catfish, mudcat, mudpout, and barbotte.

The black bullhead is much rarer than the brown and is also called the stonecat, the tadpole madtom, and the brindled madtom.

Bullheads are an unattractive fish, with their barbelled heads and eel-like

TIM HALSTROM/SASKATCHEWAN ENVIRONMENT

Brown bullhead

Black bullhead

TIM HALSTROM/SASKATCHEWAN ENVIRONMENT

tails. The front ray of the dorsal fin is a sharp spine, as are those at the front of each pec-
toral fin. Bullheads have a leathery skin that is scaleless.

Bullheads inhabit warm, sluggish, even stagnant, waters. They spawn in spring, fanning
out a nest depression in the mud. Eggs are guarded by the male.

Bullheads eat insect larvae, vegetation, crustaceans, worms, small fish—in short, just
about anything they can get.

Anglers can stillfish for them, primarily at night, using everything from cheese to meat
to worms and frozen minnows. A traditional "pickerel rig" or a simple hook and sinker are
all the tackle needed for this fish.

Because of its limited range, small size (usually under a half-kilogram), unattractive
appearance, and often strong "fishy" taste, the bullhead is seldom the target of recreational anglers.

BURBOT • (Lota lota)

TIM HALSTROM/SASKATCHEWAN ENVIRONMENT

If the Arctic grayling takes the
prize for most beautiful fish,
then the burbot sits at the other
end of the attractiveness scale.
A freshwater member of the
cod family, the burbot is also
known as ling, ling cod, maria, black maria, loche (its French Canadian name) and methy
(its Cree name). It is also colloquially known as "dogfish" and is often spurned by anglers
for its appearance and for its reputation as a strong, bad-tasting fish. That is unfortunate
because almost everything about the burbot's reputation, except its appearance, is unde-
served.

The burbot has the front end of a cod and the rear end of an eel, is yellow-brown to
dark brown in colour and heavily mottled. Although the skin is finely scaled, it is so covered
in mucous that it is hard to tell that there are any scales at all.

Burbot spawn any time from early winter through to early spring, usually before ice-out.
Ice anglers can look forward to a late winter bonanza as burbot move into shallow water to
spawn and feed. Eggs are laid in the shallows or in tributaries, and simply left on their own.

Although its appearance has led to the belief by some anglers that this fish is a bottom
feeder, quite the contrary is true. The burbot is a cold-water fish, highly predatory, and feeds
mostly on other fish, including substantial walleye and perch. They also eat crustaceans,
insects, fish eggs, and plankton.

Burbot are most commonly caught by ice anglers stillfishing with jigs or pickerel rigs
tipped with frozen minnows. But they are also caught as incidental catch by walleye anglers
during the open-water season, fishing live-bait rigs tipped with leeches and crawlers. In fact,
the largest burbot I have ever seen, easily weighing in the 6-kilogram (13-pound) range, was
caught on a live-leech rig during a fishing tournament on Lake Diefenbaker. Burbot are
tough fighters, with an aggressive bite, great fun to catch on light tackle.

While the average size for burbot is 1 to 1.5 kilograms (2 to 3 pounds), the current
provincial record fish tipped the scales at 8.43 kilograms (18 pounds, 10 ounces), taken
from Candle Lake in 1993.

Burbot are reputed to be bad tasting, strong, fishy. They aren't. Some old-timers refer to them as "freshwater lobster" or "poor man's lobster." The quality of water in which they are caught will do much to determine the taste. Burbot can be easily skinned, the two fillets removed from the skeleton. These can be soaked in milk or salted water for an hour or so, then rinsed in cold water to remove any strong taste, but this is rarely necessary. Burbot can be pan-fried in butter or good quality oil and seasoned to taste. They can also be boiled, cut into chunks and then dipped into a melted butter and garlic mixture—poor man's lobster.

CARP • (Cyprinus carpio)

Another much maligned fish, the carp is coming into its own as a pre-eminent sport fish in Saskatchewan, where there are abundant wild stocks and low fishing pressure. The carp is an invader species, one that continues to expand its range. Carp are actually members of the minnow family, sharing their family tree with shiners and chubs. They are distinguished by large, coarse scales, teeth located in their throats (pharyngeal teeth), and variable colouration that depends on habitat.

TIM HALSTROM/SASKATCHEWAN ENVIRONMENT

Carp are native to Asia, and in some parts of the world, notably China, have been farmed for food for many years. The common carp is coloured a dark yellowish green along the back, fading to whitish yellow on the belly. The carp was first introduced to Europe during the time of Henry VIII and to America in the early 1800s, primarily because it was easy to pond-raise for food. Varieties include the mirror carp, the leather carp, and the grass carp. Only the common carp occurs naturally in Saskatchewan waters.

Adult carp spawn in shallow water, from spring through to early summer, probably depending on water temperature. Mature females can deposit anywhere from 35,000 to over two million eggs in weedy backwater bays or the shallow margins of rivers and creeks. During the mating season, male and female fish can be seen thrashing through shallow water, with so little depth that much of the carp's body can be seen clear of the water's surface.

Carp are omnivorous—they will take cottonwood seeds off the surface, insects, crustaceans, larvae, worms, aquatic plants, even algae. Many carp anglers use corn as a bait, first "chumming" an area with a sweetened corn that they distribute across the bottom of the area they wish to fish. Then "whisker rigs" are tied using corn as bait, cast out and allowed to sit on the bottom where chumming has taken place.

Carp can be fished from shore using specialized rigs—long rods (12 feet or more), reels with a free-spool setting, and hefty monofilament line. The bait is cast out and allowed to settle, and the rod placed in forked supports on shore. The technique is called ledgering. However, fly anglers have recently discovered that flies duplicating certain seeds and insects, even kernels of corn, will fool carp quite nicely, allowing these big powerful fish to be taken on relatively light fly tackle. Carp are one of the finest fighting fish in the freshwater world. In Europe they are prized as sport fish. In fact, European carp anglers will travel thousands of kilometres for the chance to hook into truly wild fish in Saskatchewan.

Carp grow to a tremendous size, exceeding 15 kilograms (30 pounds), and are common throughout south and southeast Saskatchewan, in the Qu'Appelle watershed and Last Mountain Lake particularly, where good populations of trophy-sized fish can be found.

Bowfishing for carp has been a popular sport in Saskatchewan for a number of years, but a successful catch invariably means the death of the fish. Increasingly, anglers are learning European techniques for carp that allow them to catch and release these fish as they would any other sport fish.

Carp can be smoked, pickled, or fried, but are not generally popular as table fare.

CHANNEL CATFISH • *(Ictalurus punctatus)*

The channel catfish is found in Saskatchewan in the Qu'Appelle River system, which is in turn connected to the Red River through the Assiniboine. The Red is home to one of the most robust populations of trophy catfish in North America. While the catfish caught in the Qu'Appelle system are certainly not as large as those found in the Red,

TIM HALSTROM/SASKATCHEWAN ENVIRONMENT

the species does occur naturally in Saskatchewan and adds to a varied fishery. Channel catfish are also called channel cats, lake catfish, Great Lakes catfish, and just plain "cat."

Adult catfish are dark grey to black along the back, fading to grey or off-white along the belly of the fish. Cats are scaleless. Four pairs of barbels border their mouths.

Mature catfish appear to like deeper water in current areas during daylight hours, but will come into shallower waters to feed at night and under low light conditions. They spawn in spring, in shallow water, the female laying as many as 20,000 eggs in a nest prepared by the male. The eggs are guarded until they hatch.

Catfish are not selective about the food they eat—everything from underwater vegetation, insect larvae, crayfish, clams, and small fish to dead or decaying material found along the bottom. Such indiscriminate eating habits are the key to techniques for anglers. Cats will respond to moving lures, but much more commonly are caught stillfishing with cut bait, balls of worm, or specially prepared stink-baits. Like the carp, catfish are strong fighters, and hooking into a large one is a bit like tying onto the back end of a moving freight train. Sturdy tackle and heavier mono lines are the rule.

Channel catfish can grow to become very large—over 70 kilograms (150 pounds) in the lower Mississippi River in the United States. The average size for a channel cat in Saskatchewan is 1 or 2 kilograms (2 to 4 pounds), but larger specimens have been reported. The provincial record kept catfish was caught in the Qu'Appelle River in 1999 and weighed 7.37 kiograms (16 pounds). The largest released fish, also from the Qu'Appelle, was taken in 1998 and weighed 6.36 kilograms (14 pounds).

Catfish are farmed commercially for food in the United States and are good eating fish when selectively harvested from wild stocks. Smaller fish are better eaters.

CUTTHROAT TROUT • (Onchorhynchus clarki)

TIM HALSTROM/SASKATCHEWAN ENVIRONMENT

The cutthroat trout, sometimes called Cranbrook trout and sea trout, is an introduced species in Saskatchewan, first stocked in 1988, and present in only very few water bodies in the province. There is no evidence of successful reproduction in Saskatchewan waters, and numbers are sustained only by stocking efforts.

There are two forms of cutthroat trout, one called a coastal cutthroat, the other a yellowstone cutthroat. They are not easy to tell apart, and to all intents and purposes, are the same fish, with the exception that some (but not all) of the coastal variety do migrate to salt water and return.

Cutthroat trout are yellow to golden-brown in colour, with black spots marking the sides. The name cutthroat derives from the orange or red slash marks on the throat below the jaw.

In fresh water, cutthroat live on fish eggs, minnows and the fry of other trout, and insects. Given this varied diet, anglers are just as likely to catch cutthroat trout on spoons as on spinners, live bait, dry or wet flies.

Cutthroat average in size between .5 and 1.8 kilograms (1 and 4 pounds) and only a few exceed 3 kilograms (over 6 pounds). The current Saskatchewan record is 3.0 kilograms (6 pounds, 10 ounces) caught in Little Raspberry Lake in 1996.

Cutthroat trout are excellent eating. Their flesh is firm and rich tasting, with a colour ranging from nearly white to red, depending on diet.

GOLDEYE • (Hiodon alosoides)

TIM HALSTROM/SASKATCHEWAN ENVIRONMENT

Both the goldeye, also known as Winnipeg goldeye, and its close relative, the mooneye, are native to Saskatchewan and are found throughout the Saskatchewan River system, as well as the west side of Lake Athabaska.

The goldeye is a small, silvery, blue-backed fish, spawning from ice-out until as late as June in river pools. They feed on insects, crustaceans, small fish, and frogs. Anglers can fish for them using fly gear or very light spinning tackle. Their soft mouths require a very light touch.

Goldeye got the name "Winnipeg goldeye" because of their gold-coloured eyes and because it was in the city of Winnipeg that it was discovered goldeye could be transformed by smoking them using willow wood. The resulting reddish-tinted fish was considered a delicacy. Up until then, the soft grey flesh of the goldeye was considered fit only for dog food.

Goldeye are no longer found in large numbers in the Canadian part of their native range. It is not known whether the decline is due to over-fishing, to bycatch in commercial nets set for other species, or to natural causes.

Smoked goldeye remains a delicacy, though it is often hard to come by, and smoking it yourself requires considerable patience and expertise.

LAKE STURGEON • *(Acipenser fulvescens)*

Lake sturgeon occur naturally in Saskatchewan, primarily in the Saskatchewan and Churchill river systems. Like sturgeon all over the world, their numbers are dwindling, and their presence as a sport

TIM HALSTROM/SASKATCHEWAN ENVIRONMENT

fish in the province is in jeopardy. Around the world, sturgeon populations are under severe stress as their habitat is degraded and they are over-harvested, often for their roe, which is sold as the expensive delicacy, caviar.

Sturgeon are the largest of Saskatchewan fish, characterized by an almost prehistoric appearance, with rows of bony plates under the skin of the back and sides. They are generally a brownish grey colour.

Sturgeon are spring spawners. They move upriver and deposit their eggs on rocks and logs in swift water, below rapids or low falls. Commonly two males accompanying each female, and the eggs are fertilized by the smaller male sturgeon. Studies have shown that a small female, one weighing about 5 kilograms (11 pounds), will deposit approximately 50,000 eggs, whereas a large fish weighing over 45 kilograms (100 pounds), may produce as many as 660,000 eggs or more.

Sturgeon are bottom feeders. While they can be taken on heavy tackle, only a small minority of anglers pursue them as a sport fish species.

Special regulations are currently in effect in Saskatchewan to protect this much-pressured species, and anglers should consult details in each year's Saskatchewan Anglers Guide.

Sturgeon can grow to enormous size. The current record for a kept fish is 122.58 kilograms (270 pounds) for a sturgeon taken from the South Saskatchewan River in 1962. The largest sturgeon caught and released in the province measured 150 centimetres (59 inches) and was caught in the Saskatchewan River in 2001.

LAKE TROUT • *(Salvelinus namaycush)*

The lake trout, found throughout northern Canada, is the only char native to Saskatchewan. Also called Great Lakes trout, salmon trout, Great Lakes char, togue, landlocked salmon, mountain trout, grey trout, and mackinaw trout, lakers range in colour from a light greenish grey to nearly black,

TIM HALSTROM/SASKATCHEWAN ENVIRONMENT

with many light-coloured markings across its back and sides. A particular subspecies, found in the depths of Lake Superior, is called a siscowet and is characterized by very high fat levels. The lake trout is also one-half of the hybrid called splake (see page 14). Part speckled trout and part lake trout, the splake is sometimes called a "wendigo."

Lake trout spawn in fall, when the water temperature falls to between 7°C and 14°C. Spawning can occur in water depths between 1 and 14 metres, usually over rocky, boulder-strewn lake bottoms. Lake trout rarely spawn in tributary rivers or streams, though some rare instances of this have been reported in a couple of rivers flowing into Lake Superior.

Lake trout are cold-water fish. After ice-out in the spring, anglers will find them shallow, over rocky reefs, but as water temperature goes up, the laker goes down, deeper and deeper as summer advances. In summer, lake trout feed mostly on other fish—ciscoes and whitefish—but in spring and fall when they are in shallower water, insects and minnows are added to their diet.

Lake trout angling techniques are seasonally dependent. In summer, when these trout are found only in deep waters, deep-fishing techniques are needed. Heavy jigs, specialized trolling rigs such as the Pink Lady, wire line, or heavy trolling sinkers are needed to get tackle down thirty metres or more where the fish are found. The spring and fall seasons bring lakers into the range of lighter spinning tackle and fly-fishing gear. Casting spoons, trolling spoons, trolling large, bright, minnow-imitating streamer flies—all work in shallow water.

The average size for Saskatchewan lake trout is 2 to 3 kilograms (4 to 6 pounds), but fish over 15 kilograms are caught in some waters each year. The current provincial record for lake trout is a 132-centimetre (52-inch) trout caught in Lake Athabaska in 1995.

Lake trout are excellent eating, very rich tasting. Their flesh ranges in colour from pale cream, through pink, to dark red, depending on diet and habitat of the fish.

LAKE WHITEFISH • *(Coregonus clupeaformis)*

Native to Saskatchewan and a favourite target fish for commercial fishing, lake whitefish are streamlined and silvery, darkening to brownish green along the back. They can be distinguished from the similar ciscoe, or tullibee, by the fact that the snout of the whitefish extends further than the lower jaw, the opposite of ciscoe.

TIM HALSTROM/SASKATCHEWAN ENVIRONMENT

The whitefish prefers deep-water habitat in lakes. It is a fall spawner, depositing eggs in shallow-water areas of lakes and streams, over rocky or gravelly bottom. Each female deposits 10,000 to 12,000 eggs for each pound of body weight. The eggs are abandoned when the spawn is complete, and the adult fish return to deep water.

Whitefish feed on plankton when they are young, but the adults are bottom feeders, scooping up mollusks and insect larvae, as well as small fishes.

Whitefish are only occasionally caught by anglers during the open-water season. Most are taken through the ice, by anglers fishing on or near bottom, with a small hook baited with a piece of minnow or mealworm or even a shiny bit of wire on the hook shank.

Lake whitefish average about 1 to 1.5 kilograms (2 to 3 pounds) in size. The current provincial record is 5.22 kilograms (about 11 pounds, 8 ounces) taken in Sturgeon Lake in 1973.

A fine food fish, whitefish are caught commercially for this purpose and can be prepared in a number of ways, including pan-frying and smoking.

LARGEMOUTH BASS • *(Micropterus salmoides)*

The largemouth bass is unique amongst Saskatchewan imports in that it is found in only one water body, and its presence is entirely dependent on human engineering.

TIM HALSTROM/SASKATCHEWAN ENVIRONMENT

Boundary Dam Reservoir, near Estevan, Saskatchewan, is used for cooling water for the Shand Power Plant. The hot-water return from the plant flows directly into the reservoir, elevating mean average temperatures to levels normally found in lakes hundred of kilometres further south.

The largemouth bass colouration varies from bright green in clear water to dark olive in muddy water. A solid black line of colour runs along the lateral line, and a line of dark splotches runs parallell to it below the lateral line.

Natural reproduction of largemouth bass is taking place in Boundary Dam Reservoir. They spawn in shallow water along shore, sometimes just on the bottom, sometimes in nests or beds. Eggs and freshly hatched fry are aggressively protected by parents, making them particularly vulnerable to angling pressure during spawning periods.

Largemouth bass may eat frogs, small minnows, crayfish, and insects. They are an exciting sport fish, responding to a variety of lure presentations.

Largemouth bass can be caught using jigs tipped with live night crawlers or plastic worms, with spinnerbaits that can be fished at varying depths, with surface-running buzzbaits and crankbaits, and with diving crankbaits. Surface strikes can be spectacular, and largemouth bass fight well, with acrobatic agility.

Largemouth bass average about 1 to 2 kilograms (2 to 4 pounds), but can grow to 4 kilograms (more than 8 pounds) in Boundary Reservoir. The current provincial record is 61 centimetres (about 24 inches).

Largemouth bass can be eaten, but their flesh is somewhat bony and oily, and they are not generally favoured as table fare.

NORTHERN PIKE • *(Esox lucius)*

Northern pike are native to Saskatchewan, and are sometimes referred to as jack, jackfish, great northern pike, grass pike, even "snake" or "slough shark."

TIM HALSTROM/SASKATCHEWAN ENVIRONMENT

Northern pike are long, slender, powerful predators, with dark green backs, mottled, lighter green sides, and white bellies. Their precise colouration will vary depending on habitat and water clarity.

Northern pike spawn in spring, usually around the time of ice breakup, in shallow bays and marshy areas. The female lays an average of about 35,000 eggs, and as many as 100,000, on soft, weedy lake bottoms, where they are fertilized by the male and then left to their own devices.

Pike are a cold-water fish. In spring they can be found in shallow bays where they spawn, and where the waters warm earliest, providing weed growth and food, which can include other fish, frogs, crayfish, small animals and birds, and their own young.

As shallow water warms, pike move deeper into cooler water, often near structure elements where other fish can be found, providing food for this top predator. Because they are such aggressive predators, pike are hard-fighting sport fish, striking at lures hard, and launching into long, fast runs in their attempt to become unhooked.

Anglers fishing for northern pike have a variety of techniques and tackle at their disposal. Casting lures, such as the Len Thompson or DarDevle patterns (red-and-white, five-of-diamonds, frog pattern, silver, brass), are traditional and effective. Equally potent are large floating and diving crankbaits. Fly fishers use large, brightly coloured streamer patterns, such as those pioneered by Larry Dahlberg, to imitate small fish that are a prominent part of the pike's diet.

Average size for northern pike in Saskatchewan is about 2 kilograms (4 pounds). However, fish over 10 kilograms (in excess of 20 pounds) are not uncommon. The current provincial record for northern pike is 19.41 kilograms (42 pounds, 12 ounces) for a kept fish caught in Lake Athabaska in 1954, and 137 centimetres (54 inches) for a fish caught and released in Lake Athabaska in 2000.

Northern pike taken from warm, silty water may have soft flesh and a muddy taste. But those caught in clear, cold, northern waters are excellent table fare. Filleting techniques designed to remove the "y bones" found laterally on the pike can result in boneless fillets that are firm and sweet-tasting.

RAINBOW TROUT • (*Oncorhynchus mykiss*)

The rainbow trout is the most pervasively stocked non-native fish in Saskatchewan, found in literally hundreds of ponds, creeks, rivers, and lakes throughout the province. A recent inadvertent release from a commercial fish farm added nearly 400,000 rainbows to the population of Lake Diefenbaker in southern Saskatchewan.

TIM HALSTROM/SASKATCHEWAN ENVIRONMENT

Rainbow trout colours are quite variable, ranging from olive green to bright silver, depending on water clarity and whether or not the fish are spawning. Their sides are speckled with black dots, and overlaid with a pinkish red blush.

While the reddish tinge to its sides gives the rainbow its name, there is in fact confusion about what a rainbow trout actually is. When a silvery steelhead returns from the salt, and regains its freshwater colours of pale green with a hint of pink, then it is once again called a rainbow trout. The Kamloops trout, when it has the distinctive greenish back, silvery sides, white belly and the distinctive pink hue, is also a rainbow trout.

Steelhead trout are generally considered to be sea-run rainbows, but just to make matters a little more confusing, Great Lakes basin rainbows that migrate from tributary stream to open water and back again are also called steelhead.

Whatever they are called, these flashing silver and green trout with the blushing pink sides are terrific sport fish, and have been stocked successfully across Saskatchewan. They feed primarily on insects and freshwater shrimp, but are caught by anglers on all kinds of tackle, ranging from casting spoons and spinners to hooks baited with worms or artificial bait such as Berkley Power Bait—a particularly effective tactic in Lake Diefenbaker—and surface flies, nymphs and streamer patterns.

Rainbows are caught by anglers casting from shore, trolling or casting from boats, fly-fishing from belly-boats, and as accidental catch when the target is walleye or pike.

Rainbow trout can grow to considerable size. The average size is 1 or 2 kilograms (2 to 4 pounds), but fish over 5 kilograms (10 pounds) are common. The current Saskatchewan provincial record for a kept fish is 12.44 kilograms (27 pounds, 6 ounces), caught in Lake Diefenbaker in 2001. The record for a catch-and-release rainbow tipped the scales at 5.85 kilograms (12 pounds, 14 ounces), taken from the same water in 1999.

Rainbow trout are an excellent eating fish and can be filleted or gutted and baked whole. As with most fish, and particularly trout species, rainbow trout taste best when kept cold and eaten fresh.

ROCK BASS • *(Ambloplites rupestris)*

The rock bass is actually part of the sunfish clan (as, by the way, are the largemouth and smallmouth). It occurs naturally in Saskatchewan, but in a very limited range—the Assiniboine and Qu'Appelle river systems in the province's southeast.

The rock bass is a small, oblong fish, with an overall greenish brown tint, marked with darker splotches. Like many fish, their par-

TIM HALSTROM/SASKATCHEWAN ENVIRONMENT

ticular colouring changes to match their habitat and surroundings, influenced particularly by water clarity and colour. Its eyes are a prominent red colour.

Rock bass spawn in late spring to early summer, on gravel beds or on sand bottoms. Females lay up to 5,000 eggs, and the nests and young are guarded by the male.

The diet of this fish is made up of insects, minnows, small perch, and crayfish. Like most bass, they strike aggressively and, pound for pound, are strong fighting fish. Because they are a lot of fun to catch, they—along with yellow perch—are a good choice for parents wishing to introduce youngsters to angling for the first time. Anglers can tempt a strike from rock bass stillfishing with worms or leeches, or casting with spinners or small spoons, jigs, or crankbaits. One of the simplest and most relaxing ways to catch small rock bass is to use a simple bobber setup with a split shot and small, baited hook.

Rock bass are small, rarely exceeding a weight of about .25 kilograms (8 ounces). The current provincial record rock bass weighed .76 kilograms (1 pound, 11 ounces), caught in Crooked Lake in 1999.

They are a firm, white-fleshed fish and, like most panfish, excellent eating.

SAUGER • *(Stizostedion canadense)*

The sauger is a close relative of the walleye, slightly smaller in size, and is often misnamed "pickerel" by anglers as is its larger cousin. Native to Saskatchewan, sauger are found in both river and lake habitat through-out the Saskatchewan and Churchill river systems and connected reser voirs.

TIM HALSTROM/SASKATCHEWAN ENVIRONMENT

Aside from their smaller size, sauger can be distinguished from walleye by rows of black spots on their spiny dorsal fin, by darker, more defined splotches on their sides, and by the absence of a white lobe on the caudal fin.

Sauger inhabit much the same water as walleye, but anecdotal evidence suggests they have a greater preference for fast water, and deeper, colder reaches of the same water bod-ies than their larger relative. They breed in spring, following hard on the heels of the wall-eye spawn, utilizing the same gravel and rock shoals. Some interbreeding does occur, the result of which is the "saugeye," as it is commonly called.

Sauger eat smaller fish, insects, leeches, and crayfish. They share with the walleye a spe-cial structure in their eye called the *Tapetum lucidum*, which enables them to hunt for prey in very low light conditions.

Sauger are most often caught in conjunction with walleye angling, and by the same techniques and tactics. Jigs (tipped with live bait or plastic), live bait rigging with leeches or worms, and trolling or casting of minnow-imitating crankbaits will all take sauger.

Sauger are smaller than walleye, and average about 1 kilogram or slightly less in weight (under 2 pounds). The current Saskatchewan record for a kept fish is 3.55 kilograms (7 pounds, 13 ounces), very large for a sauger, caught in the South Saskatchewan River. The largest caught and released sauger in Saskatchewan, measuring 56.5 centimetres (about 22¼ inches), was caught in Tobin Lake in 1993.

The meat of the sauger, similar to that of walleye, is white, firm, and sweet, and is excel-lent table fare when kept fresh and pan-fried.

SMALLMOUTH BASS • *(Micropterus dolomieu)*

Regarded by many anglers as one of the best freshwater sport fish, the small-mouth bass has yet to be successfully introduced to Saskatchewan (see Chapter 2 on the history of stocking).

Smallmouth bass are a moderately sized fish, most not exceeding 38 cen-timetres (15 inches) in length. Colour is

TIM HALSTROM/SASKATCHEWAN ENVIRONMENT

variable, depending on water clarity or colour, habitat, and the size of the fish.

Smallmouth bass spawn for a period of 6–10 days in late spring and early summer, in water temperatures ranging from 12°C to 20°C (54°F to 68°F), but with egg deposition at a much narrower range, between 16°C and 18°C (61°F and 64°F). In fact, recent studies indicate that spawning success in smallmouth bass is highly temperature dependent, and that a successful spawn may only occur about one year in three.

Eggs are laid by the female in a nest made by the male. Once the eggs are successfully fertilized, the female leaves the nest in the care of the male and may spawn in another nest with another male. The male guards the eggs and the young after they hatch.

Females may lay from 5,000 to 14,000 eggs, but survival rates are not high, with about 2,000 fry resulting from successful nests.

After the spawn, smallmouth are found in relatively shallow sandy and rocky areas of a lake. As water warms, they move deeper. They prefer the shelter of rocks or shoals or submerged logs, and are not found nearly as often in the dense stands of vegetation favoured by largemouth bass.

Insects, crayfish, and other fish form the bulk of its diet, and the smallmouth bass feeds near the bottom, in the midst of the water column, or at the surface of a water body.

Because of their quality as a hard-fighting sport fish, smallmouth bass are much valued by sport fishers wherever they are found. They can be fished for in a variety of ways: stillfishing with bait; casting live bait; casting spinners, soft baits or plugs; trolling with live bait or artificials; or fly-fishing with either wet or dry flies.

Smallmouth bass are flavourful, their flesh white and flaky, making them as popular a panfish as they are a sport fish. Smallmouth bass are also called black bass, brown bass, green bass (usually reserved for largemouth bass), and even white or mountain trout in southern regions of their range.

SPLAKE • *(Salvelinus fontinalis x Salvelinus namaycush)*

One of the "artificial" trout, the splake is a fertile hybrid cross of the milt of speckled or brook trout (*Salvelinus fontinalis*) and the eggs of lake trout (*Salvelinus namaycush*). The result is a grayish green trout with numerous bright spots on its sides, and usually lacking the pronounced forked tail of the lake trout.

TIM HALSTROM/SASKATCHEWAN ENVIRONMENT

Splake are actually classified as char rather than trout. They are fall spawners, but in Saskatchewan waters, their numbers are only sustained through stocking programs. They feed on freshwater shrimp, insects, and small fish.

Angling techniques range from fly tackle to casting small spoons or spinners with spinning gear. Splake are strong fighters and an excellent sport fish. The provincial record splake weighed 6 kilograms (13 pounds, 4 ounces), caught in Fern Lake in 1988.

Like most char, splake are rich tasting and excellent table fare.

TIGER TROUT • *(Salvelinus fontinalis x Salmo trutta)*

The tiger trout is another exotic hybrid, a cross between a male brook or speckled trout (*Salvelinus fontinalis*) and a female brown trout (*Salmo trutta*).

The result is a very aggressive sport fish that is uniquely marked with gold vermiculations over its brownish yellow sides.

Tiger trout are stocked on a very limited basis in Saskatchewan. There is a high mortality rate for both eggs and fry. There is no known natural reproduction of tiger trout in Saskatchewan.

Tiger trout feed on forage typical of all trout insects, minnows, small fish, freshwater shrimp—and are caught by anglers using fly-fishing gear, or casting spinners or small spoons with spinning tackle.

TIM HALSTROM/SASKATCHEWAN ENVIRONMENT

The average size for a tiger trout is less than 1 kilogram (1 to 2 pounds) and the current provincial record is 4.04 kilograms (8 pounds, 14 ounces), taken from Little Jackfish Lake in 2000.

WALLEYE • *(Stizostedion vitreum)*

Saskatchewan's most popular and pervasive sport fish, the walleye is native to Saskatchewan and its range has been expanded throughout the province by extensive stocking. Along with northern pike and yellow perch, it is highly valued for its accessibility as a sport fish, its dogged fighting spirit when hooked, and its excellent taste.

TIM HALSTROM/SASKATCHEWAN ENVIRONMENT

Walleye are various shades of yellow and green, darker on top, shading to creamy white on the belly, with a distinctive spiny dorsal fin and a white spot on the lower lobe of the caudal fin.

Walleye are spring spawners. For optimum spawning habitat, they need rock or gravel beds with current moving over them, providing oxygenated water. Walleye will often migrate from lakes into tributary streams to find spawning habitat, or will seek out windswept shores with rock cobble bottoms when current is not available.

Finding walleye is often a matter of understanding their patterns of movement in major bodies of water. In large lakes and reservoirs with an abundance of underwater structure—points, reefs, sunken islands—they will move from place to place following baitfish that may be moved around by the wind. On lakes lacking such structure, walleye will follow drop-off edges, weedlines, and even slight depressions in lake bottoms—anything that might offer them cover or hold their preferred foods.

Walleye feed on crayfish, minnows, leeches, the young of other fish such as yellow perch, frogs, and aquatic insects. In bodies of water with large hatches of mayflies (sometimes called fishflies or shadflies), these large insects will form a significant portion of a walleye's diet while a hatch is on.

Anglers seeking walleye have a wide range of tactics and tackle at their disposal, from jigs to live-bait rigs, crankbaits, spinner rigs, worm harnesses, and fly patterns. Live leeches and night crawlers are the live bait of choice in Saskastchewan, since it is not legal to fish with live minnows in the province.

Walleye average about .5 to 1.5 kilograms in size (1 to 3 pounds), but Saskatchewan is graced with a number of waters—notably Lake Diefenbaker, Last Mountain Lake, and the Saskatchewan River system—that boast an extraordinary number of walleye weighing in at over 5 kilograms—in excess of 10 pounds.

The current provincial record walleye was caught on the Saskatchewan River on the reach between Tobin and Codette Lakes, in 1997. It was live-released, and weighed in at 8.2 kilograms, or just over 18 pounds.

Walleye is an excellent food fish, particularly in smaller sizes below 2 kilograms (4 pounds). It is excellent pan-fried, and recipes for it abound, including some in Chapter 8 following.

YELLOW PERCH • *(Perca flavescens)*

Yellow perch are one of the most common and popular sport fish in Saskatchewan. Small-bodied and "football"-shaped, they are often brilliantly coloured, ranging from bright yellow and green to gold and orange. Their spiked dorsal fins are a clear indicator that they are a first cousin of the walleye and sauger, other members of the perch family of fishes.

TIM HALSTROM/SASKATCHEWAN ENVIRONMENT

Because they spawn in spring, moving into shallow weedbeds before ice-out, perch are a favourite target of late-season ice anglers. Strings of eggs are laid over weeds and sunken wood, where they stick until they hatch. Young-of-the-year perch are numerous, and are often the principal food of larger predators—walleye and pike.

Perch themselves are aggressive feeders, foraging for insects, crustaceans, and smaller fish. I have had 6-inch-long perch strike at trolled crankbaits that are an inch longer than they are.

Perch are most commonly caught, both in open water and through the ice, with a vertical presentation. Small jigs on light spinning tackle, tipped with a minnow head, a mealworm or maggot, a bit of night crawler, or a fish eye will tempt a perch strike. They are light biters, and scrappy when hooked. Perch is a favourite fish for parents wishing to introduce their kids to the sport of recreational fishing. They are relatively easy to catch, and school in significant numbers. Find one perch, and you'll find more. Schools are often all of a size.

Perch are small fish, averaging less than half a kilogram (less than 1 pound). The current Saskatchewan record perch was a giant of its kind, weighing in at 1.11 kilograms (just over 2 pounds, 7 ounces). It was caught in Pagan Lake in 1991.

Perch are an excellent eating panfish, with sweet, firm, white meat that is great fried or poached.

CHAPTER TWO
FISH STOCKING IN SASKATCHEWAN

Pete Edwards, supervisor of the Sport Fishing Division of the Fisheries Branch, Department of Natural Resources, shows how pike fingerlings, hatched in a hatchery, are orientated to and then dumped into Buffalo Pound Lake (May 1958).

During the past century, more than 1.6 billion fish of thirty different species have been stocked in Saskatchewan waters. Some are indigenous species introduced to new waters, expanding their range in the province. Among these are whitefish, walleye, perch, northern pike, grayling, and lake trout, along with some minnow species. Exotic species have been introduced to the province over the same period, not all with successful results. Those that have shown evidence of naturally reproducing populations are largemouth bass, smallmouth bass, brook trout, brown trout, and rainbow trout. Others, such as the American eel, kokanee, splake, American smelt, blue gill, and alpine char have failed to thrive, or to survive at all.

When fish are transplanted into new habitat, many factors affect their survival. These include temperature and quality of water, levels of oxygen, stability of water levels throughout the season, availability of appropriate areas for spawning and suitable forage, predation by native fish, and the health of the stocked newcomers.

Fish culture, the breeding and stocking of fish, has been practiced by government management agencies in North America for more than a hundred years and is common practice throughout the continent.

In practicing fish culture, governments have had a number of objectives over the years, most of which are still applicable to varying degrees. Stocking is carried out to enhance or expand the range of indigenous species or to restore species native to a particular watershed where some factor has caused a major decline in stocks. Stocking is used to improve and enhance recreational fishing opportunities—so-called "put and take" fisheries; it is used to introduce new or "exotic" species, not native to the territory in which stocking is to take place, for commercial or recreational reasons.

Occasionally, stocking is done for specific technical and experimental reasons. For example, in the late 1990s, white amur, or "grass carp," were introduced to Loch Leven in Cypress Hills Provincial Park to help control heavy weed growth. Amur are known for their insatiable appetites for underwater vegetation. In fact, there are those who oppose their introduction simply because of their capacity to fundamentally change habitat. What they eat they pull up by the roots, ensuring it will not immediately regrow, as do weeds that are mechanically harvested. The amur stocked in Loch Leven are sterile, triploid fish that cannot reproduce. In this case, their activity is intended to improve habitat and to enhance recreation, from swimming and canoeing to fishing for another stocked—and exotic—species: brook trout.

While Saskatchewan was the last of the Canadian provinces to engage in fish stocking and fish culture, these activities date back as far as 1887, when there was active discussion about stocking smallmouth bass.

The first actual stocking activity dates to 1900, when 8 million whitefish were brought by rail and wagon from Selkirk, Manitoba, more than 300 miles, to Pasqua, Crooked, and Round lakes on the Qu'Appelle River system. Apparently the trip was not all that good for the whitefish, which arrived in poor condition.

By 1913, the Canadian government had begun construction of a fish hatchery at Fort Qu'Appelle, whose main purpose was to stock whitefish in lakes where populations had been depleted. Sixteen million whitefish eggs were reared at the hatchery in 1914–15, and nearly 11 million of these were distributed to lakes in the Qu'Appelle

Above left, Dominion Government Fish Hatchery on Echo Lake, c. 1920; above right, the same hatchery after some renovations; left, the new fish hatchery building at B-Say-Tah in September 1957, shortly after its completion.

system. While whitefish culture dominated the hatchery in early years, by the 1920s, perch, bass, walleye, brown trout, and rainbows were added.

In 1930, the Province of Saskatchewan took over the hatchery from the Dominion of Canada—it was at this time that the province began to manage its fishery and set regulations of its own. Up to this point, all fishing regulations and management were governed from Ottawa. The hatchery was renovated a number of times and finally rebuilt in 1956. It was further renovated and expanded in the 1980s. Over the years, the Fort Qu'Appelle Hatchery, located on the south shore of Echo Lake between the town of Fort Qu'Appelle and Echo Lake Provincial Park has provided more than 2 billion fish to Saskatchewan waters, greatly enhancing the quality of the resource for both recreational anglers and commercial fishermen.

The following are just some of the species handled by the hatchery during the past century.

ARCTIC GRAYLING

The natural range of the grayling lies mostly north of the fifty-sixth parallel, in remote areas which are often difficult to get to. In order to expand the range of the grayling further south to improve access for anglers, spawn-taking operations were initially carried out at a place called Rocky Falls, not far from Reindeer Lake. Later, spawn was taken from the Fond du Lac River near Black Lake.

Well over 11 million grayling have been introduced to a number of sites, selected for their similarity to the original habitat of this beautiful fish, with clear, cold water, rocks, lots of fast water, and rapids or falls nearby. Some grayling were stocked in more southerly Shield lakes, bodies of water that were more like brook trout habitat. A few sites south of the Shield were also stocked.

It is notable that the greatest success in establishing a good population of grayling actually occurred in a relatively small, landlocked lake on the edge of the Shield not far from La Ronge. Stocking began in the early 1950s in 29-hectare Downton Lake, and real success in establishing a grayling population took place after competing native species were eliminated in 1959. In other small lakes containing pike and perch, grayling do not do well. But in Downton, there was a sufficient spawn in some years that it was used as a source of eggs for hatchery rearing. And in some years, the spawn has resulted in viable offspring.

While other competitive and predatory fish are a major limiting factor in successful stocking of grayling, so is water quality and climate. While grayling are found in the northern reaches of the Churchill River drainage, for example, they are not found in the southern reaches, in spite of the fact that other factors, such as the presence of other fish species, are similar.

SAB RB 8365 (1)

Three men sort fish in a fish trap at the spawning camp on the Potato River, twelve miles south of Lac La Ronge (May 1958).

BLUEGILL

One of America's favourite panfish, the bluegill has met with little success during two attempts to stock it in Saskatchewan waters. In 1928, forty-two "large sunfish" were stocked in Coyote Lake, in southeast Saskatchewan. During low water levels experienced between 1931 and 1938, no bluegill were captured in test nets during the time period. In another try during the early 1950s, thirty bluegill brought in from Montana didn't make it through the winter in hatchery holding ponds.

BROOK TROUT

Brook trout are native to eastern Canada, but may have been stocked in the Cypress Hills as early as 1928. The first documented stocking took place in 1933, when 13,600 brookies from Alberta were put into Cold Lake and four streams in the Cypress Hills. Between that date and 1953, brook trout were imported from Alberta, Montana, Oregon, and Washington. During the 1950s, fry and fingerlings from naturalized Saskatchewan stocks were used in addition to imports. Planted in waters primarily between forty-nine and fifty-six degrees north latitude, brookies have naturalized most successfully of all the exotic species brought into the province.

Brookies have been stocked in both streams and still waters, mostly smaller ponds, with the majority in streams. Streams in which brook trout are most successful feature plenty of shade, fairly constant water levels and temperatures (streams are often spring-fed), clean, gravelled spawning areas, and lack of major predator fish.

Even in small northern lakes where no natural reproduction takes place, decent brookie fisheries are maintained by stocking. Shallower, southern lakes, with higher summer temperatures, appear more suited to rainbow than brook trout for stocking or other fish farming efforts.

BROWN TROUT

During the 1920s, brown trout were introduced from Banff, Alberta, to Saskatchewan waters. Later stockings had their source in both Alberta and Montana. Early stocking efforts in the Cypress Hills, in twenty-one streams and sixteen standing waters, were successful, and browns are caught in streams there to the present day.

CRAPPIE

Another popular item on anglers' lists as close by as Manitoba and Northwestern Ontario, the crappie has not fared well in Saskatchewan. In the mid-1920s about 1,400 crappie were imported from North Dakota and planted in a number of lakes in southern Saskatchewan. No fish survived. A second effort was made in 1950, when both black and white crappie were brought in from Montana, but they failed to survive the winter in rearing ponds. Later stocking in more northerly waters around Meadow Lake and Hudson Bay proved to be unsuccessful.

LAKE TROUT

The natural range of lake trout in Saskatchewan is in the Precambrian Shield, north of fifty-five degrees north latitude, with few exceptions. Typical lake trout lakes are deep, cold, and rocky.

In an attempt to expand the range of the lake trout, a number of lakes were stocked, beginning in the 1920s, but none of these early efforts met with any success. The most likely reasons for these failures was that too little dissolved oxygen was present in the stocked waters, and summer temperatures were simply too warm for these cold-loving fish.

SAB RA 5272 (1)

Makwa Lake, 1941: above, nets in the lake at the egg collecting station; below, spawning walleye.

SAB RA 5272 (2)

Attempts were made again starting in the 1960s, this time in deep, cold lakes that have since shown sustainable populations of lake trout. In more recent times, Lake Diefenbaker, one of the largest fisheries in the southern part of the province, was stocked with lake trout. While no scientific tests have been done to determine how successful these stocking efforts have been, anecdotal information from anglers confirms occasional lake trout catches in the reservoir.

LARGEMOUTH BASS

Unlike the smallmouth bass, which has struggled to gain a foothold in Saskatchewan waters, the largemouth bass ("old bucketmouth" as she is affectionately called) has found a niche in the waters and in the hearts of anglers in southern Saskatchewan. Things didn't get off to a great start. All seventeen attempts to stock the largemouth bass prior to the 1950s failed, indicating the fish could not survive here.

But one man-made habitat made all the difference in the world. The Shand Power Station on Boundary Dam Reservoir just outside Estevan is a coal-fired generating station that uses water for steam to drive turbines and for cooling. Water that comes from the reservoir cold is returned warm as toast. The result is a mean average temperature in Boundary Dam Reservoir that is well above what you would expect for a shallow, eutrophic lake at this latitude.

And for largemouth bass, it turns out to be just about perfect. During the 1990s they did well alongside pike, perch, walleye, sucker, and other species. They are reproducing naturally, and bass up to 3.6 kilograms (nearly 8 pounds) have been caught. A reduced limit of two bass, and angler education resulting in a strong catch-and-release ethic, has helped to maintain and enhance a good population of largemouth bass in a place where you would never expect to find them.

NORTHERN PIKE

This most aggressive of predators was not always a popular sport fish. In the first decade or so of the twentieth century, stocking was discouraged, in part because the pike was regarded as a poor quality game fish. Fortunately for recreational anglers, attitudes change, and by the end of the second decade, pike were being stocked into the central and southern parts of the province—to date, well in excess of 28 million eggs, fry, fingerlings, and adults have been stocked into waters that were previously without them. Some of these waters were barren; some had small pike populations and were supplemented. In some cases, pike were stocked in lakes that had overpopulations of stunted perch. With the introduction of a peak predator like the pike, perch populations would drop, and the average size of individual fish would normalize to a level permitted by available forage.

Studies have indicated that northern pike do a lot better when stocked as fingerlings or adults. For example, a 1971 report by T. Lawrence Marshall and Ronald P. Johnson for Saskatchewan Environment (Fisheries Report No. 8) quotes an unpublished study (Royer, 1971) in which natural reproduction was compared to hatchery stocking. The results were quite dramatic. Natural reproduction resulted in a count of between 1,000 and 1,600 progeny per acre of marsh over four years, while hatchery stocking produced fewer than two fingerlings per acre over two years.

PERCH

Another widespread native species in Saskatchewan, perch have been moved around to various waters in the province since the early 1920s. Hatchery propogation beginning in 1925 saw ten million perch collected at Fort Qu'Appelle and subsequently distributed to lakes in southern and central Saskatchewan. Since then, several million perch have been planted in various waters. However, most have been transplanted from lake to lake, and it is rare now for perch to be hatchery raised.

In some situations where little or no competition is present, perch will have a tendency to overpopulate the waters and become stunted in size. The best cure for this problem is the introduction of northern pike into the same waters. Once this predator is present, perch populations tend to regain a more natural balance.

RAINBOW TROUT

Saskatchewan's most commonly stocked trout was first introduced from Alberta in 1924, on a limited basis. Not until the 1950s, however, were rainbow strains from Alberta, British Columbia, Washington, and Montana widely distributed in the province. Since the 1950s, well in excess of four and a half million rainbows have been stocked in Saskatchewan. In addition, rainbows are available commercially to private landowners who are able to stock them in their own ponds. They are the most successfully stocked exotic species in the province, found in waters from the furthest southern reaches of Saskatchewan all the way to northern waters. In the late 1990s, Lake Diefenbaker benefited from one of the largest unintentional stockings of rainbow trout ever carried out. An escape of a large number of fish from an aquaculture net pen near the town of Riverhurst was estimated at well over 400,000 rainbows. Anglers fishing the area have reported excellent rainbow trout fishing in the subsequent years. What the long-term effects on the lake may be is uncertain at present.

SMALLMOUTH BASS

Attempts to stock smallmouth bass in Saskatchewan go back to the 1920s and, to date, all have met with limited success. Smallies were stocked in Prince Albert National Park between 1931 and 1942, but failed to become a sustaining population. In the early 1970s Parkbeg Reservoir was stocked with smallmouth, but the stocking effort failed when the reservoir suffered a winterkill. In the early 1990s an effort to stock Oyama reservoir, supported by the Flatland Fly Fishers club of Regina, also failed.

Current efforts to introduce the smallmouth into Saskatchewan waters began in 1996, when 195 adults, imported from Manitoba and certified free of parasites, were stocked in a lake called Chopper Lake in the Cub Hills. The intent was to create a brood stock population that would later be used to stock selected lakes in the province. In 1998 North Dakota approached the province because they had a surplus of smallmouth bass fingerlings left over from a rearing program. Five thousand fingerlings were stocked in a strip-mine pond near Estevan, Saskatchewan, that year. A few hundred more were placed in Parkbeg Reservoir, where once again they winterkilled. The fish placed in the strip-mine pond are now doing pretty well, with a couple of years of natural reproduction behind them and good growth rates.

In the same year (1998), another 25,000 fingerlings were brought into the province, and stocked in Konuto Lake. All the lakes into which smallmouth bass have been placed to date, including Konuto, are landlocked lakes, so no accidental escape of stocked bass is possible.

The entire smallmouth bass stocking program is still experimental. Saskatchewan Environment is monitoring growth and reproductive success. One-year-old bass have achieved a length of 14.5 centimetres (5¾ inches) in Konuto Lake, and 14 centimetres (5½ inches) in the strip-mine pond. Compare this to Lake Simcoe in Ontario, a lake in which smallmouth bass are native. In Simcoe, year-old smallmouth are 10.7 centimetres (4¼ inches) long, and in another Ontario bass lake, Opeonge, yearlings are only 5.5 centimetres (about 2 inches) long. The difference can be explained partly by the fact that in the Saskatchewan lakes in which they have been stocked to date, smallmouth face no real competition. Three-year-old smallies in Konuto measure out at an average of 27.3 centimetres (10¾ inches), and in the strip-mine pond, at 28 centimetres (11 inches). Three-year-old Simcoe bass average 21 centimetres (8¼ inches) and in Opeongo, 19.6 centimetres (7¾ inches).

While the smallmouth bass in experimental reservoirs are showing excellent growth rates, it will be at least another five to ten years before a sport fishery can be established in the province. When it is opened, it will most likely begin strictly as a catch-and-release fishery.

SPLAKE

The first splake were bred in Saskatchewan in 1969 when the eggs of a lake trout from Whelan Bay were fertilized with sperm from a brook trout from McDougal Creek. Of the 4,500 eggs taken, 3,870 fingerlings were produced; they grew rapidly. Splake have been stocked in a number of small lakes. While the hybrids have survived, no natural reproduction appears to have taken place.

WALLEYE

As far back as the early 1920s, a few walleye were moved from lake to lake in Saskatchewan. But stocking began in earnest later the same decade. In 1924, eggs from Manitoba were reared at the Fort Qu'Appelle Hatchery. Since then, annual spawn camps have been conducted to collect eggs and milt at a number of lakes around the province, from Prince Albert National Park to Mission Lake near Fort Qu'Appelle. For most of the last decade, spawn camps have been held at Coteau Bay on Lake Diefenbaker, one of the most prolific walleye spawning areas in the province.

More walleye have been put in more Saskatchewan waters—at an average rate of 35 to 50 million fry and fingerlings per year—than any other species. Over the years, walleye eggs from Saskatchewan have been traded for trout, salmon, and bass from other provinces and states. While a number of shallow bodies of water have proved inhospitable to walleye stocking due to periodic winterkill and low summer oxygen levels, many have proved capable of sustaining a recreational sport fishery.

It is interesting to note that a number of studies have shown that, in waters with a naturally sustaining walleye population, supplemental stocking makes little difference to the abundance of fish stocks. A series of test nettings carried out in a number of lakes during the 1960s clearly indicated that years in which classes of fish were supplemented by stocking were no more abundant than years dependent on only natural reproduction.

Although walleye can survive in shallower, warm-water environments, they do best in larger, cool-water lakes, reservoirs, and rivers.

WHITEFISH

Whitefish are one of the most important commercial species in the province. They were originally stocked to supplement natural reproduction in "depleted" waters. However, studies soon showed that such tactics did not work, that hatchery-raised eggs and fry did not improve the strength of native populations. From the early 1950s, whitefish stocking has been primarily to introduce the species into new territory and to help maintain non-reproducing populations.

One of the critical factors affecting the survival of stocked whitefish is salinity. Levels of dissolved salts higher than 19,000 parts per million are lethal to whitefish. But even in lakes with lower levels—anything higher than 3,100 parts per million—natural reproduction does not appear to take place.

STOCKING PROS AND CONS

The environmental, economic, social, and scientific soundness of stocking as a fisheries management practice has been debated as long as the activity itself has been carried out. Some argue that the introduction of exotic species (non-native fish) is a good thing because it enhances the fishing experience for anglers, provides angling opportunities that have not previously existed, and makes use of waters that may have been unsuitable for native stocks. Others maintain that it is undesirable because exotic stocks compete too well with native fish. There is some concern that the genetically limited stock available from hatcheries puts the genetic strength of wild stocks at risk.

In recent years, occurrences such as the serious outbreak of "whirling disease" in U.S. mountain-state waters, an epidemic whose origins can be traced back to hatchery roots, has called into question the use of hatchery stocks on a widespread basis. A number of studies have indicated that adding stocked fish to natural populations seems to have little or no effect on their abundance, and is probably wasted effort.

It is equally true that a number of Saskatchewan waters—due to periodic winter-kill, occasional climatic disruptions, or other environmental causes—would be fishless if they were not stocked. These are providing good quality angling experiences to recreational anglers of all ages. Fish are also stocked in Saskatchewan for so-called "put and take" fisheries, where catchable-sized fish are stocked for purely recreational angling purposes, or where fingerlings are stocked to provide limited recreational opportunities with no intention of establishing a self-sustaining fishery. In both cases, continued stocking activity is necessary to provide anglers with year in, year out angling. Such stocking activities continue in Saskatchewan and are popular, particularly with local anglers who owe their easy access to an enjoyable day of fishing to such efforts.

CHAPTER THREE
COMMERCIAL FISHING IN SASKATCHEWAN

SAB RA 11,778

Workers clean and fillet fish in the fish filleting plant at Lac La Ronge (no date).

There are three significant uses of the fishery resource in Saskatchewan; recreational angling, First Nations subsistence fishing, and commercial fishing. The latter has a long history in the province, with its roots going back to about 1885, when rail transport first came to the Qu'Appelle Valley in what was then part of the Northwest Territories. The commercial target species in the early years of the commercial fishery was whitefish, and the industry was based on export to markets primarily in eastern Canada and—until the 1930s when concern over parasite infestations created restrictions—the United States. After more than a century, a commercial whitefish fishery is still carried on in Last Mountain Lake. Today, most of this whitefish harvest is kept for personal use or sold locally. Very little is sold through the Fresh Fish Marketing Corporation, the primary vehicle for the sale of commercially caught fish. The commercial fishery has moved progressively northward.

As the availability of rail transport improved in the province, so the commercial fishery expanded. What began as a southern whitefish fishery moved north, and other species—pike, walleye, lake trout, the favoured species of recreational anglers—were also fished for commercially. By 1900, Prince Albert had rail service, and twenty years later, the commercial fishery had expanded to include Lac La Ronge and Dore, Churchill and Montreal lakes. Over the next thirty years, fish processing plants were built across northern Saskatchewan, at such places as Big River, Dore Lake, Buffalo

SAB RA 11,785 (2)

Commercial fishermen dry and repair nets, Turtle Lake (no date).

Narrows, Cree Lake, Reindeer Lake, Amisk Lake, and Wollaston Lake.

Prior to 1930, for some twenty-five years after Saskatchewan became a province in 1905, control of the commercial fishery in Saskatchewan rested with the federal government and was regulated and managed from Ottawa. During these early years of the commercial fishery, the industry was dominated by southern businesses, by commercial companies from Alberta and Manitoba; few First Nations or Metis people were involved in the industry. The fur trade was much more important to the economy of northern First Nations peoples. After the province took over regulation of the fishery, it continued to be dominated by southern commercial interests, with little participation by local residents of First Nations communities in the north.

In the early years of the commercial fishery, there was no significant sport fishing industry in Saskatchewan. First Nations subsistence fishermen and commercial companies had the same approach to the resource: get as many fish as possible for the least cost in time, effort, and money. As a result, the two became competing interests, often targeting the same productive lakes, or even the same areas of a single lake. The consequences were all too predictable. With this kind of pressure on fish stocks, the most popular places soon suffered decline. In northern waters, fish grow slowly. Once the spawning fish, generally larger females, are reduced in numbers, it takes little time for an entire population to drop in size to critically low levels. For First Nations subsistence fishermen, who depended on their success for food for themselves and their dogs, the effects of such fishing pressure were severe. For commercial fishing companies, the need to make a profit dictated that they set more and more nets to maintain a supply of fish for their markets.

Between the end of World War I and the beginning of World War II, commercial harvest of fish in Saskatchewan more than doubled. Whitefish production increased from less than 1 million kilograms (over 2 million pounds) delivered prior to 1921 to just under 2.5 million kilograms (5.5 million pounds) in 1941. Walleye jumped from a 1921 level of about 100,000 kilograms (over 200,000 pounds) to nearly 750,000 kilograms (over 1.5 million pounds). Lake trout and northern pike showed similar trends in harvest levels in the years between the two world wars. While local residents and First Nations people expressed concerns about the depletion of fish stocks, it seems little action was taken for much of the first half of the twentieth century.

The history of management of the commercial fishery is similar in one way to the management of recreational angling—it is a history of gradually increasing management by regulation. For commercial fishing, the primary regulation involved quotas that governed the harvest of the resource from each lake. The first quotas imposed were the simplest—they were overall harvest limits for an entire lake. A set number of kilograms was set for a lake, one that included all species of fish caught. No separate species limits were imposed under this system. Until 1949 this was the management tool used on all lakes in Saskatchewan.

When lake quotas work well, they offer commercial fishermen the greatest flexibility and the greatest likelihood that the entire quota from a lake will be harvested. The system assumes a kind of random fishing, in which all species are caught, and all populations are fairly represented in the total catch for the lake.

SAB RA 5267 (1)

SAB RA 5260

Men in oil skins fishing with nets,
Turtle Lake, c. 1948.

George Selinger of Dilke removes fish
from net, before they are trucked to
weighing stations and then to the filleting station at Dilke (circa 1950).

However, if one species is valued more highly than others, fishermen may target that specific species above all others, and this "high-grading" approach can take its toll rapidly on the targeted species, which are soon over-harvested and their numbers depleted.

By about 1950, "tolerance quotas" were set up to establish limits based on the percentage of fish caught that could be game fish. The balance of quota would usually be whitefish. For instance, on a given lake, twenty-five percent might be allocated to northern pike, the balance to whitefish. Once the northern pike quota has been caught, however, all fishing ceases, so the total quota on the lake might never be reached. Tolerances are applied on a daily basis, and if a tolerance is exceeded, the fishery is closed. On some lakes, the tolerance for game fish catch is zero percent. On these lakes, all incidentally caught game fish are to be turned over to conservation officers. If too many game fish are turning up in nets, the fishery is reviewed. By 1970, about eighty Saskatchewan lakes had tolerance limits imposed on them. By the mid-1990s that number was reduced to about thirty. In most cases, species limits have replaced tolerance limits.

Species limits apply specific quotas to each species harvested in a particular body of water. They were first imposed for lake trout on Cree, Wollaston, and Reindeer lakes. In today's commercial fishery, individual species limits are the most common management tool used to control harvest by commercial fishermen. In a 1996 report, the provincial government clearly identified the context in which limits and quotas imposed on commercial fishing would be managed. They identified the priorities for use of the fishery resource as follows:

1. Conservation: the first priority is to ensure that sufficient breeding fish are available to maintain the population. If the fishery is badly depleted, no fishing is allowed.

2. Treaty Indian fishing: if a surplus is available, the first users considered must be Indians taking fish for food pursuant to treaty rights.

3. Subsistence fishing: mainly in northern areas, disadvantaged local residents who need fish for food are given access to the resource.

4. Sport fishing by Saskatchewan residents: all residents with valid sport-fishing licenses have access to all public waters for angling purposes, subject to seasons and catch limits.

5. Commercial users: this includes sport and commercial fishing and tourist outfitting. Preference in allocating the resource to these uses is based mainly on past fishing history on the lake in question.

SAB RB 2435 (2)

Commercial fishing with nets through the ice on Last Mountain Lake, c. 1954.

In the mid-1960s, commercial fish production (delivered weight) of all species totaled 6,802,000 kilograms (15 million pounds). By the mid-1990s, the best estimates of delivered weight of commercially caught fish in the province had fallen to 2,427,000 kilograms (about 5 million pounds), a drop of nearly two-thirds in three decades.

And that's not all that had changed. An industry once dominated by southern commercial enterprises had moved entirely into the north, and was, and is, primarily conducted by First Nations people, the vast majority of whom had been excluded from the industry in its earlier years.

By the mid-1990s there were about seven hundred licensed commercial fishermen in northern Saskatchewan, and about the same number again of helpers, operating primarily north of the fifty-fourth parallel. About 250 lakes were fished per year, with a total harvest between 3 and 4 million kilograms (about 6 to 9 million pounds), at least a million of that in whitefish and nearly another million in suckers or species such as carp, goldeye, sauger, tullibee, or perch. The vast majority of fish caught are sold to the Fresh Fish Marketing Corporation. About 200,000 to 300,000 kilograms (400,000 to

SAB RA 11,675

Fish put up to dry, Stony Rapids, Saskatchewan.

CHAPTER THREE

Left: Metis worker cleans fish in preparation for crating and transporting to the fish filleting plant, La Ronge (no date).

Below: A First Nations woman and child make a fishing net in northern Saskatchewan, c. 1948.

600,000 pounds) are sold directly to consumers or to fish dealers in the province.

The majority of commercial fishing now takes place, as it did in the beginning of the industry, in the winter, when cold temperatures simplify the storage of the fish until they can be delivered. Summer fishing requires either quick delivery or freezing facilities close at hand to avoid problems with spoilage. The last statistics available, from the 1990s, indicate that the average commercial fisherman earns less than $5,000 per year from fishing activities.

SAB RA 818

Fish on the ice at Regina Beach, 1942.

CHAPTER FOUR
FISHING IN SASKATCHEWAN

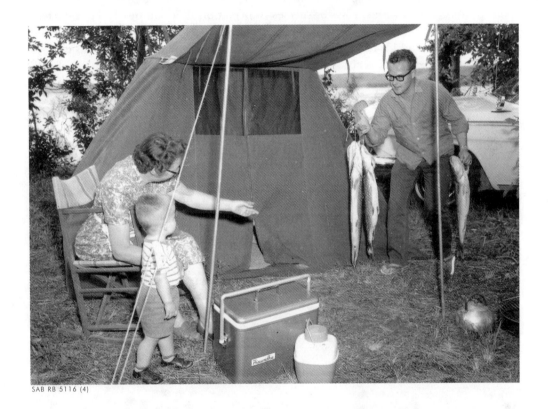

Dad, proud of his catch, returns to the family campsite at Echo Lake, summer 1962.

There is no such thing as a foolproof method for catching fish. Fishing pressure, weather conditions, seasonal variations, the availability of natural food sources, fluctuating populations through natural cycles of growth and decline—all play their part in determining just how successful a given fishing trip will be. And while there is always something new to try in the angling world, there are also tried and true approaches to catching fish have proven themselves to generations of anglers. For each of the terrific sport fish species in Saskatchewan, there are particular presentation techniques, lures, baits, and other fishing tackle accessories that have been shown to be most effective. This chapter provides anglers—regardless of how much time they have spent on the water—with species-by-species information they will need to get started. The techniques described here are for use with spinning and casting tackle, in open water. Fly-fishing and ice fishing are covered in the two chapters following this one.

Fishing tackle—rods, reels, lures, lines, and accessories—are as much a part of fishing as the fishing itself. Show me an angler and I'll show you a collector. Every one of us has his or her favourite fishing gadget, or well-worn and much beloved fishing reel or fishing rod. It's part of the fishing culture.

MICHAEL SNOOK

Part of the author's collection of fishing reels, including Abu Garcia Cardinal (A); Abu Garcia CD Series (B); Mitchell 300X Gold (C); two antique Mitchell reels (D); Abu Garcia Eon (E) and a pair of Abu Garcia Ambassadeurs (F).

SAB RA 11,634 (2)

Willie Cole, well-known radio personality from Regina, tells this story about one of his favourite pieces of fishing tackle—his first rod and reel. As a youngster, Willie fished Cook's Creek, a small creek that runs into the Red River near Selkirk, Manitoba. As Willie tells the story:

[Cook's Creek] was the swimming hole of choice for early residents in East Selkirk and it laid claim to some of the best perch fishing in the area. For most of the summer it was just a quiet stream that grew its share of cattails and lily pads. In those lily pads lay some of the best perch fishing anywhere. My first memory of fishing was shortly after my uncle gave me a reel he no longer wanted (didn't want to repair). My older brother Pat had won an aluminum fishing rod that just lay in the corner. He had no interest in fishing, so I claimed it and repaired the reel as best I could. My uncle believed that the heavier the line the less likely the big one will get away—we're talking 50-pound-test nylon—strong enough to tow a truck out of a swamp. But at the age of 7, who cared? We were goin' fishin'.

My buddy Brian and I went into the garden, dug a soup can full of earthworms, and away we went to an old footbridge that crossed Cook's Creek. We baited our hooks, laid on the small broken bridge and pretty much followed the perch we wanted to catch around the lily pads. We filled our pail with perch and left for home feeling like Buffalo Bill after a hunt. We experienced many more great catches along the Red River near Selkirk. I used that aluminum rod and old reel until one day when the BIG ONE got away—with everything. While we were fishing the Red for catfish in front of the Manitoba Hydro Steam Plant, a storm approached. Brian and I hid under some old driftwood logs piled up on shore by that spring's flooding. While the storm was drenching us, our lines remained in the water. I watched as my rod bent as far as an aluminum rod can bend. Then I could hear that 50-pound test screaming off the reel. It unwound until there was no more. My uncle must have tied a knot on the reel that was never going to give. That was the last I saw of the rod and reel, and I never saw the fish that took it. I miss that old rod and reel 'til today!"

Willie is not alone. On the bottoms of lakes and streams across the country, there are collections of old, much loved fishing tackle, museums of fishing settled on the silt and the rocks of our favourite fishing holes.

A couple of phrases have come into the angling world in recent years, which provide a little insight into the difference between those who catch fish even when conditions are not ideal, and those who suffer more fishless days than any of us would like to admit to. The first is "pattern fishing." This phrase, coined by tournament anglers, refers to the fact that, in a given set of conditions, fish will behave in a certain way. Figure out that "pattern" of behaviour, and you'll definitely catch more fish.

Walleye, for example, can be a finicky fish at the best of times. When a low pressure system blows in, they can be downright moody. But they will still bite if you have patience and can figure out the pattern. There are some known clues—low pressure systems seem to drive walleye into deeper water, away from the shallow shoreline flats and the edges of weeds that they prefer when they are actively feeding. They are more likely to be found at the bottom of the main drop-off in the lake than at the top. And they are more likely to respond to slower presentations—vertical jigging or very slowly drifting along with a simple, live-bait setup—than to quicker ones such as trolling with minnow-imitating crankbaits. Figuring out the details of the pattern is up to the angler. It is like solving a jigsaw puzzle, gradually figuring out where things fit—which is where the second phrase comes in: "the fish will tell us what they want."

A significant part of figuring out the "pattern," or puzzle, that fishing often poses is the concept of "structure." At its simplest, this consists of finding the obvious physical features in a lake—the points, islands, reefs, sunken points and islands, saddle-shaped depressions between an island and the shoreline—that may attract and hold fish of various species. At its best, this idea has evolved to include an understanding of how specific species relate to the physical features in a lake, how this changes with the seasons, with water conditions (wind and wave action), and with the movement of bait fish or other forage that fish prey upon.

In a relatively featureless lake, where the predominant structural element is the edge of the weedbed that rings the lake, a wise angler will fish the weeds. If the only spot in a shallow lake that holds cold water in summer is directly above some groundwater springs on the lake bottom, a pike angler will find these springs and fish them. If schools of minnows are driven into the back of a small bay by prevailing winds, then the fish that prey upon them will soon follow. While traditional structural elements do play a part in locating fish, they are not the only factor to be considered, and are part of a larger picture that, taken as a whole, constitutes a pattern.

By experimenting with different techniques, by moving from place to place, and by observing the response of the target species of fish, it is possible to put the clues together that will eventually provide you with the pattern you need to catch fish. For example, in low pressure conditions, the walleye on a particular lake may respond very well when fished with a light, ⅛-ounce jig, green or blue in colour, tipped with a live leech, fished vertically in 7 metres (22 feet) of water off a major point that comes well out into the deepest part of the lake. On the next lake over, the pattern may be completely different. Figuring out what works, how, and when, is as much a part of the fun of fishing as the catching itself. The most successful recreational and tournament anglers are the ones who solve these puzzles best. It takes time on the water, patience, and a willingness to experiment, observe, and analyze the results. But it works.

ARCTIC GRAYLING

Grayling are found in clear, cold northern waters, often in fast-moving sections of rivers and streams or at the inlet or outlet of a stream or river where it meets a lake. Grayling feed extensively on insects, as well as small minnows, and this is the biggest clue to the techniques and tackle best suited to catching them in open water.

Grayling are small fish, very active, with soft mouths, so light tackle is a must. Ultralight is even better. Typically, a spinning rod and reel, five feet long or a bit longer, rated for 4- to 8-pound-test line or lighter, with a light to ultralight action, is ideal for anglers casting tiny lures or jigs. (See illustration, right).

If you are heading north to fish for grayling, be sure to stock your tackle box with lots of small jigs, lures, and spinners. How small? I find that ¹⁄₁₆- and ¹⁄₈-ounce jigs are ideal. They cast well on ultralight rods with light, 4- to 6-pound-

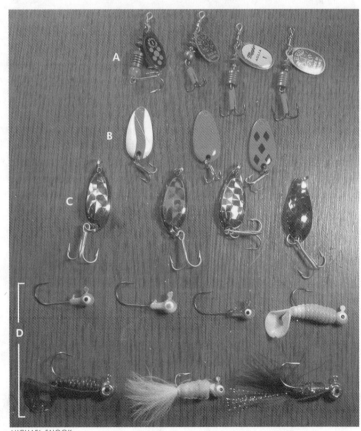

Typical grayling fishing lures—Mepps spinners, size 1 (A); small (1-inch) Len Thompson spoons (B); small Krocodile spoons (C); various ¹/₈- and ¹/₁₆-ounce lead-head jigs (D).

MICHAEL SNOOK

Sportsman uses a hand net to land an Arctic grayling in Careen Lake, c. 1940.

test line, and are the right size to imitate insect life when dressed with artificial plastic bait. Small plastic tails or grubs a couple of centimetres (one inch) long or less, in white, yellow, black, brown, and red, or in combinations of these colours, is an effective way to fool grayling into thinking they are slurping the larvae of one insect or another that floats by them on the current. Jigs of this size have small hooks, ideal for the soft mouth of the grayling. But a word to the wise—sharpen your hooks before using them. Very few jigs, or lures of any kind, come sharp out of the box. The quickest way to lose a small, agile fish like a grayling, which you will be fighting in fast current most of the time, is to use a dull hook.

Cast a light jig to fish the eddy that forms on the downriver side of a rock in the current. The pocket of still water that forms behind such rocks is an ideal resting place for grayling, and a spot where they will sit protected from the current, waiting for food to drift in to them. If you can cast just upstream of a rock so that the current carries your tiny jig right into the pocket, it will be mimicking nature at its best. If you see grayling coming to the surface to take insects there, then use the lightest jig you have, so that it floats higher in the current. If there is no evidence of surface feeding, go heavier, since the fish are probably taking nymphal or larval forms of the insect below the surface.

Since grayling also feed on small minnows, appropriately sized shiny spoons and in-line spinners of various colours are also effective lures for grayling. Appropriate sizes are the smallest you can find—smaller than two centimetres (one inch) long, and as light in weight as you can get away with. Spoons should be bright—silver, brass, and gold colours will work. The light glinting off their surfaces will suggest the shiny scales on the sides of minnows, attracting strikes. Spinners seem to work best if their blades are in the same shiny metallic colours, or in black, yellow, or orange. Cast both spoons and spinners upstream and across the current, and retrieve back through the current. Depending on water conditions and how actively feeding the grayling happen to be, both steady and erratic retrieves will work.

You are going to be fishing for grayling in rocky fast water a lot of the time, so snags are inevitable. Take extra jigs, lures, and spinners with you because you are going to lose some along the way.

For the angler who prefers to fish with the lightest tackle possible, grayling are an ideal Saskatchewan sport fish.

BROOK TROUT

Like the grayling, the brook trout (or speckled trout) prefers clear, clean, cool to cold water. While it is found in small ponds such as those that form behind beaver ponds, it is more likely that you will be fishing for it in moving water—often in streams small enough to jump over in a single bound.

In some waters (particularly in isolated northern waters such as those found in northern Quebec and Labrador) brook trout may grow to considerable size—five-pounders are caught consistently in such waters. But with a few remote exceptions, the brookies caught in Saskatchewan will be smaller fish taken from small waters. They feed on all sorts of aquatic insects in both their adult and larval form, on terrestrial insects that have the misfortune to fall into the water, on small minnows, crayfish, aquatic and terrestrial worms, and even on frogs.

Look for brook trout in the shadows beneath undercut stream banks or overhanging vegetation. They prefer the deepest water available to them in their small stream habitat, so will often be found in deeper pools rather than in shallow, fast-water riffles. Where the flow is large and fast enough, brook trout can also be found seeking shelter on the downstream side of boulders in the midst of the flow.

The small waters they are found in, and the size of the prey they feed on, suggest that, like grayling, brook trout are best fished for with light and ultralight tackle. In fact, most of the techniques used for grayling will work equally well on these trout. But there are some differences to take into account. Brook trout will most often be found in quiet waters, where the splash of a larger lure or jig hitting the surface may well frighten easily spooked fish.

So, casting small jigs, spoons, or spinners upstream and allowing them to drift down to the fish is a better technique than casting directly to the fish. And brook trout are more responsive to live-bait presentations as well. My first trout-fishing outfit, one that I fished with as a youngster, consisted of a light, five-foot fiberglass rod, a small spinning reel loaded with 6-pound-test monofilament. Lures? None. A small lead weight (a split shot sinker works best) a couple of feet up the line and a small hook (No. 8 to No. 12) tied directly to the end of the line and baited with a small piece of night crawler completed the entire outfit. Pennies spent on tackle, worms caught in the back garden by hand, and a simple presentation—a young angler's dream outfit.

This simple rig was fished using the current. Cast upstream, or upstream and across the current, and allowed to drift down with the flow, it caught plenty of brookies for me over the years. With the invention of new products like Berkley Power Bait, the live worm can be replaced with a bit of smelly goo moulded over a hook or a small plastic worm or grub that looks like the real thing and smells like something only a trout could love.

Brook trout are also lovers of the still water in beaver ponds. But beaver ponds are full of logs, branches, twigs and other potential "snags," so that anglers fishing on or near bottom will get their hooks hung up more often than not. The solution is to use a bobber, a float from which you can hang your line, sinker and hook, or lure at the depth you want to, from just off the bottom—safely out of the way of all the snags to be found there—or close to the surface if trout are coming up to feast on insects near or on the top of the pond.

You can hang a tiny jig below a bobber, or the lightest and tiniest of spoons, or just a plain hook with a small sinker a bit higher on the line. Hooks can be baited with night crawlers, leeches (a very effective live bait for pond trout of all species), frozen minnows, or artificial baits such as Power Bait.

Brook trout are light biters, with lightning fast reflexes. The ideal trout rod is a bit more flexible, with a softer action, than one used for walleye or perch. Fibreglass rods, with their soft, slow action, are ideal trout rods. Spinning outfits are preferred over bait-casting ones, because they are generally more available in the small sizes and light to ultralight designs that suits this kind of trout fishing best.

Brook trout are feisty, acrobatic fish, stocked in a number of suitable waters throughout Saskatchewan. They are also amongst the finest table fare of all freshwater trout species.

BROWN TROUT

Brown trout are European immigrants that have taken well to the few Saskatchewan waters where they have been stocked. They are more tolerant of warm water that is not so clear and clean as that preferred by brook trout. They are found in lakes and larger rivers as well as in classic trout streams and smaller ponds. And they can grow to a significant size—up to 8 kilograms (over 17 pounds)—in Saskatchewan waters.

But be warned. Of all the trout species, this one has a well-deserved reputation for being the hardest to catch. Any other species of trout, any perch or pike, even the moody walleye, is more likely to end up on the end of your line than a brown trout. While it is possible to cast a spinner or spoon for browns, particularly in larger waters, and catch them occasionally, most are caught by fly fishers.

While they are not the most plentiful sport fish to be found in Saskatchewan, brown trout are worth the effort if you like a challenge, enjoy a good game of wits, and have the patience and determination to keep trying. But anyone who has fished for them will understand if you take a break to try your luck for splashy rainbows instead.

BURBOT

The burbot, also known as black maria, ling cod, or colloquially as "dog fish" or sometimes just "ugly fish," is a fine sport fish found in many Saskatchewan waters and more commonly caught through the ice than in open water.

Burbot are most often caught by walleye or perch anglers fishing with bait. Live worms, leeches, frozen minnows, and locally caught crayfish will all attract the interest of burbot. I have caught them stillfishing with a jig, drifting slowly with a live-bait setup for walleye, and trolling at a reasonable speed with spinner blade rigs baited with night crawlers.

If you do catch one, burbot are energetic fighters. They are tough enough to stand up well to the rigours of catch-and-release—which is what most anglers do when they catch sight of one.

CARP

The carp also has a reputation for being one of Saskatchewan's homeliest fish. And the truth is, it is not the world's prettiest. But as a sport fish, it may well be one of the finest fighting fish you will ever have at the end of your line.

Imported from Asia, carp have invaded virtually any watery habitat that is warm enough and provides enough food. They are pervasive in the Qu'Appelle watershed, where they do well and grow to sizes up to 15 kilograms (over 30 pounds). Carp are occasionally caught incidentally by anglers fishing with bait for walleye or perch. But they can be specifically targeted as a sport fish by anglers who have learned to use European techniques and hardware designed just for this fish.

Carp are most often fished for from shore, using a technique called "ledgering" ("bank fishing" is the British term). The gear consists of a long, very limber fishing rod; a rod holder that looks like a forked stick about 30 inches (nearly 1 metre) tall; a strike alarm that beeps at you when a carp picks up your bait and spools line off your reel; "boilies" and "whisker rigs" or "hair rigs" at the business end of your line. Add to this a wide-brimmed hat, good sunglasses and a comfortable folding seat, and you are just about equipped. But not quite. Carp are often pre-baited with "chum" for several days

MICHAEL SNOOK

Bank-fishing gear for carp fishing.

The author with 31-pound carp, caught and released in Last Mountain Lake, July 2002.

KEVIN DEWALT

prior to angling. Sweetened, softened corn—the chum of choice—is scattered over the water and sinks to the bottom in the area where you plan to fish. The carp discover the tasty treat waiting for them and hang around, so that you have fish at hand when you show up with rod and reel. It's a time-honoured tactic that works. Now that you have the general picture, here are the details.

A long fishing rod, 12 to 15 feet in length, is commonly used. A "bait runner" reel that can be set to spool freely is loaded with at least 12-pound-test line, more commonly 17- or 20-pound test. A large spinning reel with lots of line capacity is needed, because carp are a hard-fighting, long-running fish. When you hook into one, it's a bit like tying your fishing line to the back of a half-ton truck!

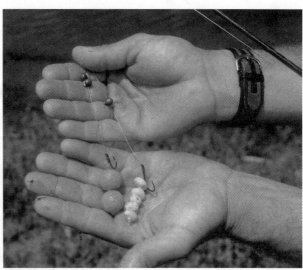

KEVIN DEWALT

Carp bait: Boilies (left) and corn on whisker rigs (right).

A heavy "bank" or "bell" sinker is slid onto the end of the line, and a snap swivel or just a swivel tied on, holding the sinker in place. To this is attached a short leader or "snell"—usually 15 to 20 centimetres (6 to 8 inches) long—with a hook attached to the end, baited with either a "boilie"—a round dough-like bait—or a "hair rig" baited with sweetened field corn. The rig is cast out to the area where the carp have previously been chummed with corn, and the rod is set into two rests, short poles or pipes with forked rod holders on top, that are stuck into the ground on shore. The line is snugged up, the reel set into free-spool mode, and the angler waits for a strike. Some anglers use alarms that sound when their line moves to indicate a strike. Some free-spooling reels, such as those made by Mitchell, have an alarm built into the reel. When the alarm sounds, the angler picks the rod up off the rests, and sets the hook. The battle is on.

Neither corn nor boilies are placed directly on the hook in carp fishing. When the hook is tied to the snell, a tag end of line is left. A small loop is tied at the end of the tag. The loop is threaded through the boilie using a needle (a small crochet needle will do the trick), a small piece of toothpick placed through the loop, and the boilie snugged up against the toothpick, which keeps it from falling off. The same technique is used with softened and sweetened field corn, except several kernels are threaded on, along with a small piece of foam that serves as a float, and once again, a small piece of toothpick holds the whole thing together.

With both a boilie and whisker-rigged corn, the hook is bare, dangling on the line beside the bait, not hidden in it. When a carp picks up the bait, she swallows it. Carp grind up their food with "pharyngeal teeth" located in their throat. While they are processing the bait, the hook is positioned perfectly to catch at the front of their mouth, where a solid hook set keeps it secure.

Fighting a carp is an undertaking requiring great patience. A good-sized fish—7 kilograms (15 pounds) or more—will make long powerful runs, usually several of them, before it tires and can be brought to the net. A truly large carp—over 15 kilograms (30 pounds)—will have you running and hopping along the shore to keep up with it as it attempts to tie your fishing line in knots around any convenient boulder or stump it can find.

In southern Saskatchewan, carp fishing is enjoying new-found popularity, especially on Last Mountain Lake, where outfitter Robert Schulz has developed a clientele from Europe as well as from the local angling population. If you have never caught a carp before, except by accident perhaps, then Saskatchewan is the place to come for a spectacular fishing experience. At Last Mountain Lake it is common for anglers to catch a couple of dozen fish in a day, ranging in size from 6 to 15 kilograms (12 to 30 pounds)—enough to leave your arms begging for a rest at the end of the day.

CHANNEL CATFISH

Channel cats have found their way into Saskatchewan by way of the Qu'Appelle River. The Qu'Appelle drains into the Assiniboine, which in turn meets the Red River in the center of the city of Winnipeg, Manitoba. The Red is home to some of the best cat fishing in the world, centred on the community of Lockport, just a short drive north of Winnipeg. While Saskatchewan cannot lay claim to the trophy fishery found in the Red River, both the Qu'Appelle and Assiniboine rivers contain catfish, and some anglers do pursue them.

Catfishing tackle is pretty much the same throughout North America. What has worked for generations in the deep American south works just as well in the northern prairies. Start with a short, sturdy, stiff, baitcasting rod, a reel that will hold plenty of 17 to 30-pound-test line (some use even heavier line than this), and a premium monofilament fishing line. Some anglers prefer to use the new super lines. Be aware however, that with the great strength of lines such as Berkley FireLine or SpiderWire, goes relatively little stretch in the line. Combine this with the stiffness of the typical baitcasting rod used for big cats, and you have an unforgiving outfit that puts all the stress on the reel's drag system and on the angler, who must know precisely how to play a big fish or risk damage to rod, reel, or both.

The most common way to rig "terminal tackle" (the hook-lure-bait combination at the end of your fishing line) for catfish is to use a three-way swivel with a sinker attached to a dropper line. Tie one loop of the three-way swivel to your fishing line. Tie a short length of line (12 to 24 inches or 30 to 60 centimetres) to the second loop of the three-way swivel and tie a heavy bell sinker or bank sinker to the end of that line. Tie a leader to the third loop of the swivel, to which is attached your baited hook. This is a stillfishing rig, since most catfish anglers anchor and drop or cast their lines into deeper holes where the catfish tend to lie.

Bait for catfish is as varied as catfishermen. Many inveterate cat anglers make up their own smelly concoctions—"stinkbaits" as they are often called, which consist of varying combinations of anise oil, ground-up fish, and rotten chicken livers. Yummy to a catfish. Such concoctions are also available as commercially made and marketed pastes. Cats will respond equally well to cutbaits—small pieces of dead fish attached to the hook. Even a wadded ball of nightcrawler on the hook will work.

While light tackle will work just fine for small catfish, most anglers set out with bigger fish in mind. For cats over 7 kilograms (15 pounds), baitcasting rods and reels are best. Use a 6- to 7-foot, heavy-action rod, rated for lines of 25-pound-test or greater. Use a baitcasting reel that will hold plenty of heavy line, has a sturdy drag, and is well built to withstand the rigours of playing big, strong fish in current.

Catfish are only caught in a few locations in southeastern Saskatchewan, and are certainly not the main reason for making the province a fishing destination. However, once established, catfish tend to endure, and as time goes on, this fishery will grow in importance.

LAKE TROUT

Saskatchewan's only native trout is found in the deep, clear, cold waters of northern lakes. Two things determine the tackle and techniques used for catching this magnificent trout—its need for cold water and its choice of forage.

Lake trout are very temperature dependent. They prefer temperatures around 10°C (50°F) and will migrate to lower lake depths and back with the changing seasons. In fall, when they spawn, lake trout may be found on shallower reefs and shoals, at depths as little as a few metres (10 feet), provided the water temperature is right. They can similarly be found shallow in spring time, but as soon as the sun starts to warm up the surface water, they begin to descend to darker, colder depths.

Lake trout are predaceous, feeding primarily on other fish—whitefish, sculpin, sticklebacks, suckers, cisco, and even grayling. They also eat insect larvae, crustaceans,

MICHAEL SNOOK

Typical lake trout spoons and crankbaits, also used for northern pike: Len Thompson spoon, size 2 (A); Northland Fishing Tackle Tiger Spoons (B); Mepps spinners, size 5 (C); Rapala floating (D) and jointed floating crankbaits (E).

leeches, clams, snails, and even mice and shrews.

In spring and fall, when surface water temperatures are icy cold in northern lakes, anglers can readily troll for lake trout using medium-sized spoons, in-line spinners, and minnow-imitating crankbaits. Three to four-inch (10 centimetre) spoons that have a shiny side—preferably silver over either brass or gold—and a coloured side, work very well. The classic "five of diamonds," the green and black "frog" pattern, and other spoons made by DarDevle or Len Thompson are excellent lake trout lures. So are diving Rapalas, 6 to 8 inches in length (16 centimetres or longer) in blue and white, blue and silver, in perch colours, and others. Larger in-line spinners, such as those made by Mepps, in bright colours and silver work very well. The surest method for trolling spoons or crankbaits for lake trout in the early and late season is to first find the depth at which the fish are located on a fish finder. Then, troll that area placing lures just a foot or two (about half a metre) above them in the water. Lake trout will strike aggressively when feeding.

For this kind of trolling, either a medium-sized 6- to 7-foot spinning rod or similar sized baitcasting rod, will serve nicely. Match the rod to a reel that will hold a

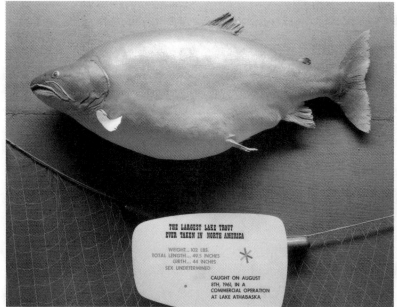

Largest lake trout ever caught in North America, taken in a commercial fishing net, on Lake Athabaska, August 8, 1961.

THE LARGEST LAKE TROUT
EVER TAKEN IN NORTH AMERICA

WEIGHT... 102 LBS.
TOTAL LENGTH... 49.5 INCHES
GIRTH... 44 INCHES
SEX. UNDETERMINED

CAUGHT ON AUGUST
8TH, 1961, IN A
COMMERCIAL OPERATION
AT LAKE ATHABASKA

SAB RB 5125 (1)

reasonable amount of 12- to 17-pound-test line. Lake trout are aggressive fish, and will make long runs taking off lots of line. Lakers can also cut your line with remarkable ease. They tend to roll over and over when caught, wrapping fishing line around themselves. The rear edge of their gill covers is razor-sharp, and if this edge should contact the fishing line, the line will be severed instantly. The antidote is to use a 12-inch (30-centimetre) steel leader when you troll for spring or fall lake trout, and keep a tight line, so that it is harder for the trout to roll.

By early summer, lake trout have descended into the depths; 80 or 90 feet (30 metres) or deeper is not at all uncommon. At this depth, different fishing methods are needed. While trolling still works, deep trolling is not the same as its shallow water cousin. There are a number of ways to get a spoon or crankbait down deep.

Traditionally, anglers would go to heavy-weighted sinkers and steel line to plumb these depths. Today there are several alternatives. One is a device called a "Pink Lady," a flat, bright-pink plastic diving plane that will take your line down to great depths, then release when you pull hard on your line to set the hook. It allows you to fish deep with monofilament line. However, it does interfere with both the action of your lure, and your ability to "feel" what is happening deep below the surface.

Another option is to use heavy clip-on sinkers with the new super lines. High-tech lines like Berkley FireLine or SpiderWire have much narrower diameters for their strength than does ordinary monofilament. The resulting drop in water resistance means they sink more easily. By clipping on a sinker weighing a couple of ounces or more, far enough away from your lure that it doesn't interfere with the lure's action, you can fish deep without sacrificing as much feel, or the natural movement of the lure you've chosen to use. As a bonus, both FireLine and Spider Wire have little to no stretch, so that when you set the hook, even far below the boat, the response of your line and lure is immediate. Other lines might experience as much as ten or fifteen percent stretching.

Lake trout in deep water do relate to structure—to underwater humps, bumps, reefs, and dropoffs. Find the fish using a depth finder, and you can drop a heavy jig (an ounce or better) dressed with bucktail, tipped with a frozen minnow or a large plastic tail. But jigging for lake trout in deep water takes boat control. On a relatively calm day you can anchor (with a long enough rope), or use an electric trolling motor to hold over your fishing spot. When the wind is blowing, though, you will find it hard to execute this kind of precision fishing strategy for lakers. Better to drift or troll, using a Pink Lady or clip-on sinker, on rough days.

Lake trout are amongst the finest sport fish in Saskatchewan. They are large (over 40 inches or 1 metre is the current provincial record), they are strong fighters, they are beautiful fish, and their flesh, ranging from pale pink to deep red depending on their diet, is a mealtime treat. Most anglers who venture into the far north to fly-in lodges do so in pursuit of lake trout. They are worth the effort.

LARGEMOUTH BASS

Found only in the Boundary Dam Reservoir, largemouth bass are favourites of anglers. Scrappy fighters and acrobats, they strike aggressively, and are relatively easy for anglers to catch. Because the reservoir in which they are found is not large, there is a limited variety of habitat for the bass to use. Anglers who figure this out can match their tackle to the fishing conditions. Although this is the furthest north that largemouth bass are found in North America, the tackle and techniques used to catch these fish will be recognized by anyone who has ever watched an American bass fishing show.

Both casting and spinning rods and reels are used to catch largemouth bass, though casting outfits are more popular, in part because, for part of the summer season, these fish inhabit the densest parts of weedbeds, and the heavier casting outfits offer greater strength for anglers trying to haul fish out of this jungle.

Largemouth bass feed on insects, crustaceans, minnows, the young of other sport fish species, and aquatic and terrestrial worms—in short, just about anything that is available to them. The lures and baits that have been developed over the years specifically for bass anglers reflect this diversity of diet.

The classic largemouth lure is the spinnerbait (see upper photo opposite), used primarily for fishing on or near the surface. These splashy, noisy lures trigger dramatic top-water strikes from hungry bass, but there are other ways to fish for Saskatchewan largemouth.

Early in the season largemouth can be found scattered along the shoreline, tucked in tight under overhanging vegetation. Anglers can use a bow-mounted electric trolling motor to work their boat along the shore, casting toward it with spinnerbaits in the ¼- or ⅜-ounce sizes, letting the lure sink just below the surface before starting a retrieve. Strikes will often come as soon as the lure moves away from the shoreline, as it is reeled back to the boat. The same technique can be used with floating, or suspending, shal-

MICHAEL SNOOK

Above, spinnerbaits for largemouth bass can be fished on or near the surface or under water.

Below, crankbaits for largemouth bass, including: Rapala Shad Raps (A); Berkley Frenzy lures (B); Berkley Frenzy surface popper (C); and a classic Fred Arbogast Jitterbug (D).

MICHAEL SNOOK

low-diving crankbaits (see lower photo opposite). Cast them in as close to shore as possible, allow them to sit still on the surface for a moment or two, then start reeling in. Pop the lure below the surface when starting the retrieve, and if there's a largemouth nearby, this is the time to expect a strike.

If for some reason—such as very clear water, high sun, or lots of fishing pressure—the bass have moved into deeper water offshore, then fishing a heavier spinnerbait (½-ounce will do) slower and closer to bottom is a better technique. The same applies to crankbaits. The deeper diving models, fished as slowly as possible, bumped off bottom, will trigger strikes under these conditions at Boundary Dam.

As the season advances and thick weed growth emerges in the back bays of the reservoir, bass may still be found along the shoreline, but will also take refuge in the thickest stuff they can find. This is where the baitcasting rod and reel come into their own. Casting a spinnerbait, crankbait, or other surface plug into the weeds, and skimming the lure back to the boat near the surface will trigger strikes from bass hiding below. Once hooked, they'll dive into the greenery and tangle an angler's line around every possible weed. A sturdy baitcasting outfit spooled with 17- to 20-pound-test line is what it takes to winch largemouth out of this watery jungle.

While spinnerbaits and crankbaits are probably the most common lures used to catch largemouth at Boundary Dam, other tried-and-true techniques work just as well. Casting a rubber-skirted jig into pockets in the weeds, or up against the rocks along the rip-rap at the dam, will produce fish. So will worm rigs fished deep and slow when the bite is off.

While live bait (night crawlers, leeches, or locally caught frogs) will work for largemouth, they are less commonly used than artificial bait. As a rule of thumb, the thicker the weed growth, the murkier the water, the larger, splashier, brighter, noisier the lure used, the better.

MICHAEL SNOOK

Skirted, weedless jigs for largemouth bass. Also useful for pike found in weedbeds.

NORTHERN PIKE

One of Saskatchewan's most popular sport fish, the northern pike, or jackfish, is found throughout the province's waters, from southern ponds and lakes to the most northerly fly-in destinations.

The pike is an aggressive predator, top of the food chain in most lakes, growing to sizes in excess of 14 kilograms (30 pounds). Its long, slender body and large square tail tell anglers all they need to know about this fish—it's fast and a fighter. The pike's mouth is large in proportion to its body, and it comes equipped with lots of very sharp teeth. This fish eats other fish, the largest it can manage, and lots of them. When caught, the pike will make fast runs away from the boat. Larger fish may hug bottom, just like walleye. You can count on one final surge of energy when a pike catches a glimpse of your boat, and you'll have to be prepared for them to swim into the shadows right under it.

Anglers seeking northern pike can take their cues from the fish itself. Use any lure that resembles a minnow or baitfish, in sizes and colours to match the local population. That includes brightly coloured spoons, crankbaits, in-line spinnerbaits, all of which can be cast and retrieved moderately quickly, or trolled at speeds ranging from a mile and a half to three and a half miles an hour. Spoons such as the Len Thompson, or DarDevle, 3 inches long or larger, in red-and-white, perch colours, "five of diamonds" patterns, with bright silver or brass on the cupped side of the spoon, or plain brass, silver or gold spoons, will imitate baitfish and small gamefish that are the prey of northern pike. Mepps, Blue Fox, or Panther Martin in-line spinners, in the largest sizes, dressed with bucktail or plain, present a similar target to pike. Mepps spinners provide an option for a trailing plastic minnow behind an in-line spinner, an approach that works well on some pike. Crankbaits from Rapala, Berkley Frenzy lures, and similar minnow-imitating plugs, are sure-fire producers for northern pike. Again, the larger-sized models—5 inches (12 centimetres) or longer—are best, and colours should include perch, fire-tiger, crawdad, blue and silver, blue and white, black and white, silver, and "natural" photographic-style finishes. And the same spinnerbaits used for largemouth bass fishing are very effective for pike, especially in spring fishing conditions, or for fishing up against weedbeds in northern lakes throughout the season.

There's nothing subtle about the strike of a pike. Slashing, aggressive, hard, more than one angler has come close to losing a rod and reel overboard to a surprise attack from a northern. While either spinning or baitcasting outfits can be used for these fish, the casting rig is preferred. Baitcasting rods, even the longer ones preferred for northern pike, are available in heavier, stiffer actions suitable for trolling large spoons and crankbaits at good speeds. The more muscular rods are better for controlling large, strong fish. And baitcasting reels are better suited to handle large quantities of heavier line—17-pound-test and stronger.

In spring, pike will be found first in shallow bays that face into the southern sun, particularly those with dark-coloured bottoms that hold the sun's heat. In these bays, the first weed growth in the lake will appear. The earliest spawns of minnows and other fish species will take place, along with the earliest insect hatches. Where there is food, there will be pike. At this early time of year, when water is often still clear, it is sometimes possible to see pike basking in the shallows from some distance away. This allows an angler to hunt for them by eye ("sight-fishing") and then cast to desirable fish. A good pair of polarized sunglasses is essential equipment for this kind of fishing. Another productive technique is to cast a floating crankbait toward the newest weed growth, let it sit on the surface for a moment, twitch it once or twice, and pull it under the water at the beginning of the retrieve. Pike will rise a dozen feet from bottom to attack a likely-looking meal on the surface. They often strike just as the retrieve begins. Casting a spoon or in-line spinner into the same area, letting it sink a few feet into the water, then starting the retrieve will often trigger the same strike response. These spring conditions are also ideal for fly-fishing for pike (see Chapter 5).

Pike are cold-water fish. The further south you are, the more they will move into deeper water as summer arrives and the water warms. They are often caught incidentally by walleye anglers trolling with spinner blade rigs baited with night crawlers, in fifteen to twenty-five feet of water. In northern waters, which tend to remain cold all summer, pike will relate to weedbeds adjacent to deep water throughout the season. Find the right weedbed, cast to it, and the pike will respond.

Pike can be caught by anglers trolling with spoons or crankbaits all through the open-water season, but it is a particularly effective approach in autumn, when big pike, sensing the seasonal changes, will go on the prowl and feed heavily for several weeks, often right up until freeze-up. At this time of year, trolling spoons or crankbaits along shore, just at the outside edge of the weeds, often in about 10 to 12 feet (3 to 4 metres) of water, can be very productive. On a cool October morning on Last Mountain Lake, near Rowan's Ravine Provincial Park, the two visitors from Ontario I was guiding that day took a dozen pike ranging from 2 to 8 kilograms (5 to 17 pounds) in just a few hours, trolling 3½-inch red-and-white and five-of-diamonds spoons at a speed of just over a mile and a half an hour. We covered several miles of shoreline, and the pike were scattered all along it, feeding actively and striking aggressively. This shoreline trolling pattern for northern pike works on many Saskatchewan lakes in autumn.

Anglers seeking pike should remember to take along a few accessories. Cotton fish-handling gloves are a must—pike can be very slimy and hard to hold onto while you are removing hooks—wet the gloves first to get a better hold on the fish and risk less damage to it. Bring along a big pair of needle-nose pliers for removing hooks. Many pike anglers like to use "spreaders" to keep a pike's mouth open while removing lures. Make sure your net is big enough to handle large, toothy fish. I have seen more than a few trophy jackfish go right through smaller nets with inexpensive cotton mesh. Some anglers prefer fish "cradles" when handling big fish. These are mesh nets suspended between two parallel wooden handles that cradle a fish in the water while you remove the hook. In theory, they allow you to release fish without handling them or removing them from water. In practice, they take a bit of getting used to, and usually it takes two anglers to deal with a big fish in a cradle net.

Always use metal leaders when fishing for northern pike. They can bite through monofilament with ease, can handle super lines with only a bit more effort, and will leave you not only fishless, but lureless as well. Amongst the best leaders on the market are Berkley's wire-wound leaders, with a ball-bearing swivel at one end and a cross-locked snap at the other. Use the 12-inch model, in black, for best results.

RAINBOW TROUT

Rainbows are the most common trout species in the central and southern part of Saskatchewan, stocked in public and private ponds, and reproducing naturally in some bodies of water that have been stocked for years. When caught, rainbow trout are acrobatic fighters. Underwater a rainbow will shake its head vigorously, make short, quick runs, and once it surfaces, it will jump, often more than once, in an effort to shake the hook. Taken from cool, clean water, rainbow trout are excellent eating.

Rainbows can be taken with a great variety of fishing techniques, from stillfishing with bait, to casting or trolling spoons or plugs, to fly-fishing. In small stocked ponds, where shore fishing is the rule, a couple of techniques are particularly effective.

Anglers can use small, light or ultralight spinning outfits to cast the smallest of spoons, spinners, or tiny crankbaits to active fish. When the rainbows in a pond are feeding on minnows or small crustaceans, these lures will prove effective. However, when the dominant food source is insects, different approaches are needed. Anglers can cast a small jig (1/8-ounce or less), dressed with a piece of night crawler, a small leech, or a bit of Berkley PowerBait moulded onto the hook. Hop and drag the jig slowly back over the bottom of the pond. Be ready for a strike each time you stop moving the bait. Rainbow trout bite very lightly, and will drop anything that feels wrong, in a flash. Soft-action rods are more forgiving for this kind of fishing than stiffer, fast-action rods. The fish may hook itself against the gentle tension of the soft, bending fishing rod, even before the angler sets the hook. Just as good as a small jig is the oldest, simplest terminal tackle ever—tie a small (No. 6 or smaller) hook on the end of the line. Bait it as above. Squeeze a small split-shot sinker onto the fishing line about two feet above the hook. Cast the rig out and retrieve as with a jig.

Small ponds can also be fished very effectively using bobbers; either fixed or slip bobbers will work. If the trout are feeding close to the surface (you can tell this when there are swirls or little whirlpools of water on top, but no visible fish), then use a short length of line below the bobber to a tiny baited jig or hook and sinker. If the trout are deep, use a longer drop of line below the bobber. The fish will tell you what depth they like, so experiment. This kind of fishing is great fun for kids or for brand new anglers who are just getting used to the sport of recreational fishing. Rainbow trout are ready biters, and the bobber is a visual clue that something is going on below the water, out of sight.

Rainbow trout in creeks and streams are caught much like other trout species. Anglers can cast small spoons or spinners upstream and across the current, and retrieve the lure so that it moves downstream with the current. Like most trout, rainbows in moving water will seek out the shelter of overhanging vegetation or creek banks that are undercut. They will also lurk behind rocks in the middle of the stream, letting the eddying current bring food to them. Small jigs tipped with either plastic tails or grubs or with live bait also work for fishing small streams. Rainbows in moving water are a favourite fish of the fly angler (see Chapter 5). And they are readily taken through the ice (see Chapter 6).

Rainbow trout in larger waters are caught incidentally by anglers drifting or trolling live-bait rigs for walleye. They can also be taken by anglers trolling bright spoons or crankbaits in areas where rainbow trout are holding. Since they feed on insects, minnows, and the young of other game fish, any lure or bait that imitates these food sources will attract the attention of rainbow trout. Lake Diefenbaker is a favourite southern destination for rainbow trout anglers, since it holds a good population of naturalized rainbows, and since a large accidental release of several hundred thousand farm fish in the mid-1990s created an unplanned stocking.

WALLEYE (AND SAUGER)

Easily the most popular sport fish species in Saskatchewan, walleye, and their first cousin, the sauger, are sought after in waters throughout the province. They are present in all but the coldest, furthest north waters in Saskatchewan, are stocked by Saskatchewan Environment to maintain numbers for sport fishing, and are the mainstay of most Saskatchewan anglers. Walleye are found in shallow southern lakes and reservoirs, in deeper, rockier northern lakes, and in most river systems in the province. Sauger prefer faster moving water, and are usually found in more northerly river systems, such as the Saskatchewan.

Walleye prefer cool water, are a schooling fish, and are often present in large numbers in many lakes and rivers. However, the fact that there are lots of them does not mean that they are always easy to catch. Walleye are quite sensitive to fishing pressure and to changes in weather or water quality, and are strongly influenced by the presence or lack of prey. They feed on insects, as well as naturally occurring populations of leeches, minnows, crayfish, aquatic worms, and the young of game fish, including their own.

In recent years, there has been an explosion of knowledge about the behaviour of this fish, and the tactics and techniques needed to catch it. Whole books have been written on the subject, and there is more information available than could ever be covered in a portion of a single chapter. The information on walleye angling that follows here is a brief synopsis, enough information to get anyone wishing to fish for walleye in Saskatchewan off to a good start. Literature on walleye fishing can be found in the reference list in Appendix F.

I first started fishing for walleye fifty years ago in northern Ontario. We called them "pickerel" back then, and many still refer to walleye by this misnomer. The pickerel, or "chain pickerel," is actually a close relative of the pike. Found in much more southern waters than those in Saskatchewan, it looks like a small northern pike, is green, and has a mottled chain-like pattern of markings on its skin, thus the name.

The walleye is a member of the perch family, and it is distinguished by the feature that, more than anything else, defines its relationship to its habitat and to the anglers who fish for it. Walleye are given this name because of their big eyes, located on the top and to the side of their heads. The large, light-detecting surface in their eyes allows them to see well in murky, low light conditions. For years, anglers believed that you couldn't catch walleye in the middle of the day, or the middle of the summer, when the high, bright sun penetrates deeply into the water column of any lake or river. This notion has long since proved to be wrong, but there is a grain of truth hidden in it.

Because walleye have a sight advantage in low light conditions, they will often feed most actively when other fish are at a disadvantage. In the early morning, around dusk, on choppy days when the wind has blown the lake into waves that bounce sunlight around and prevent deep penetration of light, in waters turned murky by algae growth or clay and mud stirred up by wind or current, or on overcast days, walleye have a feeding advantage. They are more likely to be active under such conditions than on days that are clear and sunny, with calm, clear waters. But nothing is guaranteed about walleye. Several of the largest fish I have caught have come on such days, at times when I expected to catch little or nothing, and certainly not a trophy over 5 kilograms (10 pounds). The habitat of a walleye is complex, and many things influence its behaviour. Light, however, is a good starting point to understanding this wary, sometimes frustrating, fish that provides some of the best table fare you'll ever enjoy.

Although it is possible in limited circumstances to fish for walleye from shore, this is one species that really is best pursued from a boat. Not only does being mobile get you to where the fish are (they move around constantly), but it provides a platform for fishing presentations, from vertical jigging to drifting with the wind to trolling with an electric motor. While it is a useful tool for fishing for any species, a sonar unit—the depth finder/fish finder—is an essential tool for walleye anglers. Walleye move with the schools of minnows they feed on. They move with changes of wind and current. They move as water conditions (temperature, oxygen content, turbidity or water clarity) change. Walleye are content at almost any depth, from a few feet of water to sixty or seventy feet deep or even deeper, if conditions are right. In order to catch walleye, you have to first find them, and sonar is the most effective way to do so. This is particularly true in southern lakes and reservoirs where classic point and bar structure is scarce, and walleye may be found at any number of spots along the edge of drop-offs or weedbeds. And in northern lakes where you can expect to find rock points, reefs and similar structures, a sonar unit will let you know just where the fish are holding on the structure and at what depth, and will assist you to keep track of them as they move throughout the fishing day. A sonar coupled with a Global Positioning System (GPS) unit provides anglers with the tools to literally map out underwater terrain by entering "waypoints," (precise points of longitude and latitude), then using these as a map, displayed on the screen of their GPS, to fish the most productive spots.

Once found, walleye can be fished for in a variety of ways, depending on fishing conditions. My first walleye was caught on a simple hook and sinker, using live minnows as bait, with the hook suspended just a few inches off the lake bottom. In this basic rig are found the basic elements of almost all live-bait presentations for walleye.

If you bring the hook and sinker together into a single lure, you have a jig. More walleye (and plenty of other fish, too) have been caught on jigs than on any other single piece of fishing tackle. Fished with a light- to medium-action rod, in lengths of 5 to

6 feet, with line in the 4- to 10-pound-test range, jigs are ideal for precision fishing a school of walleye that is relating to a specific structural element under the water. As a rule, the lighter the jig and the lighter the line, the better. A ⅛-ounce jig, fished on 6-pound-test line, tipped with a live leech, is ideal bait for vertical jigging walleye in still water. Fishing jigs in river currents is a different matter. While the lightest possible jig is still the best, it is likely you'll be

LOWRANCE CANADA

A Lowrance 480M, an ideal sonar unit for walleye anglers, with excellent sonar, GPS and mapping capability.

fishing with ¼-ounce or heavier in river current. In the Churchill River in north-central Saskatchewan, for instance, the following has produced literally hundreds of walleye. Fishing a current edge, or washout hole created when the river drops over an underwater ledge or large rock, requires getting your jig down near the bottom in stiff current. Use a ⅜-ounce jig head, tipped with a 3-inch single or twin tail grub, and a frozen minnow. Set the jig right on the bottom, then lift it just off the rocks. The moving water will usually do the rest. Walleye in these circumstances will sometimes jump on a bait with a vigorous strike that is easy to detect. But sometimes the only way an angler knows that a fish is there is to lift up on the jig and feel the extra weight of a fish. Either way, a quick set of the hook is a must. Walleye can detect that something is wrong and spit out a jig in less than a tenth of a second!

In smaller rivers such as the Saskatchewan River, particularly the stretch between Codette and Tobin Lake, jigging with a live leech is effective. Here, boat control is essential. The best way to present a jig in current is to drift downstream, but steer your boat into the current and use an electric trolling motor to slow your drift so that the boat is moving just a bit slower than the current. This technique is called "slipping," and it is useful for keeping your jig as close to vertical beneath the boat as possible. Again, bites can be very subtle, sometimes just a slight increase in weight on your fishing line. When in doubt, set the hook.

In southern lakes and reservoirs, walleye may hold off shoreline points, working their way up and down the drop-off into deep water, coming shallow to feed, going deeper for rest and safety. Casting a jig into shallow water high on the point, then gradually lifting and dropping it a few inches at a time while moving it into deeper water, catches walleye. Jigs can be drifted or slow-trolled along a drop-off or "break-line"—the edge of a weedbed or the line where a shallow shoreline flat drops into deeper water. The jig can be dragged along the bottom, or hopped in short jumps of a few inches, lifting and dropping the jig across the bottom as the boat drifts along.

Jigs come in many shapes and colours. The traditional round-head jig is perfect for vertical jigging. Bullet-shaped jigs may be more efficient for casting and retrieving, particularly in weedy areas. Wedge-shaped "stand-up" jigs will sit on the bottom with the hook and bait sticking upwards a couple of inches. Fishing a live leech or small frozen minnow on a jig requires only the single hook that the jig comes with. But fishing with long night crawlers is another matter. A night crawler can stretch easily to eight inches behind a hook, leading to "short bites" by cautious walleye—the last inch of the tail of

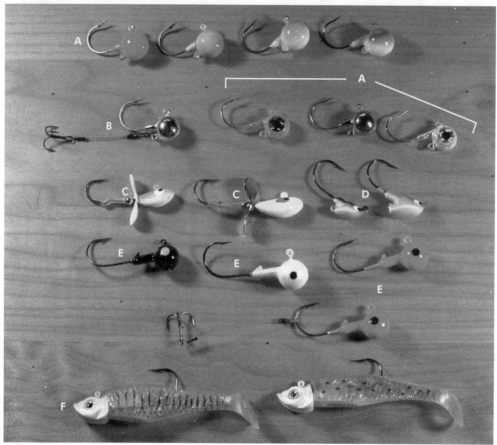

MICHAEL SNOOK

A selection of jigs, including: Northland Fishing Tackle Fire-Ball Jig (A), with an attached stinger hook (B); Northland's Whistler Jig (C), Stand-Up Jig (D), Gum-Ball Jig (E), and Mimic Minnow Jig (F).

the crawler is bitten off, the angler sets the hook on—nothing. Northland Fishing Tackle makes a jig that solves this problem—the Fire-Ball Jig (see photo opposite) has as second "eye" for clipping in a "stinger" hook. This second hook trails behind the main hook and can be hooked into the night crawler further down its body, to snag those short-biting walleye.

As effective as they are, jigs don't always work on walleye. The best invention in recent years as an alternative fishing method to the jig is the Lindy rig, also called a live-bait rig, a slip-sinker rig, or just plain "rig" (see photo right). This approach separates the hook from the sinker by as much distance as the angler wants, and the sinker slides freely on the fishing line—it "slips," so that when a walleye picks up the bait, the angler feels the bite and lets line go to slide through the eye, or hole, in the sinker. The walleye doesn't detect the weight of the sinker, starts to swallow the bait, and the angler sets the hook.

Here's how the system works. Slide a slip sinker (several styles available) onto the end of your fishing line. Tie a small snap swivel to the end of the line. Take a second piece of monofilament line (6- to 10-pound-test is typi-

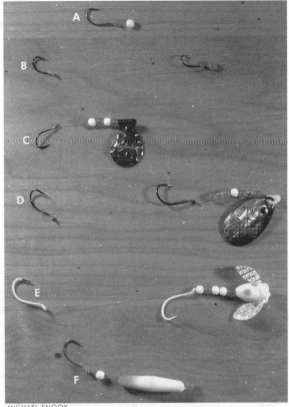

MICHAEL SNOOK

Live-bait fishing rigs, sometimes called Lindy rigs or just "bait rigs": a single-hook rig with a bright yellow attractor bead, suitable for use with leeches (A); a double-hook rig for night crawlers (B); a rig with a small, No. 1 blade, for use with leeches (C); a night-crawler rig with a larger, size 3 spinning blade (D); a night-crawler rig with an in-line Spin-n-Glo (E); and a single-hook rig for frozen minnows, larger leeches, or night crawlers, using an in-line float to keep bait off the bottom (F).

cal), the length that you want to use. The more finicky and wary the fish, the longer this piece of line, called a "snell," needs to be. Fishing big trophy walleye in fall—a time when lots of anglers on the water can put a lot of pressure on the fish—can call for snells as long as ten feet. On one end of the snell, tie one hook if you plan to fish with a live leech, or two hooks a few inches apart when fishing with night crawlers. Hooks should be in the No. 4 to No. 8 size range. The next step in the process depends on how you wish to fish. For the subtlest live-bait presentation, nothing other than a hook and bait is needed. Some anglers will thread on a small orange, yellow, green, or glow bead as an attractant or strike target. Floats can be threaded on to bring your bait up off the bottom. Alternatively, a shorter (up to four feet long), heavier (10- to 12-pound test) snell can be used, with a free-spinning blade on a clevis threaded on to make a "blade rig." These are useful for trolling at higher speeds for active fish, and are the live-bait equivalent of trolling with a crankbait.

An adaptation of the Lindy rigging system, particularly useful when fishing blade rigs, is the replacement of the slip sinker with a "bottom bouncer." This is basically a sinker with a long wire tail on the bottom end, and a loop at the top that allows an angler to clip it onto the fishing line. The wire tail bounces along the bottom, keeps your gear off the rocks and other bottom junk that can snag fishing lures and hooks, and imparts a jerky motion to the lure as the tail of the bouncer catches and releases from rocks, gravel and other obstacles. Bottom bouncers, which can be as light as ¼-ounce and as heavy as 3 or 4 ounces in weight, come in various sizes and designs. A recent innovation by Northland Fishing Tackle provides anglers with a heavy-duty plastic clevis, or clip, that slides on the line and bottom bouncers of varying weights that can be clipped on and off the clevis as fishing conditions vary—heavier weights for windier conditions or heavier current. This turns the bottom bouncer into a "slip sinker," and the angler using a rig like this can fish with greater finesse than with a traditional, fixed bottom bouncer that clips to the end of your fishing line.

Bottom bouncers can be used to pull any live bait right through rough terrain on the bottom of the lake or river, but they can also be used with crankbaits, as a kind of poor man's downrigger, to get floating or neutral-buoyancy lures down to the depth you want to fish at and keep them there. Running a minnow-imitating lure such as a Rapala or Berkley Frenzy lure five, ten, fifteen feet or more behind a bottom bouncer is a common technique used by walleye anglers in prairie lakes and reservoirs.

Walleye can also be caught trolling such lures in a more traditional manner. Again, a depth finder and knowledge of the behaviour of your favourite crankbait lure are essential. If walleye are found in twenty feet of water, holding just off bottom, then getting a lure down to that depth, and keeping it there, depends on the diving ability of the lure (most are rated right on the package they come in), the fishing line used (heavier pound test lines are thicker and tend to float up in the water), and the trolling speed used. A diving crankbait rated down to twenty feet, trolled at a mile to a mile and a half per hour, on 8- or 10-pound-test line (or on a super line such as FireLine that will give you line strengths in the 20-pound-test range with the thickness of 8-pound-test monofilament) should be nosing into bottom regularly as you troll along. If you can feel the lure bumping bottom, it's working right. If not, it needs some adjustment. Let out more line, clip on an in-line sinker, twenty-five feet or so ahead of your lure. Until its nose is kissing the bottom, it's less likely to catch walleye.

Particularly in fall, walleye anglers in Saskatchewan will troll crankbaits in depths from 12 to 30 feet (4 to 9 metres), searching for big trophy fish that are feeding heavily prior to winter. Anglers fishing in deeper waters should be aware that the walleye cannot adjust the pressure in its air bladder voluntarily as pike or lake trout can (these fish can "burp" air from their bladders as they rise in the water). Bringing a walleye up suddenly from thirty feet or deeper to the surface will result in the overinflation of the swim bladder and will likely injure the fish. Either retrieve more slowly to allow the fish to adjust, or simply avoid the problem by fishing in shallower water.

In some larger reservoirs, such as Lake Diefenbaker and Last Mountain Lake, walleye may be suspending in mid-lake, twenty feet down or more, in ninety feet of water. They are feeding on suspended, migratory schools of baitfish. It is possible to take these fish using downriggers or, alternatively, in-line weights, to take crankbait lures down to the precise depth needed to troll just above schools of feeding walleye. The techniques for fishing walleye this way have been pioneered on the Great Lakes, where huge schools of mid-lake fish can be found feeding on suspended baitfish. It is an approach less frequently used in the west, where schools of suspended fish are smaller and harder to locate. But it does work if you have the gear and the patience.

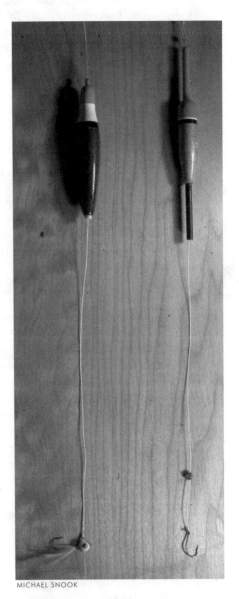

MICHAEL SNOOK

One more method for catching walleye is worth mentioning—bobber fishing. Traditionally, bobbers were of the clip-on variety. They attached firmly to your line, making them awkward to use in any depth greater than a few feet of water. Trying to cast out a bobber with ten or twelve feet of monofilament dangling below it, complete with hook, sinker and bait on the end, leads to a comedy of errors. Enter the slip bobber (see photo right). This bobber has a hole down the center of it, through which line flows freely. A rubber or knotted "bobber stop" is attached to your fishing line just above the bobber. By sliding it up or down the line, the depth at which you fish can be adjusted. And when you reel in, the bobber slips down the line all the way to the hook or jig at the end, so casting is a snap. Bobber fishing usually involves live-bait presentation. On Saskatchewan lakes, the

Slip bobbers.

most common bait used with slip bobbers is the ribbon leech. A very small jig, or a hook with a split shot crimped on the line a few feet up, sinks the leech into the water. The line stops at the bobber stop, and you're fishing. When the bobber dips into the water, it's time to set the hook. This is a particularly useful tactic to use when walleye are feeding in shallow water, where running a boat or casting larger lures might spook them. It's also useful when fishing for walleye in the weeds.

The vast majority of anglers will fish for walleye with jigs or live-bait rigs or by trolling minnow-imitating crankbaits. Success with any of these methods will be affected by the factors that influence walleye the most: seasonal variations and migration of fish, weather, and light levels. These three interact to determine whether the fishing is easy—or frustrating—on any given day.

Walleye migrate throughout the seasons, often traveling significant distances. Walleye were tagged in Coteau Bay of Lake Diefenbaker, at the most northerly end of the lake, for several years. This is a spawning area for walleye, and Saskatchewan Environment staff make use of it each spring to harvest eggs and sperm that is then used in their annual stocking program. The spawn harvest gave Sask Environment staff an ideal opportunity to tag and track fish movement. Fish tagged in the bay were found to have moved as far as 45 kilometres (over 25 miles) in just fifteen days. And some fish were found to have moved as far as 147 kilometres (over 90 miles) over the course of the summer. What drives the fish to move in this matter is not fully understood, but some things are known.

Walleye, like all living creatures, depend on food and shelter to stay alive. Their food consists of everything from hatching mayflies in late spring, to minnows, crayfish, and aquatic worms. Shelter for a walleye is a place to hide from potential predators—birds such as pelicans or cormorants—or larger predator fish like northern pike. It's also a place out of the current to rest and to lie in ambush for forage. Water temperature, too, is critical to walleye habitat. They seem to prefer water 18°C to 25°C (65°F to 75°F) and will seek this temperature in whatever body of water they inhabit.

There is a well-defined migratory pattern in Last Mountain Lake, a narrow, natural lake in southern Saskatchewan stretching 65 miles (110 kilometres). In spring, the two extreme ends of the lake are spawning areas. As spring breakup approaches, more and more walleye can be found in these areas. Post-spawn, the walleye will slowly move from spawning areas into large, shallow flats found at both ends of the lake, where the water warms quickly and where both forage fish and insect larvae can be found in late spring. As the water on these shallow flats warms and as the weed growth thickens, the fish begin to migrate north and south towards the cooler, deeper waters in the central reaches of the lake. They can be found off points and bars along the shoreline as they move, and their progress can be tracked by angler success at various points along the lake. The speed with which they move varies from year to year, depending on weather conditions. And their movement is always influenced by the presence, or absence, of forage in a given area. But the pattern is quite consistent. By mid to late summer—anytime after the last weekend of July—good concentrations of fish are found in an area of the lake centering on Rowan's Ravine Provincial Park. Fishing in this area will be good right through first ice, but by early January, the fish are on the move and ice anglers have to be mobile to find them. By late winter, they are starting to concentrate at the ends of the lake once again. Knowing this migration pattern can be a big help to fishing success on this particular lake.

On a day-by-day basis, walleye are influenced by light levels, wind, and other weather factors. Not much is known about the effect of weather on walleye, but observations by experienced anglers provide some insight. Several days in a row of stable summer weather, with light winds, a sky filled with puffy summer clouds, and consistent temperatures, appears to produce excellent walleye fishing. Unstable summer weather usually comes with a passing low pressure system, accompanied by heavy cloud cover, a change in wind direction (often from south or southwest to north or northwest), and thunder storms. It is not unusual for fishing to be very difficult immediately following the passage of such a low pressure system. Within a few days, if the weather returns to stable patterns, the fishing improves. There are plenty of theories about this, but no one can tell us why it happens.

Light levels influence walleye behaviour significantly. On overcast days with a reasonable chop, walleye can be caught in just a few feet of water, feeding on schools of minnows near shore. When the water surface is choppy, sunlight is diffused, and light levels below the surface are reduced. Overcast skies have the same effect on light levels. The darker it is below the surface the more advantage goes to the walleye. With its large, light-sensitive eyes, it can see better in low light conditions than both the fish it preys upon and those which prey upon it. Thus it's safer, and more productive, for walleye to feed in shallow water on windy, overcast days than on clear, calm ones. A steady wind from one direction will create currents that move baitfish to one side or one area of a lake, and walleye will follow the food. Although walleye can be caught at any time of the day or night, there is no question that the low light periods just before and after dawn and dusk, are peak feeding times for this fish. Again, walleye have adapted to take advantage of their superior sight in low light conditions. The early morning walleye bite is a great time to be on the water. Cool temperatures, usually light winds, and often great fishing, make it a peak time of day for anglers, one no one should miss.

YELLOW PERCH

The perch is a close cousin of the walleye, and one of the most popular game fish in Saskatchewan. Although it is occasionally found in moving water, the perch is most commonly found in lakes and reservoirs, and has been stocked by Saskatchewan Environment in a number of ponds in southern Saskatchewan that are managed as recreational "put and take" fisheries.

If the walleye is the largest member of the perch family, the yellow perch is on the smaller end of the scale. However it is a great panfish, with 8- to 10-inchers commonly caught, and perch over a foot long taken every year, particularly through the ice in winter. Perch is the species most sought-after by Saskatchewan ice anglers.

In open-water fishing, the perch is generally found deeper than walleye, and relating strongly to classic structure—points, reefs, deeper holes. Like the walleye, it prefers cooler water, so finding a deep, cold spring in summer means finding perch. Although it is often caught incidentally by walleye anglers fishing with live bait using Lindy rigs, the most common technique used for catching summer perch is to anchor over a school and jig.

Perch are a schooling fish, and the schools are often large. Find one and you find many, which makes perch fishing a natural for beginning anglers and young children. Any light- to medium-action spinning or casting rod with a spinning, baitcasting or spincast reel spooled with 6- to 10-pound-test line will work fine for perch. Lighter line, lighter rods and reels, and light jigs make perch fishing more fun. The ideal perch fishing rig would consist of a five-foot ultralight spinning rod, spooled with 4-pound-test line, using a ⅛-ounce jig for a lure, tipped with a live leech, a small chunk of night crawler, or a bit of Berkley Power Bait moulded onto the hook. As they do for pond rainbows, some anglers will use cheese, marshmallow, corn, or small slices of liver or other organ meats as bait for perch. When they are biting, they will take almost anything—including jigs tipped with plastic grubs, with no edible bait attached at all.

Any number of styles or colours of jig will work for perch, but bright colours, particularly combinations of yellow and orange, yellow and green, black and white, or red and orange, seem to be more attractive than single colour jigs. (The same, it should be noted, is true for walleye). Small jigs, up to ¼-ounce in size, are preferable.

Perch can be very aggressive feeders. I was trolling just before dusk on one of the lakes on the Qu'Appelle River, using a 6-inch Rapala for walleye. The first fish I caught on this lure was an 8-pound northern pike. The second was a 5-inch perch, slightly smaller than the bait itself. In case you think this was an accidental snag, that little perch had the head of the crankbait in its mouth and was caught on the front hook of the lure. That's no accident. That perch had great ambitions. I was able to release it without harm, but if it continues to be that aggressive, it won't survive long anyway—it will end up on someone else's hook when it's a couple of inches longer and be on its way to the frying pan. Perch are excellent eating, with a firm, sweet, white flesh (they're not called "panfish" for nothing), and once they reach a size of about 20 centimetres (8 inches) or longer, are easy to clean and fillet.

Perch can also be extremely light biters, with very sensitive mouths. Thus it's best to fish for them with smaller jigs with smaller hook sizes. In addition to traditional round-head jigs, a number of tackle manufacturers make small spoons that are effective perch lures. These include the Hawger Spoon, Deadly Dick, and Northland Tackle's Buckshot Rattle Spoon, Thumper Jig, Feathered Whistler Jig, and Gypsi Jig. Many of the same small jigs and lures that are effective in summer are equally potent lures for ice anglers (see Chapter 6). In either summer or winter, electronic sonar is an indispensable tool for finding schools of perch, determining what depth they are at, and keeping track of them as they move about.

Perch are spunky fighters for their size—fun to catch, great to eat, and well worth fishing for.

TACKLE BASICS FOR FISHING IN SASKATCHEWAN

No one likes to spend money on tackle that isn't going to be used. Many anglers try to get by with just one, all-purpose fishing rod. If this is your preference, the one to have for fishing in Saskatchewan is a 6½- to 7-foot, two-piece, medium-action spinning rod, rated for line from 6- to 12-pound test, with a spinning reel sized to match the rod and line. This will be a bit too big a rig for small trout, smaller perch, and finesse presentations. It will be a bit on the light side for the really big pike and lake trout of our northern lakes—those weighing 11 to 13 kilograms (25 to 30 pounds). But it will work pretty well for everything in between.

It makes little sense, though, to travel a long distance, or spend a lot of money and time on a fishing trip, and skimp on the gear you need to catch fish. Rod and reel combinations tuned to each species you're fishing for would be ideal, but may take some time to acquire. The following three combinations will cover most of the fishing situations found in Saskatchewan: an ultralight spinning rod, about 5 feet long, with a small spinning reel to match the rod, and 4- to 8-pound-test line—for panfish, small trout, small walleye; a 6½-foot medium-action spinning rod, with a reel sized to match, and 6- to 12-pound-test line—for walleye, smaller pike, larger rainbow trout; and a medium to medium-heavy, 7-foot casting rod, with a baitcasting reel sized to match, spooled with 12- to 17-pound-test line, for trolling for larger walleye, lake trout, pike, or for casting heavier spoons.

A multi-species tackle box should contain jigs in various weights from ⅛ ounce up to ½ ounce, in a variety of colours; trolling and casting spoons such as DarDevle or Len Thompson, 3 to 5 inches in size, in various colours (be sure to include red-and-white and five-of-diamonds patterns); crankbaits ranging in size from 3 inches to 8 inches or longer, some floating, some sinking, some shallow diving, some deep diving, in various colours (be sure to include perch, crawdad, firetiger, and some combination with blue as a dominant colour); pre-tied live-bait rigs (Lindy Rigs), including blade rigs, in both single- and double-hook styles, in various lengths—or better still, materials so that you can tie up your own as you like them; plastic tails of various sizes from tiny grubs to 6-inch worms (particularly scented brands, such as Berkley Power Bait); spare swivels, snaps, and leaders; bottom bouncers in weights from ½-ounce to 3 ounces; slip sinkers in various sizes from ¼ ounce to 1½ ounces; slip bobbers and bobber stops; spare spools for your fishing reels, some spare line, a good pocket knife, line clippers, and a good pair of long needle-nose pliers for hook removal. There are lots of other bits and pieces to include, but this is a good start to a basic tackle box. (See specific tackle lists in Appendix C and Appendix D).

The most complex and most expensive piece of fishing tackle you'll ever own is a fishing boat. They come in all shapes, sizes, colours, and materials. The cost of a fishing boat can range from a few thousand dollars for a twelve-foot tin cartopper and motor suited to protected bodies of water of modest size, to tens of thousands of dollars for a twenty-foot tournament boat rigged with a motor of 150 horsepower or larger, trolling motors, and several depth finders. Between these two extremes, there is a modest boat that will serve most of your needs.

To fish most waters in Saskatchewan, a boat no smaller than 5 metres (16 feet) long is recommended. Prairie waters are exposed to the wind—most summers, a cartopper will spend more time on your car top than in the water. But a 16-footer, equipped with at least a 25-horsepower motor, is enough boat for a cautious and practiced boat driver to handle most Saskatchewan waters on all but the roughest days. All boats, no matter how big or small, must be equipped with the necessary safety devices: life jackets for all aboard, a manual bailing device, a signaling whistle or horn, a rescue throw rope that floats, and on larger boats, signal flares and fire extinguishers.

Boats are more than just a dry ride to and from your favourite fishing hole. A good boat is a fishing platform, an essential part of your strategy for presenting bait or lure to the fish in the best way possible. Whether you're anchored, drifting, or trolling, controlling the position, speed, and maneuverability of your boat is critical to a successful day fishing. One of the best tools available for controlling your boat is the electric trolling motor. An electric trolling motor—matched in size to your boat and bow-mounted, stern-mounted, or, preferably, both—allows precision boat control in any direction in all but the windiest conditions.

Anchors aren't often thought of as tools for boat control, but they can be invaluable if you are trying to fish precisely over a small area with lots of fish. One anchor lets you stop your boat where you want to. Two anchors lets you position it so that the wind doesn't swing you away from where you want to be. A good sonar unit (Lowrance, Eagle, Garmin, Humminbird) in combination with a GPS receiver will enable you to find the fish, and stay on them.

All of this, with the addition of some rod holders, a livewell to keep your fish in, and downriggers if you need them, finishes the list. In southern waters, where lake bottoms are more likely to be sand and silt than rock, and where sand beaches are easily found, anglers use a wide variety of both aluminum and fibreglass boats. The further north you travel in Saskatchewan, the more rocks you're going to encounter, both in the water and on shore. In northern waters, the aluminum boat is king. The most popular boat on the water in Saskatchewan, no matter where you travel, is the well-respected Lund aluminum boat, from utilitarian guide boats at a northern fishing camp to high-tech tournament boats on the Saskatchewan Walleye Trail. Regardless of what model you choose, a well-equipped and properly rigged, well-maintained fishing boat is a safe boat, a joy to fish in, and a comfortable way to spend a day on the water.

CHAPTER FIVE
FLY-FISHING IN SASKATCHEWAN

GARY PARÉ

The author fly-fishing on Last Mountain Lake.

W hen the words "fly fishing" are spoken, the images that come to mind are mountain streams, lakes tucked between snow-capped peaks, freestone creeks and rivers, spring creeks, and blue-ribbon rivers like the Bow or the Yellowstone. In a province most often thought of as flat, dry, and dusty, you might be tempted to hang up the old fly rod, taking it out only on those rare occasions when you travel to greener and wetter pastures. But if you overlook the fly-fishing opportunities in Saskatchewan, you will be missing some of the finest fishing the province has to offer.

From the southern reaches of Saskatchewan, where it's possible to take largemouth bass on popper flies and streamers, to the farthest northern outpost, where grayling sip surface flies and quick-moving nymphs, fly-fishing gear will serve you well throughout the province. Most of the descriptions of where to fish in Saskatchewan are to be found later in this book, but because of the special nature of our fly-fishing destinations, some are described in this chapter.

There are plenty of places in Saskatchewan for fly fishers to practice their sport in a traditional manner, applying well-known techniques to catching the usual trout species. However, there is no reason for fly fishers to restrict themselves to these conventional pursuits. Many of the sport fish in Saskatchewan can be taken on fly-fishing gear with just a few modifications to tackle and technique. There are a myriad of books written on the subject of taking trout with flies, and not much need for me to add more than a few words to the collection. But non-typical species are another matter, and they are half the fun of fly-fishing in Saskatchewan.

BROOK, BROWN, TIGER, CUTTHROAT, RAINBOW, TIGER TROUT AND SPLAKE

As mentioned above, trout species, the most commonly sought by fly fishers, have been the subject of entire volumes of fishing literature. Books by renowned anglers such as Roderick Haig Brown, Lefty Kreh, Ernie Schwiebert, Lee Wulff, and J. Edson Leonard are particularly recommended for anyone wanting to learn more about the art of fishing for trout with flies. Several of these publications are listed in Appendix F.

These trout species have been stocked in various water bodies in Saskatchewan (see details later in this chapter), and a few general notes on tackle used to fish them here will assist both the visiting and resident angler in gearing up for a fly-fishing trip in this province.

Fly anglers are well advised to carry two fly rods with them. Because many of our stocked waters are small streams in heavily wooded or brushy areas, a small, 7-foot, 4-weight (or less) fly rod for casting in tight quarters will be useful. However, these species are also found in more open settings, in small lakes and ponds that are subject to significant prairie breezes. On windy days, a 9-foot, 7-weight fly rod, loaded with weight-forward line, is essential gear for casting light flies.

Trout, and particularly brown trout, are easily spooked by either movement or vibration. Many of Saskatchewan's trout streams are small, intimate places to fish, and demand stealth and patience from the angler. When fishing from the bank, keep low—I know anglers who belly-crawl up to the edge of a stream to keep their shadow off the water, and move with a light step. A clumsy footfall will panic skittish trout away from the pool you want to fish before you even get there.

If you are wading a small stream, always work upstream, against the current, and fish to undisturbed trout in the pool above you. The stuff your wading boots kick loose from the bottom will drift downstream, away from the trout you are fishing, and back into the pools you've already worked.

As every fly fisher knows, there are days when trout simply do not show their noses on the surface of the water. To reach these fish, which are feeding on nymphs, larvae or small minnows below the water's surface, anglers have to get down to where the fish are.

MICHAEL SNOOK

Various flies used in Saskatchewan, including: streamer patterns (A); caddis pattern dry flies (B); ants (C); small wooly buggers (D); humpy patterns (E); marabou leech patterns (F); muddler minnow (G), and generic nymph patterns (H).

In small streams, a floating line rigged with a sinking leader and tippet, or a lightly weighted fly, will do the trick. In larger waters, where the trout may be lying several metres deep, sinking-tip fly lines are a must.

Some of Saskatchewan's trout streams are so small and overgrown that casting is virtually impossible. In this case, anglers may have to break the "fish upstream" rule, and enter each pool at its upstream end from the bank. Let out a few metres of fly line and use the length of the fly rod to lift and drop the fly onto the surface, letting the current carry it downstream. Or, working upstream, reach out as far as your arm and the fly rod allow, drop the fly on the water, and let it drift back down to you. This "dapping" technique lets an angler fish uncastable waters very thoroughly.

More has been written about the selection of flies for trout than any other fly-fishing subject. In general, anglers chasing these trout species in Saskatchewan should have with them a selection of dry flies in sizes No. 12 to No. 22 that include Caddis flies, Humpies, mosquito imitations, and similar patterns. A number of nymph patterns, such as the Doc Spratley and Carey Special, are effective. In larger bodies of water where trout may be feeding on leeches, patterns such as the Wooly Bugger or Marabou Leech, in dark brown, black, and dark olive, will take trout when everything else fails.

SAB RA 5370

Fly casting for Arctic grayling on the Black Birch River near Careen Lake in northern Saskatchewan (June 1954).

ARCTIC GRAYLING

Arctic grayling are a dream fish for fly fishers. Like trout, they feed heavily on insects: mayflies, caddis flies, the nymphal stage of several insects, even hoppers and ants, are welcome fare. And so are the flies that imitate them. I've had the most luck with a generic nymph pattern tied mostly with pheasant tail feathers for grayling feeding below the surface, and there are days on northern waters when a tiny mosquito imitation is just the right thing to tempt a grayling to strike. Olive, black, and grey are attractive colours. Casting to pocket water—a still spot in the middle of the stream behind a boulder or other obstacle, or to current edges—will find grayling if they're in the neighbourhood. Some of the best fishing I've had for grayling has come in the early morning just after dawn, and around twilight, particularly when fishing for these beautiful fish in the still water of northern lakes.

SAB RB 848

Fly casting from a rock at Hunt Falls (or Lefty's Falls) on the Grease River (June 1954).

CARP

Carp are a relatively new sport-fishing phenomenon in Saskatchewan. European anglers have long known the virtues of this fish that, while not the most photogenic creature, fights like a cross between a northern pike and a freight train. Introduced to Saskatchewan in the last century, carp have adapted very well to its waters.

It was a near perfect June day when I took my first carp on fly-fishing tackle. The water was like glass—calm, clean, and clear—and all morning I had been watching carp—big carp—swimming by the spot on the shoreline where we had set up for the day. The fish would come by in twos and threes; every few minutes or so a new group would come into view. These carp were migrating along the

Rob Schulz (left) and the author (right) netting a large carp caught with fly-fishing tackle on Last Mountain Lake, July 2000.

shoreline, probably heading into the shallow back bay behind us where, in a frothy, showy, splashy way, the spring spawn was underway.

I was there with friend and outfitter Robert Schulz. Robert runs the marina at Rowan's Ravine on Last Mountain Lake in southern Saskatchewan, a less-than-forty-five-minute drive from Regina. Two of the other anglers present that day had come a lot further. Their plane had landed at the Regina airport late the previous evening, the end of a long flight from the United Kingdom. This father and son had come across the Atlantic and more than halfway across Canada to fish for carp in a prairie lake that most locals take for granted.

Carp are common throughout both the South Saskatchewan and Qu'Appelle river drainages in south Saskatchewan. And because they have been viewed by anglers for so long as "trash fish," they have been pretty much left alone. A few archers keep their eyes keen by bowfishing for carp in the shallows in spring. A few anglers have learned the European techniques for bank fishing and ledgering for these big brawlers (see page 43), but carp are not exactly subject to a lot of fishing pressure.

Carp are a superb fighting fish and in Saskatchewan, if you get on the water at the right place at the right time of year, you stand a good chance of catching multiple fish each day in the 10- to 15-kilogram (20- to 30-pound) class. That, to a dedicated carp angler, is a bit like the average walleye angler catching a half-dozen walleyes over 5 kilograms (10 pounds) in a day's angling. The right time is late spring and summer. The right place is shoreline adjacent to shallow sloughs or inlets connected to the main lake.

The carp found in Saskatchewan is the common carp, *Cyprinus carpio*, big-scaled, barbelled at the corners of his mouth, broad shouldered, and inordinately fond of muddy-bottomed, weedy water. He's one of several carp family members, including the mirror carp and the grass carp (or amur). The carp was first introduced to North America from Germany in the 1870s. Stocking continued in the United States, and carp spread almost universally across North America. Whether the fish in southern Saskatchewan are direct descendants of these original imports is impossible to know. What is clear is that carp like it here. They do very well indeed, their range limited only by their intolerance for much colder water temperatures in the more northerly reaches of the province.

Carp migrate along shorelines. If you can get their attention so that they stop and eat, then you have a chance of catching one. The mythology about carp is that they are garbage fish, sucking feed off the mucky bottom of the lake. The truth is that carp are omnivorous. They are a top predator that will browse on minnows, insects, fish eggs, crayfish, leeches, larvae, even cottonwood and thistle seeds—and sweetened kernels of corn lying on the bottom of the lake. If these fish will eat larvae, flying insects, beetles, bugs, and seeds, then they'll take a fly—some kind of fly.

Fly-fishing is a game of matching the hatch. There has to be a hatch to match of course, and on this particular fine June day, there was no sign of life on the surface or under it. No hatching mayflies, no beetles, ants, hoppers or backswimmers on the surface. I tied on a cottonwood seed imitation, but had seen no carp sipping anything on the surface. A leech pattern proved ineffective, as did a crayfish imitation and a streamer. Carp would swim by and stop to drop their noses to the bottom where they inhaled kernels of corn from the last bit of chumming by the outfitter.

Match the hatch. If the carp are feeding on corn, then feed them corn. In my flybox, I had three experimental flies, tied from a simple pattern using bright yellow chenille, ribbed with white thread and lightly weighted. I tied one on and cast it into the chummed corn and waited—a corn-fly hiding in the midst of the real thing, a hook in corn clothing.

A group of three carp swam slowly along the shoreline. One ran well over 15 kilograms (30 pounds), one about 10 (20 pounds), and the third was a small fish, in the 5-kilogram (10-pound) range. All three stopped and started slurping up corn. The middle one veered to the right, to the area where I had cast my fly, and picked it up.

Fighting a carp is a patience game, especially with a fly rod. A 10-foot, 8-weight rod has plenty of power to turn a fish, and plenty of flex to take up the shocks, but a tippet of only 8-pound test means taking your time, going slow, not forcing anything. Each run was a straight line away from shore, no turns, just a fast, strong fish headed where it wanted to go. Three, four, five, six runs. Still, the fish was too green to turn. Finally, it came near the surface, splashed a bit, and came in the direction of the rod tip. After fifteen minutes, the carp came to the net. It weighed in at just over 9 kilograms (a hair under 20 pounds), and swam briskly away when we released it.

Some of the carp in the shallow inlet behind us were feeding with nose down and tail up—called "tailing." Still others were sipping something off the surface. Carp are often compared to saltwater bonefish. Both species will feed on or near bottom, both tail when feeding in shallow water, both are very wary, and when caught, fight like mad. We moved to try our luck with the carp in the inlet.

This time a seed pattern fly elicited several near misses. Carp are smart and easily spooked. They will scare easily with just a bit of splash from your leader or fly, and the shadow of your line cast overhead is enough to turn them. If you are false casting a lot, you are probably spooking more fish than you'll catch. Because carp have good eyesight, they can probably see the angler on the bank, they can almost certainly see the angler's movement, and if the shadow of your line spooks them, your own shadow certainly will. Like most fish, carp are also quite sensitive to vibration. If you are wading and casting, move slowly and quietly. Carp have a highly developed sense of taste and smell, so avoid contaminating your bait, your tackle, or your hands, with strong or sharp smelling substances like gasoline, insect repellent, tobacco, or sunblock. Use a no-scent soap before handling your gear.

By the end of the day, several carp have come to the fly. One has come to the net. Another has broken me off. All will swim away to see another day.

Useful flies for carp include scud patterns, leech patterns, terrestrials, generic mayfly larvae, and imitations of seed such as cottonwood and thistle. For a good selection of fly patterns, along with great information on carp and their behaviour, see *Carp on the Fly* by Barry Reynolds, Brad Befus, and John Berriman (1997). To find out more about fly-fishing for carp on Last Mountain Lake, contact Rob Schulz at G & S Marina Outfitters, at 306-725-4466.

LAKE TROUT

Most anglers pursue lake trout with trolling spoons or minnow-imitating lures like the Rapala, or Berkley's Frenzy lures. In summer, when lakers go deep, heavy jigs, lead-core line, or diving aids like the Pink Lady, get baits and lures down to where the fish are.

But lake trout can be taken readily with flies at certain times of the year, adding yet another species to the fly fisher's repertoire. In spring and fall, when northern waters are cold near the surface, lake trout can be found in shallow water as little as 2 or 3 metres (6 or 8 feet) deep. A few years back, I was fishing Close Lake in northern Saskatchewan with a few friends. It was a cool, blustery, fall day in early September, and the lake trout were moving into shallow water. We found them in less than three metres of water along a rocky shoreline. After a couple of hours of casting and trolling Len Thompson spoons, I surprised our guide by putting down my spinning rod and rigging up a 9-foot, 9-weight fly rod that I also use for northern pike. A 9-foot, 8-pound-test leader, tipped with 30 centimetres (1 foot) of light, plastic-coated wire, was attached to a full-sinking line. I tied on a fly usually used for pike—a big streamer, made with red and yellow synthetic bucktail hair, about 15 centimetres (6 inches) long—and cast the line out behind the 16-foot Lund we were fishing from. These big streamer flies are usually tied on No. 1 to 1/0-sized hooks, and it's a good idea to use two hooks tied in tandem.

I trolled the big fly behind the boat, pumping the line occasionally to give the fly a bit more movement in the water. The guide's opinion was that I was wasting my time, but an hour and a half and sixteen lake trout later, I set the fly rod down and took a break. It was the first time fly tackle had been used to take lake trout at that particular fishing lodge, but I suspect it wasn't the last.

The principle that makes this tackle work is simple. Lake trout feed on minnows and small fish. Anything that imitates this natural source of food is likely to arouse a trout's interest. That's why shiny and brightly coloured metal spoons, or minnow-imitating baits such as the Frenzy, work. A large streamer fly, tied in similar colours, has the same effect, and the flowing, rippling movement of the synthetic hair through the water is an even more lifelike lure.

The lake trout I caught that day were all between 3.5 and 5.5 kilograms (8 to 12 pounds), a treat to catch on fly tackle. The wire tippet is essential gear, because lake trout will often roll over and over when caught, wrapping your line around themselves, and the razor-sharp rear edge of their gill covers cuts through most fishing line in a flash. A soft, plastic-coated wire tippet will keep the fly on your line and the fish on the hook.

I strongly recommend barbless hooks when fishing for lake trout, because it makes releasing them much easier. Just keep a tight line and the barbless hook will hold the fish as well as a barbed one.

MICHAEL SNOOK

Large streamer flies used for northern pike and lake trout.

NORTHERN PIKE

Fly fishermen have been taking northern pike on light tackle for years, and fly patterns for northerns are readily available, not that difficult to make if you tie your own, and very effective.

In the same way that you can cast a floating crankbait into the shallows in spring and get a northern to come charging up from the depths to get it, you can entice them to strike a large streamer-style pike fly. One of the most productive times to fish for pike with flies is late spring, when the waters of south-facing bays and shallows are producing new weed growth, and young-of-the-year minnows are present. Casting a Dahlberg Diver, or similar pattern, towards the new weed growth from deeper water will often catch the attention of a hungry northern. Don't be overly concerned with technique—the slap of these big flies on the water is part of their appeal. Cast out, let the fly sit for a bit, then twitch across and under the water on the retrieve. Northern pike will come powering up from the depths to take these flies, so be prepared for an explosive strike.

As lake water warms, pike head for cooler depths, and anglers switch techniques to trolling with plugs and spoons. The same techniques work with fly-fishing gear. Use a full sinking line and big streamer patterns made up in the same colours as your favourite pike spoon or plug. These are large, sparsely tied bugs, 10 to 15 centimetres (4 to 6 inches) in length, meant to imitate baitfish and young-of-the-year sport fish. Trolling big flies in productive pike waters is just as effective as any other technique.

WALLEYE

Walleye, too, can be taken with fly-fishing tackle, though they're more difficult than other non-traditional species. In spring, when they are still schooled up and before their post-spawn dispersal throughout the lake or river they live in, walleye can be caught in good numbers by anglers casting leech imitations and fishing them—as always with walleye—near bottom. A weighted Wooly Bugger pattern, cast on a sinking tip line, will probably be enough to get down to the fish during the spring of the year. The leech imitation should be swum in short jerks across the bottom, with pauses between retrieves. Strikes will most often come during the pauses, or just as the next short retrieve starts.

GEARING UP

RODS, REELS, AND LINES

The following list of basic gear for fly-fishing under varied conditions, and for both typical and non-typical species, is a start. Many of the smaller trout-holding creeks in the province are small enough to leap across, and many run through heavily brushed sections. Light to ultralight tackle shines under these conditions. A 6-foot rod, rated for 4-weight line or lighter, with a reel sized to match, allows an angler to work tight quarters, or drop a cast with the lightest touch on small waters. For fishing a dry fly on clear, shallow waters, fine, long (9- to 12-foot) leaders on double-tapered floating lines are ideal. Sinking tips and shorter leaders meet the demands of deeper running waters and nymphing techniques. Where tight cover prevents even a good roll cast from working, fly anglers may have to "dap"—drop the fly on the surface of the water and allow the line to follow it downstream with the current—in order to get their fly to the fish.

Fishing ponds or open sections of streams in the southern prairies often means fishing in the wind. Here, an 8- or 9-foot, 6- or 7-weight rod, equipped with a weight forward line, allows fishing to continue even in a stiff breeze.

Fishing for larger, non-traditional species like trout, pike, or carp, requires equipment adapted to the task. If you are going to chase big bruisers with fly-fishing tackle, a 9- to 10-foot, 9- or 10-weight rod, with a large reel capable of holding 150 metres (500 feet) of backing, is a wise choice. This heavier tackle lets you take on big, hard-fighting fish, but it also makes it possible to fish the large, open, windy lakes where these species are found. Heavier leaders (at least 6-pound tippet, preferably stronger) are needed if you're going to try for trout or carp, and light steel wire tippets tied into the working end of a stiff leader will keep northern pike from biting off your favourite streamer fly.

You may find yourself casting to surface feeders, trolling deep, or trolling shallow for these species, so floating, sinking-tip and full-sinking fly lines are all necessary equipment.

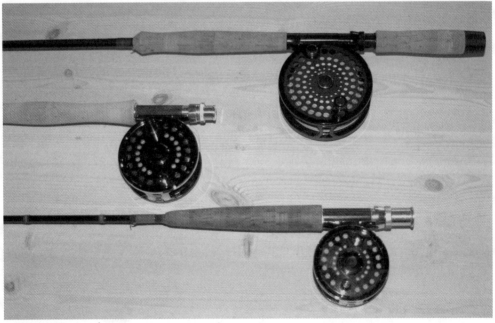

MICHAEL SNOOK

Fly reels made by Fenwick: the reels match the rod size; the largest is suitable for catching lake trout and northern pike, the smallest is ideal for a 7-foot, 4-weight rod used for small stream trout.

FLIES

Since I moved to Saskatchewan from Eastern Canada nearly two decades ago, my collection of flies has grown immensely. The reason for this excess is simple—a broad range of fishing conditions, and species to fish for, calls for a wide-ranging choice of sizes, types and patterns of fly to fish with.

Here are a few patterns that no hopeful fly fisher in Saskatchewan should ever be without. At the top of the list is the Marabou Leech, in black, dark brown, or olive. Rainbow trout will take this pattern; so will brook trout, so will browns. Get them in the right mood and you can take a largemouth bass or a walleye on a leech pattern. And while northern pike tend to prefer large, more brightly coloured flies, at the right time, a big Marabou Leech will fool a northern as easily as anything else you might toss its way.

The Wooly Bugger, the Carey Special, and the Doc Spratley are all extremely effective nymph/wet fly patterns that work as well in moving water as in still. The Humpy and Elk Hair Caddis will suit many of your dry fly needs on Saskatchewan waters.

Give a list like this to any dedicated fly fisher, and you'll get an argument, or another list, in no time at all. If you are a fly-tyer, the recipes for tying these flies follows. If not, they are readily available by mail order or through local tackle shops that carry fly-fishing gear.

CAREY SPECIAL

Like many modern fly patterns, this one has been adapted to various fishing habitats and situations. It can be tied as a large nymph or small minnow imitation, or to fool a trout into thinking it is an emerging caddis. Here is the recipe for the nymph pattern, which should be fished across and downstream:

Hook:	1X or 2X long wet fly hook, sizes 8–14
Thread:	black, orange/red, brown
Tail:	ringneck pheasant tail fibres
Rib:	oval gold tinsel
Body:	3 wound strands of peacock herl
Hackle:	ringneck pheasant rump

This fly can be tied in a weighted version, with a few wraps of lead tied around the hook in the thorax area of the fly, as an underbody.
And here it is tied as an emerging caddis. Fish to imitate the emerger, which rises quickly from the bottom towards the surface:

Hook:	1X or 2X long wet fly hook, size 8–14
Thread:	black
Rib:	medium silver tinsel
Body:	chenille, green, or to match the hatch
Hackle:	grizzly

DOC SPRATLEY

There are a number of versions of this tried and true nymph pattern that is effective on rainbow as well as Brown Trout. The version here is popular and easy to tie.

Hook:	1X or 2X long wet fly hook, size 6–14
Thread:	red/orange, olive, or black
Tail:	grizzly hackle fibres
Rib:	flat silver or gold tinsel
Body:	black dubbing or wool
Wing:	ringneck pheasant tail fibres
Hackle/legs:	grizzly neck, tied back along sides and bottom
Head:	peacock herl

GENERIC NYMPH

Hook:	1X or 2X long wet fly hook, size 6–16
Thread:	black, dark brown, olive
Tail:	pheasant tail fibers
Body:	olive or dark green mohair wool
Rib:	none, or fine peacock herl
Legs:	a few pheasant tail fibres
Head:	peacock herl, or thread

MARABOU LEECH

This effective pattern imitates a ribbon leech, food source for trout species wherever the two are found together. This is particularly effective in beaver ponds and stocked ponds, which are ideal leech habitat.

Hook:	3X or 4X long nymph or wet fly hook, size 4–12
Thread:	black, dark brown, olive
Tail:	marabou, same colour as body
Body:	black yarn, chenille, dubbing, with marabou tied in clumps to form "wing"
Beard:	optional, red hen hackle fibres, Crystal Flash, Flashabou

Fish this fly to swim it with the undulating motion of a ribbon leech. In some waters, dark or reddish brown is a better colour than black.

WOOLY BUGGER

This pattern imitates many insects and crustaceans, from dragonfly nymphs, to leeches, to crayfish.

Hook:	2X or 3X long, size 2–14
Thread:	To match body colour
Tail:	marabou, same colour as the body
Body:	chenille, yarn or dubbing, various colours
Hackle:	usually grizzly, palmered through the body, tied in by the tip

The wooly bugger is commonly fished on or near the bottom, fished in an undulating manner, with alternating short and long tugs of line. The fly can be tied in either unweighted or weighted versions.

HUMPY

This is a high floating, very durable dry fly that is particularly suited to rambunctious currents and rough water. It can be equally well fished in quiet waters.

Hook:	standard dry fly hook, sizes 6–16
Thread:	yellow, orange, green, white, black, 6/0
Tail:	moose body hair
Underbody:	match thread
Body/Wing:	deer or elk hair
Hackle:	grizzly

There is a trick to tying the deer or elk hair body and wing of this fly. Once the moose hair tail fibres have been tied in, select a bunch of deer or elk hair, cut to twice the length of the hook shank. If you use too much, the fly will be too bulky and tough to tie. Too little, and it will look sparse, thin. Trial and error will give you a feel for quantity. Clip the butt ends of the hair square, and tie in the clump, tips extending out over the tail, leaving about a quarter of an inch of space behind the eye of the hook for finishing the head of the fly. Wrap the hair with thread to the bend of the hook, tie in the floss for the underbody. Return the thread to the butts of the deer hair. Wrap the floss to create the underbody. Bend the deer hair so the tips come forward. Tie the fibres to the hook shank, just in front of the butts. Bend the hair tips up and wrap in front of them to keep them in place. Tie the grizzly hackle in front of the wing, wrap a few turns, then tie it off. Complete the fly with a thread head. This is the only method that allows for the deer hair to be held securely, to form the humped body, and the "wing".

ELK HAIR CADDIS

A dry fly to imitate the tent-shaped wing of a caddis fly on the surface.

Hook:	dry fly hook, sized 10–18
Thread:	black, brown or tan
Rib:	fine gold wire
Body:	dubbed tan, brown, olive, gray, or yellow
Hackle:	brown or dun
Wing:	elk hair or fine deer hair for smaller flies

Effective for most trout species when caddis flies are hatching, and resting on the surface.

GETTING AROUND

Fly fishers tend to get closer to their favourite species—especially trout—than most other anglers. Whether you use waders or float tube, float boat or canoe, or whether you walk along the shore—getting there can be far more than half the fun.

The simplest way for a flyfisher to get to the fish is on foot—walking the banks of a favourite stream or pond. No fancy gear required here—running shoes, hiking boots, rubber boots—whatever suits the terrain and keeps your feet comfortable for a full day of fishing will do. Best, though, to remember the advice of experienced fly fishers everywhere—walk very lightly, and keep your shadow off the water if you want to catch fish. I know anglers who will crawl the last twenty metres to their favourite stretch of creek on hands and knees to avoid casting their shadow on the water. And every heavy footfall you make will send vibrations streaming out through the water you haven't fished yet, spooking wary trout.

Waders—neoprene for cold water, lightweight Gore-Tex for the hot days of summer—will put you right in the water with the fish. They allow you to explore water in a way that looking at it from the bank never will. Most wading anglers work their way upstream, in order to be walking through and disturbing, water they've already fished. Tread lightly, but tread carefully. Whether you are wearing boot-foot waders or wading shoes, a loose or algae-covered rock on the bottom can turn an ankle as quickly as a trout can scoot for cover. The long hike back to your vehicle can become an arduous expedition in a split second.

When venturing out into deeper waters or quick currents, wise waders carry a wading staff. An adaptation of the walking stick, the staff not only helps you keep your balance; it also gives you a probe to check the bottom just ahead for obstacles and depth. If you fish water that is big, fast, and deep, wade only with great caution, wearing a life jacket or personal flotation device (PFD) and carrying a wading staff. Anyone who wades deep or fast-water streams or rivers without scouting them first and learning as much as possible about them from more seasoned anglers or locals is asking for trouble of the worst kind. Wadeable waters in Saskatchewan range from small and safe to big, boisterous and dangerous. If the water looks too tough to handle, it probably is, and this calls for more suitable gear.

For ponds and lakes too big to work properly from shore, there's nothing like the float tube (or belly boat) to get you to

MICHAEL SNOOK

Regina angler Robert Skinner fishing from a float tube.

the fish. Basically an inner tube wrapped in a cover that includes a seat for the angler, the belly boat is propelled by your two legs and a pair of swim fins. A good float tube will have enough built-in pockets to carry your gear, will be large enough to float you at the water's surface, and will be shaped so that finning through the water doesn't feel like swimming the English Channel after only a few minutes. Float tube safety issues are obvious—a big wind will blow you where *it* wants, not where *you* want, and a hole in that inner tube will sink you fast. Wear a life jacket at all times and keep an eye on the weather.

In situations where deep water and river current make a float tube impractical, the float boat comes into its own. Little more than a platform perched on a couple of pontoons, these craft are light enough, tough enough, and mobile enough to be pushed around beautifully with a small pair of oars. They keep you out of the water (think dry and warm) and let you go where no belly boat dares to float. The good ones strip down to their component parts for easy transport, and they have enough pockets onboard for all the little doodads that make fly-fishing such a joy to the gadget addict. Safety issues are, once again, obvious. If the current is too fast or the waves too big, then don't go there. You can fall off any boat, anytime, so live in your life jacket. And always keep your eye on the weather.

A float tube or a pontoon boat will take you to some great fishing when your own two feet and a pair of waders just won't do, but for some of the most interesting fly-fishing in Saskatchewan, you need a little more help. For small northern lakes, I like nothing better than to fish from a canoe. It is a quiet, comfortable, sleek, and beautiful platform for a fly fisher, once you get used to the balance and handling of the craft. If you are going to pursue pike, trout or walleye with a fly rod, you'll probably need to be fishing from a boat. But for smaller northern waters and access to some terrific rainbow and speckled trout angling, the canoe will do just fine. Safety rules are mostly common sense—know the limitations of your boat and your paddling skills, keep an eye on the weather and water conditions, and always, always, wear a life jacket.

There are many waters to fly-fish in Saskatchewan. The following are some of the best known, and best loved waters in the province, most of which have been managed as trout-fishing waters for years.

THE CYPRESS HILLS

Tucked up against the Alberta border in the southwest corner of Saskatchewan lie the Cypress Hills. Mostly contained within an interprovincial park, the hills are an unusual landform, with their greatest height equivalent to that of Canada's first National Park—Banff, in the Rocky Mountains, with an elevation of about 1,300 metres (over 4,000 feet). Some of our finest trout streams flow from these hills out onto the rolling plains of the southwest. Most of the streams in the area are spring fed. The region is sparsely populated, and the land is as close to wilderness as you could expect in a settled, agricultural province.

Some of the streams in the Cypress Hills have been managed since the 1920s and 1930s, including Battle, Bear, Belanger, Bone, Calf, Conglomerate and Sucker creeks.

Map 1. Creeks in the Cypress Hills

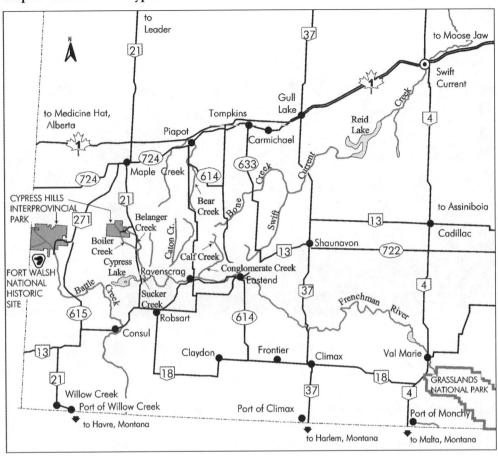

Boiler Creek has been managed since the early 1970s and the upper reaches of Swift Current Creek since the late 1960s. Canton Creek has come under provincial management only in recent years.

The lands through which all of these creeks flow is a blend of private, leased and crown lands, and access to a number of these waters requires landowner permission. Landowners have cooperated to provide parking areas and access at a number of points along the creeks in the region. Fly fishers should respect landowner rights by obtaining permission, staying on trails, and parking where parking areas have been established. If you have to open a gate to get where you are going, make sure that it is securely closed behind you. And when you leave, leave no trace that you were ever there. Anglers wishing further information about fishing in the Cypress Hills should contact the Provincial Park office (306-662-5411).

BATTLE CREEK's spring-fed waters flow from the West Block of the Cypress Hills and on to Montana's Milk River. Its cool water nurtures populations of both rainbow and

View of the Cypress Hills Provincial Park buildings from across the lake, c. 1954.

brown trout. Rainbows have been stocked since the 1920s, and average half to one kilogram (one to two pounds) in Battle's upper reaches. The easiest way to get to the creek is by way of Highway 271, about 50 kilometres (31 miles) southwest of the town of Maple Creek. It is worth noting that beyond the turnoff to the historic park of Fort Walsh, the road is usable in dry weather only. In this part of the province, that is a caution to be taken seriously. Most of the creek can only be accessed on foot within the park. Public transport is available in season from the Fort Walsh Visitor Information Centre, running down towards Farwell's Trading Post. Many anglers choose to take the ride and fish their way back on foot to the parking lot at the visitor centre. There are three wilderness campgrounds along Battle Creek, including one, the Equestrian Campground, which provides facilities for horses.

BEAR CREEK was first stocked with brown trout in the mid-1920s. Since the 1950s it has been managed for brookies. Natural reproduction does take place in the creek, supplemented with occasional stockings. The creek is on the north-facing slope of the Cypress Hills, about 24 kilometres (15 miles) south of the town of Piapot. Some reaches of the creek are heavily overgrown and difficult to fish except with light tackle and spinner rigs or still fishing. But in its open reaches, it is a creek well suited to ultralight fly tackle—if you have a 2- or 3-weight rod this is the place for it.

BELANGER CREEK flows south from the Cypress Hills into the Frenchman River. Brown trout were first stocked here in the early 1920s, and brookies since 1933. Both species have done well in these waters, and a good population sustained itself for a number of decades. More recently, rainbow trout have been added to the mix, and all three are maintained by a combination of natural reproduction and periodic stocking. Because brown trout prefer slower moving waters, you'll find them predominantly in the lower reaches of the creek, near a control structure for diverting water into Cypress Lake. Rainbows, some of them of significant size, are found in the central reaches of the creek. Brookies, which like cooler, faster water, are found in the creek's upper reaches near the Davis Creek Grid Road. A number of beaver dams and open areas provide ideal circumstances for the fly fisher. To find the creek, drive south of the town of Maple Creek on Highway 21, and start fishing south of the Davis Creek Grid Road. Parking is provided at a number of access points along the creek.

BOILER CREEK is located right within the boundaries of Cypress Hills Provincial Park's Centre Block. Surrounded by lodgepole pines and secluded from the Park's busier sections, it is a good place to fish just minutes away from excellent camping or condominium and hotel accommodation in the park. A series of beaver ponds and connecting reaches of the creek are managed as a brook trout fishery, and anglers can expect to land pan-sized fish. The creek has been stocked annually since 1971. You can hike into the creek using a footpath located by the picnic shelter that is just to the northwest of Loch Leven, in the centre of the park's built-up area. Or you can drive there by taking the dry weather trail to the Boy Scout Camp. Park officials can provide detailed directions.

BONE CREEK runs for more than 45 kilometres (28 miles) and eventually empties into Swift Current Creek. First stocked in the 1930s, it soon became known as Saskatchewan's premier brown trout stream. Browns taken from this creek have ranged in size from 1 to 4 kilograms (2 to 10 pounds), and the creek is stocked annually to supplement natural reproduction. In recent years, collaboration between local wildlife federations, local landowners, and Saskatchewan Fisheries staff has resulted in considerable habitat restoration along the stream. Good angling is provided above and below access points at these road crossings: the Klintonel reach is located about 26 kilometres (16 miles) north of the town of Eastend on Grid Road 614. Tompkins Crossing is 30 kilometres (19 miles) south of the town of Tompkins (located on the Trans-Canada) on Grid Road 633. Garden Head Bridge is 20.7 kilometres (13 miles) south of Tompkins on Grid Road 633, then 6.7 kilometres (4 miles) east. Carmichael Bridge is 16 kilometres (10 miles) south of the town of Carmichael (located on the Trans-Canada) on the municipal grid road.

CALF CREEK is a short run of cool clean water over cobble beds, leading to downstream beaver ponds, that makes for ideal brook trout territory. In winter, trout hold in the deeper water the ponds provide. The creek flows into another significant trout stream in the area, Conglomerate Creek. Surveys of Calf Creek indicate that it is sustaining a naturally reproducing population of brookies in sizes up to 1 kilogram (2 pounds). To fish Calf Creek, travel 18 kilometres (11 miles) on Grid Road 614 north from the town of Eastend, or 46 kilometres (29 miles) south from Piapot. There is a parking area at the junction of Calf Creek with Conglomerate Creek, and you walk through pasture to get to the former.

CATON CREEK has its headwaters northwest of the town of Ravenscrag. The creek flows south from the hills high above the Davis Creek Grid Road; it's home to pan-sized brook trout that hold in beaver ponds, and in pool and riffle runs. Fly-fishing is tough on this overgrown creek, but there are open areas that reward the angler with ultralight tackle. Caton Creek is 35 kilometres (22 miles) south of Maple Creek and a few kilometres (2 miles) east on the Davis Creek Grid Road. Parking and access are available throughout the Spring Valley Guest Ranch.

CONGLOMERATE CREEK flows out of the Cypress Hills and drains into the Frenchman River. Locally known as Little Frenchman's Creek, it is brown trout habitat. The browns were originally stocked in 1924, and brookies were added in 1952. Browns are still stocked in the creek to supplement naturally reproducing populations. Conglomerate Creek features open pasture lands along its entire length, making it very accessible to fly fishers. To fish it, drive 8 kilometres (5 miles) north of the town of Eastend on Grid Road 614. There are several access points with parking areas.

SWIFT CURRENT CREEK, also known as Pine Cree Creek, rises above Pine Cree Regional Park, flows through a steeply walled and scenic valley, and ultimately drain into the big water of Lake Diefenbaker about 9 kilometres (6 miles) east of Saskatchewan Landing Provincial Park.

While the reservoir is home to walleye, big pike, perch, rainbow trout, burbot, and a host of other species, the creek is home to stocked brook trout within the boundaries of the Park. First stocked in 1967, the population is maintained through a combination of natural reproduction and regular stocking. Pine Cree Regional Park is located 54 kilometres (34 miles) south of Tompkins, (located on the Trans-Canada) on Grid Road 633. Anyone wishing to fish outside the park needs permission of local landowners.

SUCKER CREEK runs through a steep-walled valley, where a series of riffles and pools provides habitat for brook trout. In the short run of stream south of the junction with Weaver Creek, anglers can find good numbers of pan-sized fish. Brookies were first stocked here back in 1931, and since the 1950s the population has sustained itself through natural reproduction. Heavy cover along the creek makes fly-fishing awkward, but fly fishers who are prepared to drift floating lines downstream can enjoy the brook trout fishing on the creek. Access and parking is located 27 kilometres (17 miles) south of the town of Maple Creek on Highway 21.

THE CUB HILLS

The Cub Hills are located about 150 kilometres (93 miles) northeast of Prince Albert. Many of the streams and lakes in the hills are within the boundaries of Narrow Hills Provincial Park. The small waters and abundant trout species make it a destination of choice for fly fishers. In fact, all seven of the trout species resident in Saskatchewan—brook, brown, cutthroat, lake, rainbow, splake and tiger trout—are found in the waters of the Cub Hills. Five of the waters in the area hold naturalized, self-reproducing pop-

Map 2. Creeks in the Cub Hills

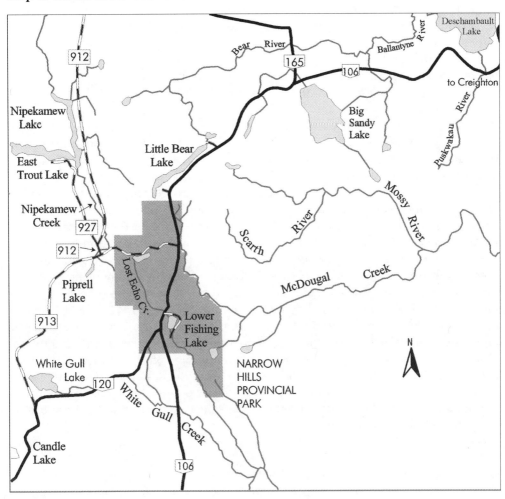

ulations of brook trout. The list of fishable waters that follows is just a small sample of the dozens of lakes and streams in the Cub Hills area. More are listed in the chapter on Fishing in Central Saskatchewan. Anglers wishing further information on fishing in the Cub Hills area should contact Saskatchewan Environment—particularly the Prince Albert office (306-953-2322)—or speak with staff at Narrow Hills Provincial Park (306-462-2622).

MCDOUGAL CREEK has its headwaters in the Cub Hills, just southeast of Little Bear Lake. It flows for about 130 kilometres (81 miles) before emptying into the Mossy River. McDougal Creek can be accessed from either Highway 106 via a side road into a picnic area, or by Highway 120 which crosses McDougal Creek. It was first stocked with brook trout in 1934, then again in the 1950s and 1960s. The result is a self-sustaining popula-tion of brook trout that can be found in the creek's deep pools and along its undercut banks. McDougal runs quick and cool, ideal trout habitat. Pan-sized brookies of 20 to 30 centimetres (8 to 12 inches) are regularly reported, but so is the occasional fish up to 40 centimetres (16 inches). Heavy cover may limit fly anglers to dapping their flies rather than casting. Some of the larger pools have a more open habitat for casting. Try a stonefly nymph pattern on these waters.

MOSSY RIVER is northeast of Narrow Hills Provincial Park, east of Little Bear Lake. Access is via Highway 106 north to the Cub Hills Road, then east to Highway 120, and north to the Mossy Creek bridge crossing. This is rough country, and foot access along the river can be difficult. The roads in the area are maintained for passenger car travel; however, having driven some of them, I would recommend doing so in a truck or sport-utility vehicle. The upper run of the river features riffle-run sections that host brook trout. Brookies were first stocked in 1979 and have become naturalized in the Mossy. Brook trout measuring 25 to 35 centimetres (10 to 14 inches) are taken regularly on flies, spinners, natural and artificial baits. Fly anglers should have wooly worms, wooly, buggers and caddis larvae and emergers close at hand for these waters.

NIPEKAMEW CREEK has its headwaters in a muskeg west of Piprell Lake. It flows into the Nipekamew River, which empties into Lac La Ronge. The creek has been stocked with brook trout since 1954. It has a naturalized population which is supplemented with stocking every couple of years. The creek features long riffle sections, punctuated with natural pools and beaver ponds. To get to Nipekamew Creek, travel north on Highway 120 and Grid Road 913 to Grid Road 912. A short distance up Grid Road 912, turn left onto East Trout Lake Road (Road 927) and follow it south to the bridge. Two additional access routes are possible—the Gem Lake Road running off Road 927, and the Sand Lake Road which can be reached from the Gem Lake Road. Thick willow cover along the banks of Nipekamew means the fly angler will be doing a lot of dapping, and you will need a short ultralight rod to fish the creek. The most open areas will be at beaver ponds. Caddis and dragonfly nymph imitations work on these waters, as do small wooly worms. Pan-sized brookies in the 20- to 25-centimetre (8- to 10-inch) range are common.

WHITE GULL CREEK has been home to brook trout since 1949. It lies near the southwest corner of Narrow Hills Provincial Park, and flows about 150 kilometres (93 miles) before emptying into the Torch River. The population of brook trout is self-sustaining in White Gull and is supplemented with stocking programs every couple of years. White Gull Creek is accessible at several points from Highways 120 and 106, via drivable roads and all-terrain vehicle trails. Anglers should check with Narrow Hills Park officials for the best advice on access. White Gull Creek holds 25- to 35-centimetre (8- to 10-inch) brook trout that respond well to stonefly, caddis fly and dragonfly nymph patterns, fished in deeper runs and pools.

LOST ECHO CREEK flows for 12 kilometres (7 miles) from Lost Echo Lake to Upper Fishing Lake, then continues on through Lower Fishing Lake, Stewart Creek, and the Torch River. Lost Echo has been a brook trout fishery since 1934, and carries a good naturalized population of brookies. The creek is accessible via Highway 106 north to the Piprell Lake cut-across road, then east to one of two trails suitable for truck traffic

Fly-fishing on the Fond du Lac River, 1950.

for part of their length and in dry conditions; otherwise travel by foot or all-terrain vehicle. Pan-sized brook trout of 20 to 25 centimetres (8 to 10 inches) are common, with a few larger specimens caught from time to time. Heavy brush along creek banks may limit fly anglers to dapping except at larger pools. Try stonefly and dragonfly nymph patterns along this creek.

RUSSELL CREEK

Russell Creek is a spring creek in southwestern Saskatchewan. The creek runs south of the town of Neville and runs parallel to Highway 43 for part of its length. It crosses gravel Grid Road 628 south of Pambrun, and is accessible by trail at a number of points. Russell Creek is a small, clear water, spring creek, stocked primarily with brook trout. It takes a delicate touch, light gear, and a quiet tread along the bank, to take nervous brookies out of water like this. Depending on what is hatching, either dry flies or nymphs will do the trick.

HIGHWAY #102

Highway 102 is a gravel highway less than 200 kilometres (124 miles) long running north into the Precambrian Shield country from La Ronge to Southend on Reindeer Lake. Along its length are dozens of small lakes, streams, and some larger bodies of water more than worthy of the fly rodder's attention. Some diehard fly anglers take a holiday by simply driving north and working their way from water to water along Highway 102. Lakes like McKay, Lynx, Mullock, Little Deer and Althouse are accessible by gravel road and trail from the 102 and are fishable by canoe, float boat, or float tube. With relative ease, the fly angler can drive into a secluded wilderness environment, with varied fishing (walleye and pike on some lakes, brook trout on others). The most popular spots are found along the most travelled section of the road between La Ronge and Missinipe on the Churchill River, but the road passes by and crosses over fishable water all the way to Southend. The smaller lakes and streams that are accessible from Highway 102 are ideal for the fly angler's craft.

CHAPTER SIX
ICE FISHING IN SASKATCHEWAN

MICHAEL SNOOK

Ice fishing shack, Last Mountain Lake, 2002.

It is −26°C (−15°F), a windy Saturday in January. Several hundred feet offshore at Last Mountain Lake, a lone angler sits perched on top of a white, five-gallon pail. Hardly moving, his attention is totally focused on an 8-inch-wide hole in the ice in front of him. He's not watching his fishing line. His eyes are glued to the monitor of a small, black-and-white camera that lies suspended just off the bottom of the lake, 25 feet below. He's watching a good-sized walleye slowly inch up to his bait, which hangs through another hole in the ice, just a foot or two to his right.

At this time of year, the water at that depth is only slightly above the freezing mark. This walleye, a cold-blooded creature, will be at a metabolic low point, all of its systems geared down to match the water temperature. But the experienced angler knows that in spite of the cold water and the slow speed at which the walleye approaches the bait, the strike, if there is one, will be lightning fast—about a tenth of a second—and so he ignores his own discomfort as the wind builds around him—watching, waiting, hoping.

The walleye edges up to within centimetres of the bait. The angler jiggles it, ever so slightly—just a tiny twitch—and the walleye stops dead in its tracks. The angler stops moving the bait. The walleye moves in closer, her mouth almost touching the bait. In a flash, she turns and is gone. Something gave the game away—a tiny bit of scent or movement or colour that this wise, old 10-pound grandmother knew wasn't quite right. The angler slumps, relaxes, pulls in his line, adjusts the bait, lowers it down again, and pours himself a cup of hot tea from his thermos. He's not new to this game either. There will be another fish, one not quite so smart. He'll wait for it.

With a solid six months of winter and plenty of lakes frozen for four months of the year or more, Saskatchewan is an ideal place for ice anglers to practise their chilly craft. Almost every species of sport fish found in the province can be angled for during the solid-water season, and in the case of some species, the biggest fish of the year will come through the ice. In southern and central Saskatchewan, perch, pike and walleye are favourite species for cold weather anglers to pursue, along with rainbow trout in some water, and burbot. In northern waters, lake trout are a welcome addition to the list.

With the availability of light, four-wheel-drive trucks, all-terrain vehicles, snowmobiles, power ice-augers, and portable shelters, ice fishing has undergone a major revolution in the last decade. Add to this the power of underwater vision provided first by depth finders, and more recently by relatively inexpensive underwater cameras and monitors, and you have a whole new world of ice angling to explore.

As in open-water fishing, the key to good ice fishing is getting "on" the fish, and that means being mobile—getting around on a lake, drilling dozens of holes, and checking out what's happening beneath the surface of the ice. In the old days of ice fishing, such mobility would have been strenuous, if not impossible. Hand augers, heavy ice shacks designed to stay in one place, and few fish finders designed for cold-weather use—all limited the ice angler's flexibility. No longer.

By understanding the movement of their favourite species throughout the winter, by reading the structural elements of a lake and by using high quality sonar or underwater video, today's ice angler can move about a lake and find fish almost as easily as in a boat on open water.

ICE FISHING SAFETY

While ice fishing extends the fishing season for anglers in Saskatchewan, it is not without its risks. Winters on the prairies, and in the northern reaches of the province, can be severely cold, windy, and unpredictable. Of course, safety begins before you leave home. It's pretty much a matter of common sense to dress for the weather—a layered system is best, so that you can remove a layer or two to avoid sweating during the strenuous work of drilling holes through the ice, then put the layers back on while you're sitting still at –25°C waiting for the fish to bite.

The first layer, the one next your skin, should be a synthetic fibre, such as polypropylene, designed to wick moisture away from you and out to the next layer of clothing. Avoid cotton and wool-based long underwear—they retain water and, once damp, are a chilling reminder of the time of year you've chosen to go fishing. In certain circumstances, they can be dangerous as well as uncomfortable, contributing to hypothermia. The second layer out should be both insulating and capable of holding some moisture (from perspiration) without losing its value as an insulator. Contemporary fleeces are perfect. Good-quality wool is almost as good. Avoid cotton blends.

The third layer should be a heavier insulating layer—thicker fleece, heavy wool, a down-filled sweater, lined or insulated pants or bibs. Pay the same attention to your head, hands, and feet. Multi-layered mitts, insulated toques or hats, well-insulated high boots with rubberized, waterproof bottoms will all keep you on the ice longer, having more fun ice fishing.

The outer layer of clothing has only one purpose—to keep wind and water away from your skin. Waterproof and windproof fabrics come in several varieties, the best-known being Gore-Tex.

With a layered system such as this, you can adjust your clothing to your activity level. If you are working up a sweat drilling holes in the ice, take off a layer of insulation and open the zipper on your outer layer to vent heat. Put it all back on when you sit down on your bucket to fish.

If you're headed out ice-fishing, someone back home should know where you are going, how long you plan to be there, and when you plan to be back home. Fishing with a group of friends is not only an enjoyable way to spend a winter day, but safer as well. Winter anglers should always be aware of the weather. High winds can reduce visibility both on the ice and on the road coming and going. High winds greatly increase the risk of frostbite to exposed skin and increase the danger of hypothermia.

Hypothermia results from a cooling of the body's core. It can happen so gradually on a cold, windy day that an angler preoccupied with fishing may not notice anything wrong until he can't stop shivering. If this happens, get out of the wind and into the warmth of your ice-fishing hut or your vehicle. Have a cup of hot tea or coffee and relax until the shivering stops and you are comfortably warm. Warming of hypothermia victims should be gradual. Someone suffering from hypothermia needs to be protected from further heat loss, even after they are in a sheltered situation. Keep the head and neck covered to reduce heat loss and make sure the rest of their clothing is dry.

The most severe instances of hypothermia occur when high winds and cold water are both involved. Getting wet on a cold winter day, or worse still, going through the ice, is definitely life threatening. Remove wet clothing and get into a dry warm space as quickly as possible. Take hot liquids and stay inside until body temperature is back to normal and symptoms have disappeared.

You should know the symptoms of severe hypothermia: lack of coordination, difficulty walking or speaking, irrational behaviour, or unconsciousness. A person suffering from severe hypothermic symptoms must be evacuated to receive emergency medical treatment as soon as possible. Treat a hypothermia victim as gently as possible—rough handling can cause the body to go into shock and pose further danger to someone who is already in a very fragile condition.

The best way to avoid hypothermia is to stay dry, warm, and well-fed. Drink lots of non-alcoholic liquids (cold weather and booze don't mix—that temporary glow you feel on the surface of your skin comes at the expense of internal body heat) and avoid thin ice.

Ice thickness varies greatly depending on temperature conditions, depth of water, current, snow cover, and season. Ice cover on rivers is rarely, if ever, safe for any kind of travel, even on foot. Even lakes with solid ice covers may have areas of thin ice due to local currents (around points and in narrows on a lake, for example) or springs. Anglers should drill test holes before venturing out on unfamiliar ice. A minimum of 10 centimetres (4 inches) of solid ice is recommended for walking. Double that to 20 centimetres or 8 inches if you're going to travel by snowmobile or all-terrain vehicle. Cars and light trucks require 30 centimetres, or at least 12 inches of ice for safe travel. Allow even more than that for heavier trucks.

There are inherent dangers in venturing out onto frozen lakes in the cold depths of winter, but if you take along a good measure of common sense, learn to read weather and ice conditions, test the ice in unfamiliar situations or after weather conditions have dramatically changed, you can enjoy a safe, if chilly, extension to the fishing season.

GEARING UP

Find a Saskatchewan ice angler and you'll probably find a couple of five-gallon plastic pails, two or three ice-fishing rods sticking out of the top, along with a scoop for spooning the slush and ice chips out of a freshly drilled hole. A small tackle box, a container of frozen minnows or a ziploc bag of mealworms or maggots, a thermos of hot coffee, a lunch bag, and a couple of plastic bags to bring home the day's catch complete the list of items you'll find inside these pails.

Ice-fishing rods and reels are the heart of an ice-fishing system that includes a power ice auger, a fish finder, and perhaps an underwater camera system. Graphite and graphite composite materials have made possible the construction of very high quality ice-fishing rods that are every bit as sensitive as their longer, warm-water cousins. High quality spinning, baitcaster and spincast reels work as well in cold weather as in hot.

These days, anglers have the choice of spooling up with monofilament line or one

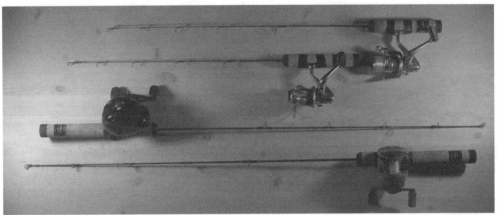

Berkley ice-fishing rods, from light action for perch to heavy action for larger walleye, pike, or lake trout.

of the new "super" lines—FireLine, SpiderWire, and their imitators. And there are as many lures, jigs, spoons, and other flashy bits of hardware to tempt the winter angler as there are his summer incarnation. Team this gear up with a portable ice-fishing shelter—part sled, part tent—and with an all-terrain vehicle, snowmobile, or four-wheel-drive truck, and you have a contemporary ice-fishing system.

The exact hardware you choose to fish with will vary with the species you are pursuing.

BURBOT

Most anglers catch burbot (also called "dog-fish," ling, black maria,) by accident while fishing for perch, walleye, or pike. Some are quickly converted by a fish that bites hard, gives a great fight, is catchable throughout the winter angling season and, when properly cleaned and prepared, is fine eating.

Burbot will feed on almost anything that resembles food, and they're opportunistic—chances are no matter what you have on the end of your line, if a burbot swims by, it will be interested. Because they are not a popular target for sports anglers, not much is known about their habits. However, in Saskatchewan waters, particularly in southern lakes, you'll find them in the same areas as you find walleye and pike. They are often caught where relatively shallow sand or gravel flats adjacent to shore drop steeply into deeper water.

One of the most productive times to catch burbot through the ice is during pre-spawn. Burbot spawn under the ice, in mid to late winter, and as they are preparing to spawn, they school up in large schools and feed actively. Anglers in the right place at the right time can experience intense action for short periods of time as schools move through. During spawn, burbot will move up from deep water to shallower sand and gravel flats or bars (less than ten feet or three metres of water) where spawning takes place.

They can be caught using tip-ups baited with medium-sized frozen minnows. Or, you can rig a minnow below a slip bobber, set up to ride just off the bottom. Jigging for burbot with lures such as the Swedish Pimple, Swedish Jig, or Hawger Spoon tipped with a minnow head is effective when schools are in the area.

Burbot bite most actively during the early hours just before and after dawn,

SAB RA 13,647 (2)

Ice fishing from the comfort of a well-equipped shack at Regina Beach, 1958.

and at dusk and into the evening. If the fish are in shallow water, it pays to get to your spot early, drill lots of holes before the fish move in shallow, so you can fish for them undisturbed by the sound of a gas ice auger.

LAKE TROUT

Northern Saskatchewan is home to dozens of lakes that hold lake trout populations. Lake trout are as catchable through the ice as they are in open water. The pull of the winter laker is irresistible. There's a chance at a trophy fish, well over 30 pounds (14 kilograms). There's the challenge of fighting a big fish on small tackle. And there's the pleasure that comes from keeping a smaller fish or two for a meal—lake trout make fine table fare.

During the open-water season, lake trout location can often be determined by water temperature. The shallower water are simply too warm for lakers to funtion at their best, and they typically inhabit the deepest, coolest reaches of the lake. Winter lake trout can be taken from depths of less than 40 feet (13 metres)—at this time of year they are not solely a deep-water fish.

In winter, because frozen lakes tend to be more uniformly cold, lake trout are free to travel more freely. What is important to lake trout in winter is food, and the presence of food is often dictated by underwater structure. Some of the same structures that walleye anglers search for are key areas for lake trout in winter. Look for a point that drops into deep water near a shallower feeding flat that may hold some remnant weed growth from the previous summer and that still holds either baitfish or young-of-the-year game fish—this will be an attractive place for a lake trout. So will any structure, such as a bar or sunken island, which has attracted the attention of baitfish or smaller sport fish that lake trout may prey upon.

Even better is a "saddle" structure—a channel of deeper water between two shallower features, such as a shoreline flat and a sunken island or bar. That channel of deeper water between structural elements will act as a funnel for baitfish moving about the lake. And keep in mind when fishing lake trout in deeper waters: if schools of baitfish suspend in mid-depths, well off the bottom, trout will often follow. Use a fish finder, and don't be shy about fishing for suspended trout when you have indications of suspended schools of bait. Find food, find lake trout.

Vertical jigging is the most effective method for winter fishing lake trout. In deep water, use heavier jigs—½-ounce or better, with large, light-coloured plastic tails or big frozen minnows or smelt. Northland Tackle's airplane jigs, Cicada lures (in the 1-ounce size), Swedish Pimples, or Hawger spoons are effective, fished either on their own or tipped with a frozen minnow. Low-stretch superlines are very effectively teamed with heavy jigs and jigging spoons for fishing in deep water. To avoid twisted line, tie in a good quality barrel swivel a half metre or so up the line. As your jig twists in the water, the swivel spins, and your main line is unaffected. When jigging in deep water, let the jig fall slowly and under control—lake trout will take a bait on the drop, and if they hit when the line is slack, it is almost impossible to set the hook quickly enough.

Because lake trout move about a lot, be prepared to drill plenty of holes, and keep moving yourself. If you have fished a hole for fifteen or twenty minutes without a bite, move to another hole. Even a few metres can make a difference.

As with all ice fishing, if you are in a group, use the numbers in your favour—one angler can fish with a jig and plastic tail, another with a jigging spoon, still a third can set up with live bait or babysit a tip-up. The same tip-up rig used for big northern pike can be used with lake trout. Set up a tip-up on one hole, then jig in another a few metres away. The fish will tell you what they prefer.

Ice anglers always have to be prepared for winter weather. Those who pursue lake trout in Saskatchewan should keep in mind that these fish are found in more remote, northern waters, where the amenities and safety of civilization may be a long trek away. The reward for putting up with the cold and the lack of nearby creature comforts is fishing for one of nature's most beautiful fish in a wild and natural setting.

NORTHERN PIKE

Northern pike, or jackfish, are found throughout Saskatchewan, from the southernmost reaches all the way to the Northwest Territories/Nunavut border. In the cold water season, pike make excellent table fare. And it is not unusual to catch the biggest pike of the year through a little hole in the ice.

Gary Folk, a veteran Regina angler and an old hand at ice fishing for pike, tells a story about the pike that wouldn't come through the hole. Gary was fishing on Mission Lake, near Fort Qu'Appelle, using a tip-up and a large smelt for a bait. His tip-up let go, and Gary gave the fish a few seconds to get the big bait securely in his mouth before reaching for the line and setting the hook by hand. The pike, obviously a good-sized

Typical ice-fishing jigs and spoons, including Northland Fishing Tackle Fire-Eye Jig (A) and generic jigging spoon (B); Deadly Dick jigging spoons (C); Hawger Spoons (D); Northland's Fire-Eye Spoons (E); Lindy Flyer (F); Tee-tot lures (G); Cicada lures (H); Krocodile spoons (J), and Northland's Fire-Eye Minnow (K).

one, stripped line on its first run, and Gary let it go, keeping just enough pressure on the line to start tiring the fish.

After several runs, the pike finally came to the hole in the ice. Gary could see its snout, but its body would not pass through the small 13-centimetre (6-inch) diameter hole his auger had cut. There is only one solution for a problem like this—make the hole bigger! A couple of friends fishing nearby rushed over with augers ready to go, but enlarging a hole in the ice, with a fishing line and a very live, very large pike already in it, is more than a little bit tricky.

By cutting a new hole right next to the original, another one next to that one, and between them with a spud, Gary's fish came unstuck, and a 7-kilogram (15-pound, 6-ounce) northern pike was posing for photos in a matter of minutes.

Gary was fishing at the outside edge of a weedbed, or at least, what was left of a summer weed flat by mid-winter. Using sonar to find remnants of weedbeds, finding their outer edge, and particularly finding the edge of a weedbed near deeper water, is a valuable skill to have when seeking winter pike. As a rule of thumb, smaller fish will come from within the borders of the weedbed. Larger trophy fish will come from the outside edge, or the nearby deeper water. Remember that pike are territorial, and it is rare to find large pike in anything resembling a "school." In fact, the area around a big pike is often devoid of other fish. If the perch or walleye in a productive spot suddenly shut off, you might want to switch to pike tactics for a while. If you catch one big pike in an area, it may be a while before another moves into the territory. Be prepared to move around.

Catching big pike on tip-up rigs is a standard ice-fishing technique. This particular pike came from a depth of about four metres, at the edge of a weedy flat that held both perch and baitfish. Where there is food, pike will sooner or later come to feed if they are in the neighbourhood, and they are happy both to scavenge anything dead lying on the bottom and to prey on live fish. A patient angler sets a tip-up, baits his 17-pound-test monofilament or heavier Dacron line with a smelt or large minnow on a quick-strike rig, puts an in-line sinker

SAB RB 5086

Jim Kierstead of Eauclaire, Wisconsin, holds a 26½-pound northern pike caught while ice fishing at Candle Lake (1962).

about half a metre above the hook, and lets the line down so that the bait is sitting on bottom, with no slack, and waits. Gary's problem pike was his only bite all day.

Since ice anglers in Saskatchewan are allowed to fish with two lines at one time, moving 20 or 30 metres (up to 100 feet) to fish for perch or walleye while waiting for that big pike to come along isn't a bad idea. Just stay close enough for the mad dash across the ice when the tip-up tips up.

The tip-up rig is not the only method for ice fishing for northern pike. Where active fish are present, jigging with a shiny jigging spoon, a jig tipped with a frozen minnow, or jigging a spoon like a Len Thompson or DarDevle, or a Northland Tackle Buck-Shot Rattle Spoon, will also tempt pike to bite. On some lakes, pike respond well to fairly active jigging presentations. On others, they seem to prefer almost no movement at all. Pike are regularly caught by anglers rigged for perch or walleye. Then the challenge is to keep the fish on without breaking ultralight line and tackle. The pike usually wins.

Big fish on small tackle pose problems for the ice angler that an open-water fisher never has to deal with. If a big fish runs hard in open water, you can let him run, following him with a boat or walking down the shoreline to keep up, let the run finish, and put tension back on the fish.

If your line gets to the fish through a 6 or 7-inch hole that is 30 inches deep, a big fish on the run pretty much guarantees that your line will be cut off against the bottom edge of the ice-fishing hole. Solution? Stick your fishing rod down the hole so the line clears the bottom edge. When the ice is thick enough, I have stuck my fishing rod and half my arm to the elbow into the water to keep the line from being broken off. It *is* cold, and I don't advise it unless you have a place to warm up and dry out afterwards, but it works.

RAINBOW TROUT

The beautiful silver rainbow trout is the most commonly stocked trout species in Saskatchewan. Found in local ponds, in stocked lakes, and in reservoirs, it is as catchable through the ice as it is in open water.

In recent years, fishing for rainbow trout on Diefenbaker Lake has been, to put it mildly, spectacular. The reason is that a number of years ago, a large number of captive rainbow escaped from a fish farm on the lake. The reservoir, which already held some rainbows, had effectively been stocked with a healthy population of adult fish. These trout are, so the story goes, sterile, and will not reproduce, so it is difficult to say how long the bumper crop will last, or what its long-term effects on the lake will be.

In the meantime, ice fishing for rainbows has become a favourite winter pastime for anglers fishing Lake Diefenbaker. Rainbow trout can be found in the classic spots off points at the mouths of bays, but the fishing is often even better at the shallow back ends of the same bays. A classic strategy is to drill a series of holes through the ice, from shallow to deep, and work them in a systematic manner. Soon enough, the fish will tell you where they are.

Brian Dygdala, who manages The Fishin' Hole tackle shop in Saskatoon, and prefers to fish for rainbows through the ice, fishes Lake Diefenbaker regularly in the winter. He looks for shallow water, 2 metres (6 feet) deep or less, and jigs with light

SAB RA 13,647 (3)

A Lebret area fisherman makes himself comfortable by the fire in a winter fishing shack on Katepwa Lake (February 1958).

tackle and 4- or 6-pound-test line, using a Backswimmer jig tipped with a mealworm or a shrimp body. Aggressive jigging action doesn't work well for rainbow trout. Jig a bit, then let the bait sit. More strikes will come when the bait is at rest than when it's moving. Shallow-water anglers are more likely to catch larger numbers of smaller fish.

Using the same tackle and techniques, anglers who fish deeper water—3 metres (10 feet) or more—have a chance at the larger rainbows (8 to 10 pounds or 4 to 5 kilograms) found in Lake Diefenbaker. But this takes patience. You might have to wait all day for a single fish.

A common way to fish for rainbows through the ice in Saskatchewan is to use a simple hook and sinker rig—light line, a small hook baited with Power Bait, and a split shot or small sinker about a half-metre (2 feet) above the hook. Yet another tackle option is to use a small, bright spoon as an attractor lure, with a dropper hook suspended a few centimetres (an inch or two) below it, tipped with a very small frozen minnow.

On smaller lakes and reservoirs holding rainbow trout, techniques and tackle are much the same, with one addition. In stocked ponds or small reservoirs, jigging with a small, bright spoon, and leaving long pauses between jigging movements, will attract aggressive strikes when fish are actively feeding. A final word to the wise from experienced anglers—shallow water angling for rainbows is best in low light conditions—early in the morning, late in the afternoon, or on overcast days.

WINTER WALLEYE

The walleye, the most popular sport fish in Saskatchewan, is elusive enough in the summer. In the winter, this species can be frustrating to find and catch, unless you have the patience to figure out their current pattern of behaviour.

Shortly after freeze-up, the best places to fish for walleye through the ice are the last places they were found during the open-water season. Chances are good that the bait and cover that kept them in that particular place during the late fall will still be around.

Find such a spot in the first few weeks of walleye fishing after a safe thickness of ice has formed and you're likely to experience some of the best fishing of the year, and perhaps your best chance at a really big fish. Walleye at this time of year are often taken in relatively shallow water (less than 6 metres or about 20 feet), and that is fortunate, because it allows the angler to release the larger female fish back into the lake, keeping a few of the smaller males for a tasty meal. Walleye caught from deep water—9 metres (or 30 feet) or more—will likely not survive release. They are unable to voluntarily expel air from an internal organ call an "air bladder," and so cannot return to the depth from which they came. The sudden decompression caused by rapid ascent from deep water may even burst the air bladder, fatally injuring the fish.

Once the ice cover thickens and snow starts to cover the ice, these concentrated schools of walleye will disappear, literally overnight. One day your favourite spot is hot; the next day, there is not a walleye in sight.

This is the time to be mobile. Try the nearest geographical structure (a point, a reef, a sunken island) or a nearby flat with remnant weed growth and nearby deep water. Fishing at a safe distance out from incoming or outflowing creeks will sometimes be key to finding fish.

In northern Saskatchewan, deeper, rocky lakes with plenty of shoreline points, reefs, sunken islands, and saddles consisting of deeper water between shallow structural elements will provide the walleye angler with plenty of choices to fish. The key to puzzling out walleye in such lakes is to stay mobile, drill plenty of holes, and use sonar constantly. If you don't get any action in one likely-looking spot, move on.

Ice fishing at Buffalo Pound, 1965.

In southern Saskatchewan, anglers are more likely to find walleye in lakes that are relatively featureless bowls—sand or muck bottomed, with little or no structure in the main lake basin, and a few shoreline points. Again, any structure that is evident should be fished and tested; if there is no action, move on to the next. On lakes with little structure, even the smallest feature can be important—a few inches of additional depth, a tiny ridge only a foot high; such seemingly insignificant features as these can attract walleye on an otherwise featureless flat.

The outside edge of a weedbed, dropping into deep water, is a prime spot for winter walleye. Even better is the outside edge of a weedbed where an indentation or a point may collect or funnel baitfish as they move around. Such places attract walleye because they are holding spots for minnows and baitfish. The presence of baitfish may be a clue to winter walleye location. If you are fishing in an area that seems to be producing a large number of small perch, it may pay to stick around until low light conditions in late afternoon to see if the walleye in the neighbourhood have discovered the same perch school that you have.

On some large reservoirs, the problem can be not too little structure, but too much, in the form of literally dozens of shoreline points. On such reservoirs as Lake Diefenbaker, walleye may be extremely mobile, and the angler seeking them must follow suit. Successful anglers will move from point to point, and use sonar to detect changes in the bottom, find the remnants of old weed beds, and locate schools of bait fish. Perseverance will eventually put an angler on walleye.

There is one pattern on southern walleye waters that is fairly certain wherever the walleye are. It's a feeding pattern, and it works like clockwork. During daylight hours, walleye can be found deep, off the drop-off at the edge of a shallower flat. As light levels drop—walleye appear to be sensitive to light levels even with a snow and ice cover—they will begin to move up the drop-off into shallower water, looking to feed. By late afternoon, just before dusk in the winter, they may have moved into as little as three or four metres of water, and for a half-hour or so, will feed actively, providing the patient angler with a premium fishing experience. Then, as suddenly as it began, the feeding frenzy is over, the walleye gone.

Find walleye on your favourite lake, determine the time that they come up to feed, and for a time in January and February, you can almost set your watch by their feeding behaviour. As with summer walleye fishing, some of the hottest action will be under low light conditions—just after first light, and just before dusk.

Best lures for walleye include jigging Rapalas, various brands of jigging spoons, spoons with dropper hooks and plain old lead head jigs. For bait, perch eyes, mealworms, and frozen minnows all work well. Almost every major body of water in southern and central Saskatchewan holds walleye. There are plenty of choices when it comes to fishing for them through the ice. And if the walleye action is slow, these same lakes hold plenty of perch and northern pike.

A final word to the wise winter walleye angler. While rivers do hold walleye in winter, the presence of current makes the ice unsafe under almost all circumstances. Assume that river ice is dangerous and look for the nearest lake as an alternative.

YELLOW PERCH

These plentiful, tasty scrappers are probably the most popular game fish for the winter angler throughout south and central Saskatchewan. They move in large schools during the winter, and the odds are good that if you catch one, you'll catch a bunch. Typical tackle for perch consists of a short graphite rod (about 2 feet), either spinning or bait-casting reel, light monofilament (4- to 6-pound-test), and a very light jig, tiny spoon, or teardrop-shaped lure at the end of the line, tipped with a mealworm, a maggot, or the eyeball of a perch that has already been harvested for tonight's supper.

Perch are highly aggressive, but very light biting. I have caught perch that are little more than minnows, just a few centimetres (an inch or two) long, on lures and bait better suited to medium-sized walleye. If these aggressive little fish are hungry, nothing will put them off. On the other hand, a handsome 33-centimetre (13-inch) perch can bite so lightly that you have no idea anything is on your line until you lift it to jig or check your bait. Sharp hooks and quick reflexes rule.

Perch typically feed just off the bottom, and most successful perch anglers will lower their favourite lure down to just touch the silt on the lake bottom, then raise it up a few centimetres. Alternately jigging, dropping the lure into the silt and lifting it, and letting it rest, will attract strikes. A trick used by many Saskatchewan perch anglers is to use a small jigging spoon with a "dropper" hook—a second hook, often a tiny treble—tied to a short piece of monofilament, hanging a few centimetres below the main lure. The jigging spoon attracts the fish with its flash and vibration, but they may prefer to chow down on something that looks more natural—a bit of bait on a tiny, almost invisible hook.

Perch are caught throughout the winter season at depths ranging from a metre or two, to twenty metres below the surface. As the weather warms in late winter, they will tend to move towards shore, particularly where spring runoff streams have started to trickle into the lake, opening the ice up a bit around the shoreline. Ice anglers who fish well back from any open water, but on the solid ice close by, can enjoy some spectacular late-season fishing.

Perch will tend to congregate near shallow points that drop off into deep water or at the deep dropoff edge of a shallow flat that still holds some remnants of last summer's weed growth. They will follow schools of baitfish that survive from last spring's hatch. If the baitfish move, so will the perch, and the wise angler will figure this out, and start moving around when the bite turns off.

Perch taken from ice-cold winter water are generally excellent eating.

Regardless of which species of fish you choose to pursue through the ice, Saskatchewan waters offer a wide range of choices. Southern and central waters hold excellent populations of walleye, perch, rainbow trout, and northern pike. Northern waters are prime destinations for winter lake trout. The province is a winter angler's paradise.

CHAPTER SEVEN
COMPETITIVE FISHING IN SASKATCHEWAN

MICHAEL SNOOK

Outfitter and organizer Rob Schulz with a trophy walleye caught and released at the Last Mountain Fall Classic walleye tournament in 2001.

Like almost every other recreational sport in North America, fishing has its competitive side. At the simplest level, it's a few friends taking bets on who will catch the first fish, the most fish, the biggest fish of the day. And no matter how competitive they are, or how successfully they compete, tournament anglers are, at heart, fishermen who love what they do.

Don Lamont, one of western Canada's most successful tournament anglers and host of his own television show—*The Complete Angler*, now in its twelfth year—got started fishing later in life than many. Fishing wasn't a significant part of Lamont's childhood. His dad, he says, was a duck hunter who didn't care much for fishing. Lamont was already in his late twenties when he moved to Prince Albert to work as a news reporter and anchor for CKBI. Here he met Al Beaver, a fire control officer for Saskatchewan's Environment Department. Al had a boat, so the two men would head out on the Hanson Lake Road to fish for walleye. Lamont bought some of his own gear, and every day before his evening shift at the station, he would head off to the North Saskatchewan River to fish from shore.

"I caught my first really big, trophy walleye in 1980," says Don, "and that really got me hooked. When I returned to Winnipeg as a radio broadcaster, I started going to seminars, reading books and magazines—anything I could get my hands on to learn more about fishing. I hated my job, and when an opening came to work as a guide at Eagle Nest Lodge on the Winnipeg River, I applied for it right away. I didn't get the job at first, but the guy who did ended up having to leave. I got the call, and it was my first full-time job in the fishing industry. I've been fishing for a living, one way or another, ever since."

For a few years, Lamont cobbled together a living by guiding, leading seminars, and fishing in tournaments. The turning point in his professional fishing career came, he says, in 1983. That year he fished a tournament at Lac Dubonnet, Manitoba, with the likes of InFisherman founder Al Linder, and pros like Gary Roach and Mike McLelland.

"I rented a little 16-foot boat, with an 18-horse motor, fished that tournament, and finished well up in the money, competing with some pretty good anglers," says Lamont, "and that really got me started in the business, with some sponsorships and industry support." These days, Don divides his time between his family, his television show, and promoting such community-based conservation efforts as Fish Futures and the Winnipeg Urban Fishing Partnership, which gives inner city kids at risk the chance to be involved in recreational fishing. One of the Partnership's activities is a one-day tournament that raises funds for its activities.

Competitive fishing events range from fundraising activities like this to highly competitive events with big money prizes for the winners. Local communities organize fishing derbies, where the whole community comes out and has a good time together. A few prizes are given out for big fish or the largest number of fish or the smallest fish caught. Traditionally, these events have featured a community fish fry at the end of the day, but this part of the tradition is waning as catch-and-release becomes more and more a part of these events.

More complex fishing tournaments have cash prizes, cash entry fees, sponsors, and detailed rules governing the contestants' behaviour. They generally last two or more days and almost always target only one species of fish. These events attract professional or semi-pro anglers who are typically supported by sponsors, as well as local amateur competitors anxious to try their luck in what is usually pretty tough competition.

Organized fishing tournaments pit competitors against each other, the elements, the fish, and the clock. Anglers fish a set number of hours each day for one, two, or three days. Before the end of each fishing day they must weigh in their catch. Some tournaments are based on individual competition, but most consist of two-person teams. The team weighing in the largest weight of fish during the tournament wins first place, and prize payouts may extend down as far as twentieth place.

It seems ironic that an activity like recreational angling, enjoyed by thousands of people as a way to relax and get away from it all, would be transformed into a competitive event, complete with the stresses and strains inherent in any competition. The attraction for those who are competitive by nature is that they are fishing with a group of people who share their passion for angling, who put more effort into learning and appreciating their chosen sport than most people do, and who enjoy every minute of their activity.

Anglers new to competitive fishing, having just come through their first tournament, often comment that they learn more in their few days of tournament angling than they do in a whole year of recreational fishing, precisely because the pressure is on to perform, to catch fish no matter what the conditions are—good weather or bad, good bite or poor—no matter how well you are feeling and no matter how well your equipment is standing up to the strain. In such hothouse conditions, the learning curve is steep and fast.

Competitive fishing benefits not only the individual angler, but the sport as a whole. Many techniques, new understandings of fish behaviour, and improvements to tackle, boats and other hardware have come as a direct result of the intense activity of tournament angling. Techniques such as bottom-bouncing and live-bait rigging for walleye have been explored and refined to a great degree as a result of their application in tournaments. The way in which we read and use sonar (or so-called "fish finders") has been revolutionized by the need of tournament anglers to get on fish fast, and be able to read underwater conditions and structure accurately. Boat control through back-trolling, the use of drift-socks and electric bow-mounted and stern-mounted trolling motors—all owe their popularity to the exposure they have had in organized competitive fishing events.

Saskatchewan has its share of derbies and tournaments, with the longest running tournament trail—The Saskatchewan Walleye Trail—and the biggest first-place cash prize for a walleye tournament in Canada—$50,000 for first place at the Vanity Cup held in Nipawin—amongst them.

Fishing tournaments concentrate significant fishing pressure into a relatively small area for a short period of time. While all the organized tournaments in Saskatchewan must operate on a catch-and-release-only basis, questions have been raised about the impact of these events on local fisheries, particularly the issue of delayed mortality at walleye tournaments, as fish are held in livewells and weighed in at the end of the tournament's fishing day before being released back into the water.

Studies conducted in Alberta, Saskatchewan, and Minnesota in the mid-1990s provided information of use not only to tournaments and competitive anglers but to recreational fishers as well. The studies indicated that certain key factors were critical in reducing the number of walleye that died after being released. The timing of tournament events was a major factor. Events that took place in mid-summer, when water temperature was at its highest, experienced the highest mortality rates. For example, at a 1994 tournament held at Tobin Lake in mid-July, the maximum water temperature reached 21°C (70°F) and 11 percent of fish released later died in holding pens used for the test. In contrast, at a tournament held on Lake Diefenbaker in May of the same year, the maximum water temperature was only 10°C (50°F) and the delayed mortality rate was less than 1 percent of the fish tested.

A combination of high water temperatures and high winds can be particularly troublesome for walleye. Holding fish in a livewell in rough water can result in physical injury to the fish, and higher mortality rates. Higher winds and rough water also make it more difficult for anglers who are handling fish in their boats.

SAB RA 11,827

A crowd gathers as fish are weighed to decide the winner at the Madge Lake Fish Derby, July 1950.

Studies also showed that the handling fish receive at the weigh-in facility further contribute to mortality. Fish are carried from the boat to the weigh scale in a water-filled box. The fish are then dumped into a holding tank, where they rest for a time while waiting to be weighed. Fish are physically handled as they are placed on a scale and individually weighed. They are then placed in another holding tank, as they await release. Studies found that the longer fished were handled at weigh-in, the more likely they were to die after release. The quality and temperature of the water in the holding tanks where the fish wait to be weighed, then wait to be released, also have a significant effect.

As a result, most well-organized walleye tournaments now aim for a weigh-in process that keeps fish out of water for less than sixty seconds. Holding tanks are commonly aerated using tanks of oxygen. Weigh-in staff wear gloves and take care not to handle fish roughly.

Individual anglers can learn from the experience of tournaments in their handling of fish. Catch-and-release is an important conservation tool, but not if the released fish are dying anyway. Recreational anglers planning to keep a few fish to eat should dispatch them quickly and keep them on ice. Leaving a fish on a stringer in warm water all day will certainly kill it and will probably make it unfit for human consumption as water temperature increases and the flesh of the fish begins to break down after its death. Anglers releasing fish should do so as quickly and gently as possible in order to ensure high survival rates. Anglers using livewells should avoid crowding the fish and should keep the wells operating so that water recirculates, is kept as cool as possible, and is well-aerated.

Some conservation-conscious anglers assume a certain percentage of what they catch and release will die and eventually be eaten by gulls, cormorants, or larger fish. Once these anglers have caught enough fish so that their assumed mortality equals a legal limit under current fishing regulations, they stop fishing for that species, or simply stop fishing for the day. Tournaments could not exist without catch-and-release, and tournament anglers are generally active promoters of the practice.

The number and location of local derbies varies greatly from year to year, but there are some long-standing events that occur each year in Saskatchewan. The longest running northern pike tournament anywhere is the Nipawin Pike Festival. The Festival is the culmination of a summer-long event that runs from early June to early October. Up to 2,000 anglers pay five dollars each to register, and that, along with a Saskatchewan angler's licence, gets you into the event. Catch and register a big enough pike and you stand a chance to win one of the big prizes—boat and motor outfits and $5,000 in cash have been given out at past events. In addition, a certain number of pike are tagged and released, and anyone catching and registering one of these is eligible for a cash prize. Interested anglers can contact the town of Nipawin at 306-862-9866 for further information.

A number of other regular tournament events are held in the Nipawin area: the annual Walleye Classic on Codette Lake; the Premier's Cup Walleye tournament, held each August; the Fish for Freedom Day, a women-only event; and the Vanity Cup, held

MICHAEL SNOOK

Tournament angler Colinda Parkinson with a nice walleye to weigh in, and release, at the Lake Diefenbaker Walleye Classic at Elbow.

in late September or early October. The Vanity boasts the highest entry fees—$500 per angler or $1,000 per two-person team—and the biggest prize structure—a $50,000 cash first prize—of any walleye tournament in Canada.

Elsewhere in Saskatchewan, the town of Riverhurst holds an annual walleye tournament on the South Saskatchewan River in June; Lake of the Prairies, which straddles the Saskatchewan/Manitoba border in the southeastern corner of the province, plays host to the Prairie Classic Walleye tournament at the beginning of June. And each year the Saskatoon-based conservation organization "Fishing for Tomorrow" holds a one-day fundraising tournament to raise money for their own conservation activities, and for charitable volunteer-based organizations such as Big Brothers.

By far the largest and most prestigious fishing tournament in Saskatchewan is the Saskatchewan Walleye Trail, consisting of five tournaments that run from late spring to early fall throughout the southern part of the province. The Trail's opening event is held at Elbow, on Lake Diefenbaker, the last weekend of May. Diefenbaker is a large, sprawling reservoir, and anglers have to contend with wind and weather as much as they do with figuring out how to fool the early-season walleye into biting.

The second event of the Trail, held in early June, is hosted by the town of Regina Beach at the southern end of Last Mountain Lake. This is the first of two Trail events that take place on Last Mountain Lake, a fishery known to produce plenty of walleye over 10 pounds. In late July, the Trail returns to Lake Diefenbaker, on the South Saskatchewan River arm at Saskatchewan Landing Provincial Park, for the third event of the season. Anglers fish many kilometres of scenic river surrounded by the steep walls of the Saskatchewan River valley.

The Qu'Appelle Valley Walleye Cup is the fourth stop on the Trail. Fished on four lakes (Pasqua, Echo, Mission, Katepwa) linked by the Qu'Appelle River, this event takes place annually on the Labour Day weekend. Its unique payout structure pays daily as well as overall winners. The Saskatchewan Walleye Trail winds up back at Last Mountain Lake at Rowan's Ravine Provincial Park on the second weekend of September.

Anglers who compete in the Walleye Trail count their best four of five finishes to qualify for Team of the Year, Angler of the Year, Mixed Team of the Year, and Youth Angler awards. Beginning in 2002, the Trail offered an opportunity for amateur anglers to compete in a separate event held the day before the tournament proper. Regular

MICHAEL SNOOK

Saskatchewan Environment staff preparing fish to be released at the Saskatchewan Walleye Trail Fall Classic.

Trail teams took out a new angler, drawn at random from all entries, for one full day of fishing. Only the amateurs were eligible to win prizes for this one-day event.

Tournament anglers are welcome to fish any one of the Trail's tournaments as single events. Contact information for the Saskatchewan Walleye Trail and other Saskatchewan tournaments is included in Appendix B.

The latest addition to the list of tournaments and derbies held in Saskatchewan is the Angler/Young Angler Walleye Championship, which teams up an adult angler with two young anglers under the age of seventeen for a day of competitive fishing. It was the brainchild of Andrew Klopak of Genmar (makers of Lund boats), who started the tournament in Manitoba. The first Saskatchewan event, organized by Bob Schlosser of the Saskatchewan Walleye Trail and Kevin Hollerbaum who operates Kevin's Marine in Fort Qu'Appelle, was held in June of 2002 on Echo Lake, and drew a twenty-boat field.

There are numerous local one-day tournaments and derbies at various locations around the province. Many derbies in northern Saskatchewan are based on the lake trout fishery. Interested anglers can contact Tourism Saskatchewan or Saskatchewan Environment (see Appendix A for contact information) for greater details on competitive fishing events.

CHAPTER EIGHT
CARING FOR YOUR CATCH

A catch of walleye, excessive by today's standards, taken from Last Mountain Lake in the 1930s.

W hen it comes to good taste, there's almost no better food in this world than *fresh* fish. But the flesh of freshwater fish spoils incredibly quickly. Spoilage can mean many things. At minimum, it means the sweet, fresh taste of your catch turns fishy, muddy, strong, and unpleasant to the palate. At worst, it can render your catch inedible, a tragic waste of a wonderful resource.

When you catch your own fish, you control the quality of the food that ends up on your table. The catching is the easiest part, and for the majority of us, the most fun, next to chowing down. But after the catching, and before the eating, how you treat your fish will make all the difference in the world.

KEEPING THE CATCH FRESH

For years I have watched as anglers treated their fish in ways that are guaranteed to harm, if not completely ruin, their flavour and quality. The first technique is what I call "drowned fish on a string." Keeping fish on a stringer and dragging them through the water all day, guarantees that those fish will not only die, but will do so fairly soon after being put on the stringer. If the water is warm, the meat on those fish will start to spoil almost right away. The first sign of that is a bleaching of the skin colour to a pale, yellowish white. If you see this, clean your fish and get it on ice right away, or you will be wasting it.

The second technique I don't recommend for storing fish is "fish in the box." This one is very common at northern fly-in camps. If the fish are coming from really cold water, if the air temperature is cool, and if the box is covered and on the bottom of the boat where it can be further chilled by the cold water that is just the other side of an aluminum hull, then they may last a couple of hours until you use them for shore lunch. They won't keep in the box all day.

If you are going to keep fish for a meal, and you have a livewell in your boat that is working properly, you can keep your catch alive until you come ashore to dispatch, clean, and prepare it. If you don't have a livewell, then killing the fish immediately and putting it on ice will keep it fresh for a reasonable period of time. A bled fish will keep much, much longer than a fish that remains whole. You can bleed a fish by cutting off its tail, stabbing a sharp knife into the rear of its head where it meets the spine, or by partially or completely severing the head by cutting up from the belly towards the spine. The method you choose will probably depend on how you plan to prepare the fish for cooking.

When a fish dies, fluids and bacteria in its digestive tract immediately begin to break down the surrounding tissue. If the digestive juices leak into the surrounding muscle, which is what we eat, then it will spoil in a matter of minutes. The fleshy portion of the fish begins to decompose very quickly after death, unless chilled or cooked quickly. Dead fish left in water will go soft and mushy in a remarkably short period of time.

If you are a shore-bound angler, and you use a creel to keep your fish in, either use a waterproof creel that can hold crushed ice, or pack the fish in moss. My father and I used to use damp grass. It didn't work. When you pull grass up, it starts to compost and can actually heat up in a closed space, spoiling fish quickly.

FILLETING 101

Unless you are keeping them alive in a livewell, the sooner you clean a fish after it is caught, the better it will keep and the better it will taste. How you clean a fish depends on how you plan to cook it, how big the fish is, and what resources you have at hand. For walleye, perch, small to medium-sized pike and lake trout, and mid-sized rainbow trout, filleting is the most common treatment.

There are many ways to fillet a fish; all of them work, and they are explained in books, videos, and even in courses offered in places such as provincial parks. The simplest, quickest, easiest way, which requires only a flat surface and a sharp knife, is one I was taught as a youngster and still use, particularly in camp when I don't have the luxuries of a real kitchen at hand.

Make an incision just behind the gill covers of the fish that goes all the way round from one side of the spine to the other. This is most easily done by holding the fish so that it rests belly up. Once you've made the cut behind the gill covers, make a slit along the belly to the anal vent, but avoid, if you can, puncturing any of the internal organs when you do this.

Remove the innards and dispose of them. At this point you have a whole, dressed fish which, with a little more work, you can prepare to be baked or barbecued or cooked in foil. If this is your choice, you will want to remove the head entirely. Then, using your thumb or a small spoon, get rid of the red vein that runs along the interior of the spine of most fish. This is the fish equivalent of a kidney, and should be cleaned out of a whole fish before cooking. This is my preferred preparation for all the trout species except lake trout, and is a particularly good way to prepare rainbow trout for cooking.

SAB RA 7071

Results of a three-hour catch from Last Mountain Lake in the 1930s—an excessive (and illegal) catch by today's standards, and a poor way to care for fresh fish.

If you wish to remove various body fins, cut around them with a short knife, and with either your hands or a pair of pliers, pull gently to separate the fin and its attached bones, from the rest of the fish. Wash the fish thoroughly in cold water, and you're ready to cook.

If you're going to cook the fish as fillets rather than as a whole fish, the rest of the filleting process goes like this:

Once the fish has been split and gutted, hold it by the head, place your knife flat against the spine, in the cut made right behind the head, and then work it back towards the tail, separating a slab fillet—skin on—from the backbone of the fish. Turn the fish over, repeat the process, and you have two slab fillets with the skin on, ready for the next stage. Remove the rib bones by slipping the knife just under the top of the rib bones, and sliding down between the bones and the skin towards the belly of the fish, until the bones are separated. Dispose of them.

Some fish, lake trout for instance, can be cooked as fillets with the skin on. Others—walleye, perch and pike particularly—need the skin removed.

Flip the fillet over so that it lies skin side down. Starting at the tail end, insert the knife between the skin and the flesh, pinch the skin between your thumbnail and the working surface, and slide the knife along between the skin and the flesh until they're separated. (A cautionary note—if you are not going to eat your fish right away, but are storing them or transporting them home, you need to leave a patch of skin and scales on the flesh—at least 2.5 centimetres (1 inch) square—so the species can be identified.

Walleye and perch have a line of small bones that follows the lateral line along the inside of the fillet. If you run your finger along the lateral line from the front of the fillet towards the tail, you can feel them. Make a long slice above and below the lateral line to the point where these fine bones stop. Remove the narrow strip along with the bones. Clean the fillet in cold water, and either get it ready for the pan, or refrigerate until you're ready to cook. Freeze for longer term storage.

Northern pike have a set of bones called Y-bones, that run parallel to the lateral line, and just above it. You can see these in larger fish, and feel them by running your hand along the inside of the fillet. They can be removed. Slide your knife alongside each side of the Y separately, and cut into the fillet so that the cut meets where the base of the Y-bone sits deep in the fillet. Remove this v-shaped section of meat and you have a completely boneless pike. In many cases, removing the Y-bones will actually separate the fillet into two parts—a long skinny section from the top part of the fillet, and a wider section tapering from the rib area back to the tail. Both will be boneless and, when taken from icy cold water, amongst the best tasting fish you'll ever eat.

An alternative method for filleting pike yields three chunky fillets free of Y-bones. Start with the pike belly down on your work surface. Make a cut right behind the head, down to the spine. Turn your knife at 90 degrees, and work it along the top of the backbone to the tail. You will now have a back fillet that you can skin. Remove the dorsal fin by cutting around its base with a sharp knife and pulling on the fin with a pair of pliers.

Now you will see the tops of the Y-bones as you look down at the fish from above. Using the tip of your filleting knife, cut a line about a half-inch deep just outside the Y-

MICHAEL SNOOK

Preparing for shore lunch near Voyageur Lodge on the Churchill River.

bones on each side of the pike. Now turn the fish on its side. You can remove the remaining side fillets by first making a cut down the side of the fish immediately behind the gills, then working deeper from the cuts you made alongside the Y-bones until you free the fillet. Slide the knife along the length of the fish from the gills to the tail, lining up with the cuts you made on the outside edge of the Y-bones. Either way, your fillets will be bone free.

Two hard and fast rules for cleaning fish. First, keep your work surface clean. Fish slime isn't good for the fillet; it imparts a strong "fishy" taste, and it's about as slippery a substance as you'll find in nature, a real invitation to cutting yourself. Second, keep your knife razor-sharp. If you are cutting through tough skin and bones, use a diamond hone between fish to restore an edge. A sharper knife is safer to use: because you rarely have to force it, it is easier to control the direction and depth of the cut.

I know anglers who guard their favourite fillet knife like the gold at Fort Knox. No one else gets to use the knife, and certainly no one else gets to sharpen it. A good fillet knife, well-made and well-sharpened, is a thing of beauty and great practicality. A poor filleting knife, and particularly a dull one, will call from the depths of your being curses you never knew were in you. Invest in a good knife. Keep it sharp. Keep it clean. Learn to use it well and safely. Keep it in a case, and in a safe place. It will treat you very well in return.

COOKING YOUR CATCH

Fish can be poached, fried, deep-fried, broiled, baked, barbecued, cooked in foil, boiled in a stew or soup, or stir-fried. When it comes to cooking them, fish have one thing in common—they cook quickly. Overcooked fish tends to be dry, tasteless, tough, rubbery, leathery, and generally unattractive. Once the translucent quality is gone from the flesh of a freshwater fish, once it starts to flake, it's done. Get it away from the heat. Red or pink-fleshed fish—trout, salmon, char—that are a bit higher in fat and oil content, take a little longer to cook than white-fleshed fish like walleye, perch, or pike. But only a little.

There are hundreds, probably thousands, of recipes for cooking fish. Here are just a few favourites.

SHORE LUNCH WALLEYE

If you fish the northern waters of Saskatchewan with an outfitter, the odds are your guide will fix you a shore lunch of fresh walleye fillets. The simple recipe that follows, or a variation on it, will more than likely be the one used. If you hear the sound of arteries snapping shut as you read on, remember, you only do this a couple of times a year. I could say "please don't try this at home," but if you want the same taste, one that takes you back to a summer day on a northern water, then you'll have to follow the script and ignore your cardiologist's dire predictions. Here it is.

> boneless walleye fillets—2 or 3 per person
> canned brown beans
> several white or spanish onions
> a couple of new potatoes per person

You'll need three very large frying pans to make this work for a group of five or six or more. In the first one, put as many cans of beans on the fire to heat as you think you'll need. In the second one, melt a half-pound of lard (yes, *lard*—no substitute tastes the same), and heat until it is smoking hot. Cut potatoes and onions into thin slices, and fry.

In the third pan, place a full pound of lard (time to deep fry), and heat until it is smoking. Meanwhile, place walleye fillets in a plastic bag with a mix of white flour, salt, pepper, and other spices to taste. Give the bag a shake to cover the fillets with spiced flour. Place into hot oil and fry until golden brown, turning once or twice.

> Note: Cooking with hot oil or melted fat of any kind can be dangerous. Avoid splashing or spilling it, and do not overhead, as hot oil is highly flammable. You should always have a fire extinguisher and a package of baking soda at hand in your kitchen for emergencies.

When everything is ready, serve with a cold drink, and ketchup or the sauce of your choice. Enjoy.

QUICK AND EASY PERCH

After a day on the ice, coming home to a hot shower, a warm kitchen, and a feed of freshly caught perch is a treat. While perch can be cooked in a number of ways, this one is quick, easy, and very tasty.

> boneless fillets of perch, enough to serve your guests
> flour
> salt and pepper
> garlic powder (not salt)
> onion powder (not salt)
> other spices to taste

Place a couple of tablespoons of olive or canola oil in the bottom of a fry pan. Add about the same amount of butter. The oil will help keep the butter from burning. Heat until the oil and butter are hot, but not smoking.

Meanwhile, mix in a plastic bag the flour and spices. Place perch fillets in the bag and shake to completely cover.

Place fillets in hot oil and cook—a matter of a minute or two per side will usually do the trick, since perch fillets are thin. If the oil is hot enough (the fish should start to sizzle the moment it hits the pan), then the outer surface of the fish, coated with flour, will sear and seal up, and the oil won't get into the tissues of the fish. It will be flaky and light, not greasy tasting. Serve with your favourite vegetables, or with eggs for a breakfast treat.

LAKE TROUT À LA PARMESAN

Willem de Lint and Hugh Taylor, both architects and occasional anglers, showed me this trick for "kicking up" cooked lake trout when we visited Hugh at his camp on an island in Lac La Ronge.

> lake trout fillets, skin on, enough to serve your guests
> canola oil, butter
> salt, pepper, garlic powder, other spices to taste
> finely grated parmesan cheese

In a cast-iron frying pan, place a tablespoon or two of butter and enough canola oil to just cover the bottom of the pan. Heat until hot but not smoking. Place the trout fillet in the pan, skin side down, and cook until the fillet is nearly cooked through. The skin may turn crispy, but it will protect the fish from burning. Just before the fish is cooked, sprinkle with spices, then top with a generous coating of finely grated parmesan cheese. Continue to cook until cheese has melted and the fish has cooked through.

Serve with your favourite vegetables. Even picky eaters who may turn up their noses at fish will enjoy this combination of savoury spices, fresh trout, and earthy parmesan.

THAI CURRIED FISH FILLETS

This one is best with flaky white-fleshed fish, rather than heavier pink- or red-fleshed fish such as rainbow trout or lake trout.

> fish fillets—walleye, pike, perch—enough to serve your guests
> a few tablespoons olive oil
> chopped fresh garlic
> onions
> coconut milk
> green or red curry paste
> mango chutney
> one fresh lime
> raisins (optional)
> sweet red pepper
> sweet green pepper
> sweet yellow pepper
> button mushrooms
> slivered or flaked almonds
> brown sugar

Quantities will vary to suit the number of persons being served.

POACHING SAUCE: Start with a few tablespoons of olive oil. In a medium-sized sauté pan, heat the oil to medium high and add about a tablespoon of finely chopped fresh garlic, and half of a finely chopped medium-sized onion. Cook until both the onions and garlic are soft and starting to caramelize. Add a 400 ml can of coconut milk, and heat until the oil in the milk begins to separate—you'll see a darker, oily liquid around the edge of the pan. Add curry paste to taste (either red or green will work—green is more authentically Thai). Stir in the curry paste until completely mixed. Taste. Add more curry to taste. Add salt and pepper to taste. If you add too much curry, you can cool things off a bit by adding some 2% milk to the mix, but too much milk will thin out the liquid more than you want. Add a tablespoon or two of mango chutney.

Place fillets or chunks of fish in the liquid to poach. Add chopped red, green, and yellow peppers, chunks of onion, and whole button mushrooms. Add a tablespoon of brown sugar. Turn heat to medium low and simmer. While the fish is poaching, take a small frying pan, heat over medium heat, dry—no oil. When pan has started to heat, throw in slivered almonds and toast lightly. They'll darken a bit and you'll be able to smell the aroma when they're done. Don't burn them—they'll turn quite bitter. Set aside and let cool.

The fish will be cooked after about five or six minutes of poaching. It should flake easily when it's done.

Serve over a bed of basmati rice, with a fresh green salad and a yogurt-based dressing. Yogurt (and milk) help to cool down the spice of the curry. Water does not. Sprinkle the dry-toasted slivered almonds over each serving. If you don't happen to have any freshwater fish handy, fillet of sole is wonderful cooked in this manner.

BATTERED FISH

Special thanks to tournament angler, occasional fishing partner, and friend Mike Coupland for showing me the secret to getting crispy battered fish—dip it in the egg last.

    walleye, perch, pike or trout fillets or chunks, enough to serve your guests
    flour
    eggs
    salt and pepper
    spices to taste
    canola or virgin olive oil

Heat enough canola or olive oil in a sauté pan so that the fish will just be covered with oil when you place the fillets or chunks in the pan.

Salt and pepper the clean, boneless fish chunks on both sides. Spice with your favourite spice mixture. Put a half-cup or more of white flour in a plastic bag. Drop the seasoned chunks of fish into the flour, close the bag and shake well. Break and whisk an egg or two (depending on quantity of fish to be cooked) in a shallow bowl. Take the fish pieces one at a time out of the flour, dip into the egg so the fish is completely covered, and place in hot oil in the pan. The oil should be hot enough that it bubbles and sizzles as the fish is placed into it.

When the battered fish has turned golden brown on the bottom, turn over with tongs to finish the other side. Remove from the oil, place on paper towelling to drain off excess oil. Serve with a fresh salad and potatoes.

This method of cooking gives you that English "fish and chips" touch.

BARBECUED LAKE TROUT (RAINBOW TROUT)

Simple recipe for trout, especially lake trout and rainbow trout, on the grill.

    fillets of trout, enough to serve your guests
    a lemon
    salt and pepper
    garlic powder

Place the fish skin-side down on a greased grill in the barbecue (skinless fish should not be cooked this way—it will stick or fall through the grill as it cooks). On the open side of the fillet, sprinkle salt and pepper to taste, garlic powder, and the freshly squeezed juice of half the lemon. Reserve the other half to serve with the fish.

If the fillet is barbecued whole, it should not be turned over as it will probably break into pieces. If the trout is larger, and cut into single serving chunks, it can be grilled on both sides. A whole fillet will cook through from the skin side. To help it along, place a piece of tin foil over the top once the fish is close to being cooked.

Serve with rice or potatoes and a salad. Sprinkle with lemon juice and fresh parsley.

TIN FOIL TROUT

rainbow or lake trout, enough to serve your guests
large piece of heavy-gauge aluminum foil
butter
salt and pepper
one lemon
soy sauce
teriyaki sauce
hoisin sauce
garlic

Place a large rainbow trout or lake trout fillet, skin side down, on a piece of aluminum foil big enough to completely wrap the fillet. Slice a lemon and place on top of the fish. Sprinkle with finely chopped garlic, salt and pepper, and place three large dabs of butter on top of the fish.

Drizzle about a tablespoon each of soy sauce, teriyaki sauce, and hoisin sauce over the fish. Wrap the foil around the fish and fold over so that it is tightly sealed.

You can place the foil in a 350 degree oven, but I prefer to cook this dish on the barbecue. Place the foil in the middle of the grill. Set the temperature on a gas grill to medium. When using a charcoal grill, let the coals burn down a bit, or raise the grill to about 6 inches about the coals. The taste is better if this dish cooks slowly.

After about ten minutes, check the fish. If it is no longer translucent, and it if flakes easily, then the fish is cooked.

Excellent when served with rice and a fresh salad.

There are literally hundreds of recipes for cooking fish. Their success depends on a few basic principles. First, use the freshest, cleanest fish you can get. There's nothing like lake trout or trout, freshly caught out of cold clean water, cleaned and put on the heat right away. Second, cook fish quickly, and don't overcook it. And third, if you are going to freeze your catch, protect it from the air and from frostburn by double wrapping it and sealing it well. Some anglers keep fish in their freezer by putting several fillets in an empty, waxed milk carton, filling the carton up with water, and then freezing the whole thing. It works. But you can't transport fish this way because the species and number of fillets can't be determined. Fish does not freeze well over the long term. Try to use it within no more than six months unless you can ensure that it is exceptionally well sealed. Fresh fish is a fine-tasting, nutritious, and healthy food, a great reward after a day's fishing, and an excellent reason to practice conservation—so that our grandchildren can enjoy the same great meals that we have.

CHAPTER NINE
GUIDED FISHING TRIPS

SAB RB 5098 (4)

Maurice Smith (left) from Winnipeg and Jimmy Robinson (right) from Minneapolis show off their catch of northern pike at Lac La Ronge.

For some, a guided fishing trip to a remote wilderness lake is a once-in-a-lifetime experience, the chance to travel to the farthest reaches of the north country for trophy lake trout and northern pike. For others, it is an annual pilgrimage to closer and less expensive destinations. Either way, Saskatchewan offers a great variety of guided fishing experiences, provided by outfitters who operate on dozens of water bodies across the province.

While wilderness fishing trips in Saskatchewan are available to those who would rather drive in than fly, odds are that the further north you are going, the more likely you are to be flying in to a remote lake and using the services of an outfitter. Any outfitted trip will cost you more than a 'do-it-yourself' expedition, so how do you go about making sure that you are getting the best value for your buck?

KNOW YOURSELF

The real secret to a successful guided fishing trip lies with you, the angler, and with anyone who is going with you. The key? Know yourself. Seems like an old, familiar saying, and hardly one that applies to a few days fishing in a pristine northern wilderness. But in fact, it remains the best piece of advice you'll ever get.

No two wilderness fishing trips are created equal. Not all outfitters offer the same services. Some trips require little more than your fishing gear, clothing, and a few personal effects. You'll be treated like a king, expected to do nothing more physically demanding than fight your fish. All your meals will be taken care of, your bedding will be fresh and well-laundered—you might as well be staying in a quality downtown hotel, albeit with an infinitely better view. Such premium trips cost more, but make your life easier—you just concentrate on catching fish and enjoying yourself.

Some trips may require you to do a little walking on well-marked trails to get to that special lake where the trout are bothered by only a dozen or so anglers a year. You may decide to take a fly-out option from base camp to a more primitive setting, where you are expected to handle the boat and motor on your own, cook for yourself, deal with camp chores, and generally take care of yourself and your friends in a wilderness setting. Still other trips may require some strenuous physical effort on your part, portaging a canoe and gear into a remote lake in order to reach your destination.

Long before you start making phone calls to outfitters or giving deposits on the trip-of-a-lifetime, then, do some thinking. What kind of trip are you interested in? What species of fish are you after? How much of a wilderness experience do you want to have? How much time do you have? What is your fitness level? What is your appetite and tolerance for adventure (which often translates into more than a little bit of adversity)? What are the seasons like where you plan to go? The further north you travel, the later spring comes, the earlier winter sets in, and summer itself can be surprisingly brief but intense—all of which has a profound effect on fishing. How well do you tolerate bad weather? Do you have the gear necessary for the trip you're considering? What is the best time of year to fish for a certain species on a specific body of water? What kind of clothing and fishing gear will you need? If something does go wrong, how will you and the outfitter deal with an emergency situation? Is there a radio phone or satellite phone in camp that allows contact with the outside world? How many people are going on the trip? What are their likes and dislikes? Do you all want more or less the same thing out of the trip? One of an outfitter's worst nightmares is a group of individuals who have completely different and incompatible expectations of the trip. No one is ever happy when this happens, and there is no easy solution when you are miles from home and the money has already been spent. The best solution is to find out about expectations before you even send in your deposit. Consult with your friends, discuss as many details of the trip as you can, and make sure you all agree on what you want to do.

An outfitter can't provide what isn't there. If you are a pike fanatic, go to a spot known for lots of pike with a good chance at catching a trophy. Stay away from lakes full of rainbow trout, with only a small pike population. While many northern lakes support good populations of both northern pike and lake trout, some of these same lakes will hold only token populations of walleye. So, if you hanker after a good shore lunch of walleye fillets, it pays to check things out in advance.

And of, course, knowing yourself includes knowing your budget. As is often the

JACK TUNNICLIFFE

The author and Chris Tunnicliffe preparing for an outfitted fishing trip on the Churchill River.

case, you get what you pay for, and the more services, the more remote the location, the more exclusive the fishing territory, the rarer the fishing experience, the more you can expect to pay for the experience. But while no outfitted trip worth doing is cheap, there are some very good values available. By value, I don't necessarily mean 'low cost,' but rather, great return for the money you spend. If you can drive to your destination lake, stay in a cabin where you do the cooking, have the option of fishing alone using your own boat, then clearly, your cost will be more modest than for a trip to a fly-in destination with all the bells and whistles provided by someone else.

DO YOUR HOMEWORK

Having given much thought to your own expectations and goals for your guided fishing trip, you can then set about finding the outfitter who will best help you to achieve those goals.

First, make use of licensed outfitters only. Licensed outfitters will usually be members of the Saskatchewan Association of Outfitters, and any outfitter who is licensed should be able to show you a piece of paper issued by the Province of Saskatchewan

SAB SB 3335

Guide Paul and tourist officer Red Wilkinson take the hook from a 27-pound lake trout at Wapata Lake, 1960. Today, a laker of this size would most likely be handled gently and released.

SAB RB 5098 (7)

Jimmy Robinson with northern pike at Lac La Ronge. His guide was Tom Venn, La Ronge.

proving their status. Individual guides, whether working on their own or for an outfitter, should have a guide card or a letter from a licensed outfitter indicating that they are employed by the outfitter.

When choosing an outfitter, you'll want to ask a lot of questions. Is the outfitter operating on a catch-and-release basis? How does the fishing vary with time of year? If guides are provided by the outfitter, are they experienced anglers who know what's going on, or are they essentially boat drivers who will get you out on the water and back to camp? If you have to hire a guide separately from the services provided by the outfitter, are there guides available locally? Can they be arranged for through your outfitter? Are they experienced? Are the fish a long boat ride from camp or close by? Does the camp provide shore lunch? Does the price you pay cover boat, motor, gas (with insurance on the boat included) as well as a guide? Are you expected to provide your own food and cook your own meals, or will all this be taken care of? Do you have to bring your own bedding, or does the lodge provide this? If the fishing lodge does all the cooking, what sort of menu is offered? The range is great, from simple but wholesome fare, to gourmet cooking in a fabulous setting. Does the outfitter offer filleting and freezing services?

If you are using the services of an outfitter for the first time, don't be afraid to ask for references. You should be able to get the outfitter to provide you with a list of names to contact. You may have friends or acquaintances who have fished with an outfitter in the past few years. When checking references, you can find out not only how the outfitter treated their client generally, but also other details that only someone who has actually been there could possibly know. You can find out if the fishing is as advertised, if the species you want to catch are actually there; you can find out about the condition of the camp itself, of the boats and motors you'll be depending on while you're out fishing; you can find out what kind of tackle was useful, and what wasn't.

When checking references, however, be fair. Remember always that no matter how remarkable a spot is reputed to be, weather, time of year, water levels, and the skill of the angler can all make a big difference to fishing success. If you do encounter a bad reference, listen carefully to what is being said. Some people can't be satisfied no matter what! A reference that is couched in generalities isn't much use to anyone. Ask for specifics when you check a reference, whether the comments you are getting are good or bad. Ask for the same specifics when you talk to the outfitter directly.

Even after you've selected your outfitter, you will still be looking for answers to ensure that your fishing trip is everything you want it to be. If a previous client or the outfitter says that spoons work best on lake trout, find out what size, what colour, what brand name, fished fast, fished slow, etc. If an outfitter says "bring lots of jigs—you'll be fishing for walleye in rocks, and the river has plenty of current," ask what weight the jigs should be, what colours, and how many you are likely to lose in a day's fishing. Find out if the outfitter stocks any tackle at his lodge or base camp. If not, you should bring extras with you just in case. Whether you're checking a reference or getting information from the outfitter, you should be able to get detailed answers to your questions.

A GUIDE TO FISHING GUIDES

Note that, when your guide is included in your package price, you're still expected to tip. A good fishing guide can make or break your fishing trip. Someone who knows the water, understands where the fish will be, and when, and how to get their attention, is invaluable. A guide who can also teach you a few tricks of the angling trade, who can take you to quiet, out-of-the-way places you would never find on your own, who has a sense of humour when things aren't going so well, is worth his or her weight in gold. Unless you're an experienced bush hand, your safety and well-being are in the hands of your guide. A guide's judgements about weather and water conditions, about whether a particular set of rapids is safe or too dangerous to run, are critical. An inexperienced, ill-informed, unskilled guide is just plain dangerous. Fortunately, they are the exception rather than the rule.

Every fishing guide I know has a story or two to tell about the impossible client—the guy who's been everywhere, done everything, caught every fish, knows everything, and isn't shy about telling you. I've collected one or two myself over the years. Wherever you're fishing, it isn't as good as some other place. Whatever you're catching, there are bigger and better fish just around the corner. Faced with such a client, a guide has only his sense of humour and his patience to get him through the day. On the other hand, a client who is a well-informed and skillful angler is a joy to work with.

Many guides working in northern Saskatchewan are First Nations people. The waters we visit as tourists, to fish and enjoy for a few days, and the land around the rivers and lakes we travel on—this is their home, the place where they live, where they earn

MICHAEL SNOOK

Tony Charles, an experienced Churchill River guide.

their living, where they raise their families. It is only common courtesy for a visitor to treat his host's home as he would his own backyard. The fact that we are on a paid fishing trip does not mean that we are free to litter or to treat the land with disrespect. The same "leave no trace" ethic that should govern our relationship to the natural world applies when we're on a guided fishing trip.

TRADE SHOWS

Many of us book our outfitted fishing trips when we attend outdoor or sports and leisure shows, most often held in mid-winter to early spring each year. Outfitters will sometimes offer special package deals at such shows, in an effort to attract attention and book their camp as fully as they can, in advance of the season.

A word or two to the wise. Never let a good deal get between you and your common sense. If someone offers you a fishing package at a great price, but on waters you don't particularly care for, fishing for species that don't particularly interest you in conditions that don't match your likes and dislikes, then the deal is no deal at all. Prepare in advance for the annual sports and leisure show. Figure out what you want to do, when, how, where, how much you can spend, and go to the show prepared to take advantage of the offer that best matches your needs. You'll have a better time, and, frankly, so will your outfitter, who wants a satisfied customer who will not only come again but who will also tell others about the good experience he's had.

Most outfitters represent themselves at show events. It is, in fact, extremely rare for outfitters or lodges to be represented by 'sales agents' or other third parties. If you encounter such a person, be cautious. I used such a sales agent once, only to find out far too late that he actually represented no one, took deposits that he never passed on for bookings he never made, and left a string of unhappy anglers and frustrated lodge owners in his wake. This particular individual was very cool, very smart, very engaging. He offered no great deals, no enticements. He set up in a small booth at the show, and offered a service—he would take bookings for several desirable fishing destinations that were not able to be present at the show, and had asked him to represent them. It was a credible presentation, very convincing, and it fooled a lot of people.

When in doubt, take down all the information you need at the show, and follow up with a booking later, dealing directly with the outfitter or lodge owner by phone, fax, e-mail, or mail. If a sales agent is involved with a particular outfitter, you can find out directly by asking the outfitter. And if anyone at a sports and leisure or outdoor show refuses to give you information that lets you deal directly with an outfitter or lodge owner, just walk away.

FINAL ADVICE

Once you've made your plans, done your research, picked your spot, made your booking and are on your way, there are still a few things to think about. No one can guarantee the weather. An early or late spring or fall can make all the difference to a fishing trip, and that's something no outfitter has control over. An experienced outfitter will know the waters in his or her territory well enough to tell you what the fish are doing in most weather conditions, but a late spring snowstorm or an early fall blizzard can put a damper on anyone's trip. Outfitters don't generally refund your money if weather spoils your trip. They take the same risks that you do and depend on the unpredictable cooperation of mother nature. Some outfitters may offer you a discount on a future trip. If a whole trip has to be cancelled—because of a late breakup in spring or an early freeze-up in fall, for instance, an outfitter may offer you alternate dates for your trip. When you make your booking, ask the outfitter about their policy on such things, so there are no surprises other than the ones dealt out by mother nature herself.

I first visited Churchill River Voyageur Lodge as a writer, doing a feature article on northern river walleye fishing for *Western Sportsman* magazine. The plan was to spend two days fishing the river—enough time to catch fish, take photos, take notes, and get to know the place.

The first day of fishing was spectacular—better than a hundred walleye caught and released in our party of four, most of them caught by my wife who put on quite a show for the guide, one of the lodge owners, and yours truly. After an exceptional day, we settled in for the evening, looking forward to a second day of great fishing and exploring another part of the river we hadn't seen yet. Nature had other plans.

That night, smoke from forest fires running out of control further upriver blew down the valley when the wind shifted. The smoke reduced visibility to a few dozen metres and made breathing a chore. We cancelled the second day of fishing, and

JACK TUNNICLIFFE

From left to right, Tony Charles (guide), the author, Chris Tunnicliffe, Benjamin Dewalt, and Kevin Dewalt, fishing near Voyageur Lodge on the Churchill River.

everyone boated out the next morning in a haze so thick it was impossible to see the shoreline as we passed. But nature has since more than made up for that one missed day of fishing. I've been back to the same place almost every year since that first trip and have had nothing but beautiful weather, clear skies, and even better fishing than on our first visit.

To enjoy good fishing in Saskatchewan, it isn't necessary to travel great distances, fly into the wilderness, and use the services of an outfitter. Good fishing can, in fact, be had in every corner of the province, from border to border, north to south and east to west. However, there is little that can match the experience of fishing a northern wilderness lake accessible only by air and guided by someone who knows the waters, understands the behaviour of the fish, and is there to make sure you have the time of your life. This is the best of what fishing is all about—not just catching and releasing fish, but doing so in an exquisite wilderness environment.

CHAPTER TEN
WHERE TO FISH
IN SOUTHERN SASKATCHEWAN

SAB RB 5116 (1)

Tourists fishing at Echo Lake, 1962.

T his is the first of three chapters identifying fishable water in the province of Saskatchewan. With over 90,000 bodies of water to choose from, it's simply not possible to list every single place an angler might want to wet a line. So, these chapters will concentrate on major watersheds, the most accessible fisheries, and locations that provide anglers with the most varied of fishing opportunities. It will also stress natural bodies of water over small, local reservoirs. These reservoirs are often stocked for put and take fisheries and may provide excellent angling. Information on stocked ponds in Saskatchewan that are available to the public can be obtained from local offices of Saskatchewan Environment. Regional parks and local parks are often associated with these reservoirs, and local information about them is readily available.

Map 3. Saskatchewan's Southern Fishing Zone

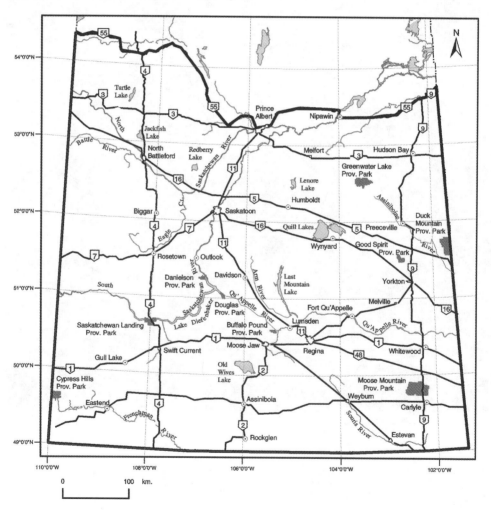

In organizing the material for this section of the book, the author has chosen to follow the lead of Saskatchewan Environment, which divides the province up into northern, central, and southern zones for purposes of opening and closing dates for fishing seasons, for special rules related to catch-and-release, and for specific species limits that apply to certain species or to specific bodies of water.

The east, west, and southern boundaries of the southern zone are defined by the province's border with Manitoba, Alberta, and the United States. The northern boundary of the southern zone is an irregular line that runs from just south of Pierceland near the Alberta border through Meadow Lake, then drops south through Big River and east through Prince Albert. The boundary then swings northeast through Smeaton and Nipawin and on to the Manitoba border at about 53.7 degrees of latitude. The northern boundary of the southern zone follows Highway 55 from the Alberta border to Shellbrook, Highways 55 and 3 through Prince Albert, Highway 55 to its junction with Highway 9, and Highway 9 to the Manitoba border. Anglers fishing near the northern edge of the southern zone should check the map provided by Saskatchewan Environment with the annual fishing guide, and consult with the local office if in doubt about which zone a particular body of water is in.

As a convenient reference for anglers familiar with the Canadian topographical map index system, the map number for the area in which each waterbody is found is listed (Cypress Hills area, for example, can be found on map 72F). Anglers wishing to obtain large-scale maps can use the Canadian Index, available through the Canadian Map Office, to find topographical maps of all regions. (See Appendix F for maps and other sources of information).

Wherever a provincial park, regional park, or licensed outfitter is associated with a specific body of water, these will be identified. Most bodies of water will be identified with the nearest community where services of any kind are located. While the majority of outfitters operate in the central and northern zones of Saskatchewan, there are fishing outfitters in the southern part of the province as well. Where these are known, they are listed here. Please consult with the Saskatchewan Outfitters Association and Saskatchewan Environment for more complete outfitter information.

ADMIRAL RESERVOIR (72F)

The town of Admiral is located in the southwest corner of Saskatchewan, about 18 kilometres west of Highway 4, at the junction of Highway 13 and Secondary Highway 638. The reservoir is located about 6 kilometres (4 miles) southwest of the town, on a gravel grid road. It contains a native population of walleye, sauger, and yellow perch. The reservoir is small—only 41 hectares.

ALAMEDA RESERVOIR (62F)

Alameda Reservoir is one of Saskatchewan's newest fisheries, the result of a damming of Moose Mountain Creek just north of where it flows into the Souris River. It is located 3 kilometres (2 miles) east of Highway 9 and the town of Alameda, on a gravel grid. Alameda Reservoir offers private camping facilities and a good launch ramp. It is a pike, walleye, and perch fishery.

ARMIT RIVER (63C)

The Armit River is one of a number of trout fisheries in the Porcupine Hills area. It runs south from Highway 3, through the town of Armit, just a short distance west of the Manitoba–Saskatchewan border in east-central Saskatchewan. It is accessible by trail, and holds a population of brook trout.

ASSINIBOINE RIVER (62M, 62N)

The Assiniboine River's headwaters are to be found southeast of Greenwater Provincial Park in eastern Saskatchewan. From there, the river flows south and east through Preeceville, past Sturgess and Kamsack, and on into the north end of Lake of the Prairies. From the south end of the lake, it flows south and east, meets the Qu'Appelle at St. Lazarre, and eventually turns east, flowing all the way to its junction with the Red River in the heart of Winnipeg, Manitoba. The river crosses Highways 49, 9, 5, 8, and 357 between its source and the top of Lake of the Prairies, affording shore anglers numerous points of access to the northern pike, walleye, and perch found in its waters.

SAB RA 13,968

Russell and Earle Short of Swift Current fish at a trout pool on Belanger Creek, Cypress Hills area (July 1958).

AVONLEA RESERVOIR (72H)

Not far from the town of Avonlea, just off Highway 334, is Avonlea Reservoir, created by a dam built in the 1960s under the *Prairie Farm Rehabilitation Act*. This local fishery, 231 hectares in size, is located at a regional park, equipped with a good launch ramp, and is a favourite destination for anglers seeking pan-sized walleye on small, easy-to-fish waters.

BARRIER LAKE (63D)

Barrier Lake is accessible by gravel road off Highway 35 at Archerwill. It has a good launch ramp, and is serviced by an outfitter—Barrier Beach Resort—offering accommodation (year-round), auto and marine fuel, and canoe and boat rentals. The store and restaurant are open from May to September. The lake holds pike, walleye, and perch.

BATKA LAKE (62N)

Batka Lake is one of several small lakes found within the boundaries of Duck Mountain Provincial Park, a full service park located on Highway 57 at the border between Saskatchewan and Manitoba. Batka Lake is 31 hectares, accessible by gravel road, with a poor quality launch ramp. It holds pike, walleye, and yellow perch.

BEAR CREEK (72F)

Bear Creek, located 24 kilometres (15 miles) south of the town of Piapot, is accessible through private land and is a managed brook trout fishery. See Chapter 5 for more details on this southwestern fishery located on the north slope of the Cypress Hills.

BELANGER CREEK (72F)

About 13 kilometres (8 miles) south of Cypress Hills Interprovincial Park on Highway 21 you'll find access to Belanger Creek, home to brook, brown, and rainbow trout. The creek is easiest to access south of the Davis Creek grid. See Chapter 5 for details.

BESANT CREEK (72I)

Besant Creek is a small creek that runs through Besant Campground, a private campground found just to the south of the Trans-Canada, a short distance west of the town of Caronport. The creek is home to stocked populations of brook and rainbow trout.

BIG SHELL LAKE (73G)

Located 12 kilometres (7 miles) southwest of the town of Shell Lake, Big Shell Lake has a private campground and access to the water at a good boat launch. The lake holds burbot, northern pike, walleye, and perch.

BIRCH LAKE (62F)

Birch Lake is a small 24-hectare lake located within the boundaries of Moose Mountain Provincial Park, a full service park. The lake is accessible by trail and holds yellow perch.

BLACKSTRAP RESERVOIR (72O)

When you drive northwest from Regina to Saskatoon on Highway 11, and just before you reach the community of Dundurn, if you look to the east of the highway you'll notice a high, cone-shaped hill. Blackstrap "mountain" is a man-made ski hill overlooking Blackstrap Lake, a man-made reservoir, and a favourite local fishing spot for anglers from nearby Saskatoon. Blackstrap is accessed from Highway 11 by a clearly marked grid road.

The reservoir, which is about 1,200 hectares in size and divided roughly in half by a causeway, holds burbot, pike, walleye, whitefish, and yellow perch. A good launch ramp at a provincial recreation site provides access to anglers with boats. The causeway is a popular spot for shorebound anglers.

BONE CREEK (72F)

Bone Creek is 45 kilometres (28 miles) of trout water accessible at several points along its length. The Klintonel reach is 47 kilometres (29 miles) due south of Piapot on Highway 614. Carmichael Bridge is found 16 kilometres (10 miles) south of the town of Carmichael on the municipal grid road, and Tompkins crossing is 30 kilometres (19 miles) south of the town of Tompkins on Grid Road 633. The creek is managed for brown trout. Chapter 5 provides more details on this excellent fishery.

BOUNDARY DAM RESERVOIR (62E)

Boundary Dam Reservoir was created by a dam built on Long Creek, just south of where it flows into the Souris River. The reservoir was built to provide cooling water

SAB RB 11,161

Aerial view of the Boundary Dam Power Station, Estevan, in operation in 1963. The river can be seen behind the building.

for the Shand Power Station. Warm water from the power plant flows back into the reservoir, creating an artificial environment that enables Saskatchewan anglers and visitors alike to experience an unusual fishery for the prairies—largemouth bass. The largemouth population of the lake is doing very well, reproducing naturally, and fish in the 7-pound range have been caught. These would rank as decent bass anywhere, but particularly in a habitat so much outside of their normal range. Access to the reservoir is on paved road off Highway 47, about 5 kilometres (3 miles) south of the town of Estevan. The relatively small reservoir—about 600 hectares in size—boasts a rich fishery because of the effect on the habitat of the warm water inflow. Besides largemouth bass, the reservoir holds a good population of perch, pike, and walleye. For anglers who are prepared to brave the cold, the warm water provides the opportunity to fish from shore into open water well into the winter months. The reservoir features a good launch ramp, barbecue facilities in a recreational area near the boat launch, and good parking. The nearby town of Estevan offers full services to visiting anglers.

BRIGHTSAND LAKE (73F)

Brightsand Lake is located 27 kilometres (17 miles) southeast of the town of St. Walburg. It is the site of a regional park which provides serviced and non-serviced campsites and a concrete boat launch. The lake holds pike, walleye, and perch.

CALF CREEK (72F)

Calf Creek is a tributary to another southwestern trout fishery, Conglomerate Creek. Calf can be found 46 kilometres (29 miles) south of the town of Piapot on Grid Road 614; access it by taking a short walk through a pasture. Calf Creek is managed as a brown trout fishery. See Chapter 5 for more details.

CATON CREEK (72F)

Drive 35 kilometres (22 miles) south of Maple Creek, and 14 kilometres (9 miles) east on the Davis Creek grid to the Spring Valley Guest Ranch, where parking is available for those wishing to fish for brook trout in Caton Creek. See Chapter 5 for details.

CHITEK LAKE (73G)

Chitek Lake is located at the north end of Highway 24, about 60 kilometres (37 miles) north of Spiritwood. The lake has a Saskatchewan Environment campsite, and Little Pine Lodge outfitters offer cabins, boats and motors, and fuel, as well as ice-fishing services in winter. Chitek Lake holds populations of northern pike, walleye, whitefish, and perch.

CODETTE RESERVOIR (73H)

Located adjacent to the town of Codette, Codette Reservoir is a man-made impoundment on the Saskatchewan River created by the building of the Francois-Findlay dam. Access to the reservoir is through the Wapiti Valley Regional Park, east of Highway 6 on the north side of the reservoir, about 16 kilometres (10 miles) north of Gronlid. The marina at the park features a boat launch in a sheltered bay, boat rentals, and a store selling tackle and bait. There is a small provincial campground just to the east of Highway 6 on the southern shore of the reservoir. Codette Lake holds burbot, walleye, northern pike, whitefish, and perch.

CONDIE RESERVOIR (72I)

Condie Reservoir is found at a provincial recreation site about 12 kilometres (7 miles) northwest of the city of Regina, just west of Highway 11. In the reservoir itself and in the waters of adjoining Boggy Creek, anglers can find walleye, pike, and perch. Fishing in Boggy Creek is generally limited to shore fishing, while anglers on Condie Reservoir favour canoes and float tubes or float boats.

CONGLOMERATE CREEK (72F)

Located 40 kilometres (25 miles) south of the town of Piapot and about 8.4 kilometres (5 miles) north of the town of Eastend on Grid Road 614, Conglomerate Creek can be accessed from several points with available parking. Conglomerate is managed as a brown trout fishery. See Chapter 5 for further details.

COWAN LAKE (73G)

Cowan Lake, located just north of Big River in a beautiful boreal forest setting, is a long thin lake that parallels Highway 55 for about 50 kilometres (31 miles). There is public access at the town of Big River with a good boat launch. The nearby regional park has camping facilities and shower/laundry/washroom facilities on site. Additional services can be found 29 kilometres (18 miles) north of Big River at Poplar Point Resort/Grizzly Hill Outfitters. Though primarily a hunting outfitter, Poplar Point has cabins to house up to forty persons, and fifteen non-electric campsites. They provide boat launch access to the lake and other services. Cowan Lake holds pike, walleye, and perch.

CYPRESS HILLS (72F)

Located south of the town of Maple Creek, Cypress Hills Interprovincial Park is home to several stocked trout fisheries. Battle Creek, in the park's West Block, is accessible by way of Highway 271, about 50 kilometres (31 miles) southwest of Maple Creek. Loch Leven and Boiler Creek are both found in the park's Centre Block, 28 kilometres (17 miles) south of Maple Creek on Highway 21. Battle Creek holds brown and rainbow trout; Boiler Creek is a brook trout fishery; and Loch Leven hosts brookies, rainbows and cutthroat trout. For more information on trout fishing in southwestern Saskatchewan, see Chapter 5.

EASTEND RESERVOIR (72F)

Eastend Reservoir is located 4 kilometres (2 miles) west of the town of Eastend. This 112-hectare fishery contains northern pike, walleye, and yellow perch.

FAIRWELL CREEK (72F)

Located just off gravel Grid Road 724, about 15 kilometres (9 miles) north of the town of Ravenscrag, Fairwell Creek is managed as a brook, brown, and rainbow trout fishery. Access to the creek is through private land, and permission should be sought from the landowner.

FISHING LAKE (62M)

Fishing Lake is a 2,800-hectare lake, located 5 kilometres (3 miles) south of the town of Kuroki off Highway 5. It features regional park facilities at Saskin Beach, K.C. Beach, and Leslie Beach, all of which have boat launches and provide other services. The lake holds burbot, pike, walleye, and yellow perch.

FRENCHMAN RIVER (72F)

The Frenchman River is a major watershed in southwest Saskatchewan that runs from the Cypress Hills through the town of Eastend and Grasslands National Park and into northern Montana. It is accessible at a number of points along its length. It is crossed by Highway 13 at Eastend, by Highway 37, which runs south from Gull Lake through Shaunavon, and by Highway 4, which runs due south from Swift Current. The Frenchman River is home to burbot, northern pike, walleye, and yellow perch.

GOOD SPIRIT LAKE (62M)

Located in Good Spirit Lake Provincial Park, north and west of the town of Yorkton on Highways 9 and 229, Good Spirit Lake is accessible by paved road. Though it is in a provincial park, it has a poor launch ramp. The 4,600-hectare reservoir holds pike, walleye, and yellow perch.

SAB RA 315

Canoeing on the Frenchman River near Eastend.

GREEN LAKE (73J)

Green Lake is located just south of Highway 55, near the town of Green Lake. It is serviced by three outfitters—Bait Masters Bear Hunting Camp, Green Lake Lodge, and Northern Field and Stream Outfitters. Bait Masters is primarily a hunting camp. Green Lake Lodge offers both cabin and camping accommodation, boat rentals and fuel, and a launch ramp. Northern Field and Stream offers hunting and fishing opportunities. Green Lake holds pike, walleye, and whitefish.

GREENWATER LAKE (63D)

Bordered by Highway 35 on the west, Highway 3 in the north, Highway 49 to the south, and by the Manitoba border on the east is a largely unpopulated and road-less area dotted with dozens of small lakes and streams and dominated by a land-form along its eastern edge called the Porcupine Hills. Much of this area is unpopulated and roadless. Within this area is Greenwater Provincial Park, which straddles Highway 38 about 50 kilometres (31 miles) north of the town of Kelvington. Greenwater Lake is the largest of the park's bodies of water at just under 1,000 hectares. The lake is accessible on paved road, has a good launch ramp, and holds populations of burbot, pike, walleye, and perch.

HAY MEADOW CREEK (72H)

Located 1 kilometre (less than 1 mile) south of the town of Lisieux on Highway 2, Hay Meadow Creek is a small, brook trout creek.

JACKFISH CREEK (73F)

Jackfish Creek has its source north of the town of Glaslyn and flows southwest, then southeast into Jackfish Lake. The creek is accessible where Grid Road 794 crosses it, about 8 kilometres (5 miles) southwest of town and through private land (permission should be sought for access through private lands). The creek holds a population of brook trout.

JACKFISH LAKE (73F)

Located 35 kilometres (22 miles) north of North Battleford on Highway 4, Jackfish Lake is over 8,000 hectares in size and is accessible from the towns of Cochin, Meota, and Aquadeo Beach. Battlefords Provincial Park provides access to Jackfish Lake with two boat launches, while adjacent Murray Lake is accessible through Lehman Creek at Cochin. The park offers all services, including campgrounds and service centres with laundry and toilet facilities. Meota Regional Park offers camping and a concrete launch ramp, as well as services in the nearby town. Walleye, perch, pike, and whitefish are abundant in both Jackfish and Murray Lakes.

JUMBO LAKE (73K)

Jumbo Lake is 1 kilometre (less than 1 mile) west of the town of Loon Lake, situated just off Highway 26, in Makwa Lake Provincial Park (see Makwa Lake). The 1,100-hectare lake is accessible by gravel road and has a good quality launch ramp. Jumbo Beach Resort offers a lakeside store, boat rentals, and a restaurant. The lake holds a good population of pike, walleye, whitefish, and perch.

KENOSEE LAKE (62F)

The main recreational lake in Moose Mountain Provincial Park, Kenosee Lake is a shallow body of water that is periodically subject to winter kill. The 835-hectare lake holds northern pike and yellow perch. Anglers wishing to launch their boats on Kenosee have access to a good boat launch.

KIPABISKAU LAKE (73A)

Kipabiskau Lake, on the Barrier River, is 19 kilometres (12 miles) east of the town of Pleasantdale, off Highway 6. It is also accessed off Highway 35 to the east, in both cases by gravel road. It hosts a Regional Park with a good launch ramp, boat rentals and fishing tackle for sale on site. The lake holds populations of pike, walleye, and perch.

LAC PELLETIER (72G)

Lac Pelletier is the site of a regional park, accessible by driving south on Highway 4 from the town of Swift Current for 30 kilometres (19 miles) then west on Highway 343 about another 10 kilometres (6 miles). A busy resort area with a store and food facilities, the park features serviced and unserviced campsites and a good boat launch. The lake, which is 6 kilometres (4 miles) long, holds burbot, whitefish, northern pike, walleye, and yellow perch.

SAB RB 4450 (1)

Aerial view of Lac Pelletier, south of Swift Current, 1959.

LAKE OF THE PRAIRIES (62N)

Lake of the Prairies is a major impoundment of the Assiniboine River. Formed by a dam at the Manitoba end of the lake just north of Shellmouth, the lake runs from just south of Highway 357, east across Highway 369 before crossing the border into Manitoba. Best access to the lake is via Highway 10, approximately 63 kilometres (39 miles) east of Yorkton. Lake of the Prairies plays host to a major walleye tournament every June and is managed under Manitoba regulations as a quality walleye fishery. It contains walleye, northern pike, and yellow perch.

LAST MOUNTAIN LAKE (72I, 72P)

Along with Lake Diefenbaker and the Qu'Appelle chain of lakes, Last Mountain Lake is one of the premier fisheries of south Saskatchewan. Located between Highways 11, 2, and 20, it is accessible at numerous points along its nearly 120-kilometre (75-mile) length. Last Mountain Lake is less than an hour's drive from the city of Regina and boasts trophy walleye and pike fishing, as well as jumbo perch and burbot, during both open-water and ice-fishing seasons. Walleye over 4.5 kilograms (10 pounds) and pike over 9 kilos (20 pounds) are caught each year in Last Mountain Lake, some of the biggest of these through the ice. Yellow perch over half a kilogram (1 pound) and over 31 centimetres (12 inches) in length are taken by anglers fishing Last Mountain Lake, again, many of these through the ice. The lake is also a world-class carp fishery, with wild carp in excess of 14 kilograms (30 pounds) caught on the lake each year.

Access to the lake can be found at many points, particularly where cottage developments have sprung up along the lakeshore. Public launch ramps are found at Regina Beach (Highway 11 to Highway 54 then north to Regina Beach); at Saskatchewan Beach (Highway 20 to Highway 322); at Rowan's Ravine Provincial

Carp taken from Last Mountain Lake on display at the Regina Exhibition, August 1956.

Park (Highway 20 to Highway 220, then due west into the park); and at Last Mountain Lake Regional Park (west of Govan off Highway 20).

Regina Beach is a resort community with full services including gas, food, accommodation, and outfitting (Regina Beach Vacations and Outfitters). The south end of Last Mountain Lake is particularly good for walleye fishing in spring (prior to the end of June), as is the far northern end of the lake accessed through Last Mountain Lake Regional Park, near the town of Govan. Walleye spawning areas at either end of the lake draw large schools, which then gradually migrate to the deeper, cooler waters of the central part of the lake as the water temperature warms.

There is a good public launch ramp at Saskatchewan Beach just off Highway 322, which also gives access to the southern part of the lake.

One of the best access points to Last Mountain Lake is at Rowan's Ravine Provincial Park, a full service park which boasts well-equipped campgrounds and an excellent marina operated by G & S Marina Outfitters. G & S operate a private marina with rental boats adjacent to the public launch ramp, a store and bait shop, a restaurant in the park, and cabin accommodations within the park. G & S offer guided walleye and pike fishing, but their specialty is finding and catching trophy-sized carp.

Last Mountain Lake plays host to two of the Saskatchewan Walleye Trail tournaments—the Spring Classic at Regina Beach early in June each year, and the Fall Classic, held at Rowan's Ravine the weekend after Labour Day each autumn (see Chapter 7).

SAB RA 9879

Fishing on a busy holiday at Valeport, Last Mountain Lake (1920s).

While Last Mountain Lake can be fished from shore (particularly for carp), it is a large lake with many shoreline points and plenty of habitat for fish that move from place to place as wind and the seasons dictate. It is best fished from a boat, and anglers should be prepared to move around until they find active fish.

Last Mountain Lake is a long, narrow lake, with shallow marshy areas at each end. At the north end of the lake is North America's oldest bird sanctuary, the Last Mountain Lake Wildlife Sanctuary, and at the south end, is Valeport Marsh. The two offer some of the best migratory bird watching in all of western Canada in the spring and fall of the year.

LENORE LAKES (73A)

Southeast of the city of Prince Albert, between Highways 2 and 35, lies a region dotted with literally dozens of small lakes, ponds, and reservoirs, many of which hold fish. The vast majority of these small water bodies are under 500 hectares, are accessible locally on gravel roads, have either no boat access or poor launch ramps, and hold populations of pike, walleye, and perch.

In the middle of this area, just north of the town of Lake Lenore, adjacent to Highway 368, lie Big Lake Lenore, North Lake Lenore, and South Lake Lenore.

The big lake is 9 kilometres (6 miles) north of the town and is nearly 5,000 hectares in size. Accessible by both paved and gravel roads, it has a good launch ramp and holds pike, perch, walleye, and whitefish. It enjoys an excellent reputation as a walleye fishery among local anglers.

North Lake Lenore (870 hectares) is just 2 kilometres (1 mile) west of the town of St. Brieux. It features a regional park, a good launch ramp, and populations of pike, walleye, perch, and whitefish.

South Lake Lenore, the smallest of the three at only 174 hectares, is 6 kilometres (4 miles) northwest of the town of Lake Lenore. Accessible by paved and gravel roads, it has a poor launch ramp and holds the same species as its two larger namesakes.

LITTLE JACKFISH LAKE (62N)

Twelve hectares in size, the aptly named Little Jackfish Lake is located in Duck Mountain Provincial Park. The park is on the Saskatchewan/Manitoba border just under 30 kilometres (18 miles) east of the town of Kamsack on Highway 57. The road access to the lake is excellent. It is stocked with rainbow and tiger trout.

MADGE LAKE (62N)

At over 1600 hectares, Madge Lake is the largest body of water in Duck Mountain Provincial Park. Accessible through a good boat launch, it holds northern pike, walleye, and perch.

MAKWA LAKE (73K)

Makwa Lake, a 3,000-hectare lake located 1 kilometre (less than 1 mile) west of Loon Lake, is the site of Makwa Lake Provincial Park. Adjacent to the park is a grocery and lakeside store. The park has a good launch ramp, and Makwa Lake resort provides cabin rentals and boat rentals. Makwa Lake holds pike, walleye, whitefish, and perch.

MARGO LAKE (62M)

Two kilometres (1 mile) southwest of the town of Margo off Highway 5 is 253-hectare Margo Lake. It is accessible only by trail and has a poor boat launch. Margo Lake contains walleye and northern pike.

MCBRIDE LAKE (63C)

McBride Lake is located on a gravel road that runs east from Highway 9, just south of the Reserve on the western side of the Porcupine Hills. This 250-hectare lake has a provincial campsite at its eastern end. It has a good launch ramp and holds pike, walleye, and perch.

MEREAN LAKE (63D)

Merean Lake (719 hectares) lies within the boundaries of Greenwater Provincial Park, about 17 kilometres (11 miles) south and west of Chelan on Highway 23. It is accessible by gravel road, has a good launch ramp, and holds burbot, pike, walleye, and perch.

MEETING LAKE (73G)

Meeting Lake is 28 kilometres (17 miles) south of Spiritwood, accessible from Highway 378. It is the site of Meeting Lake Regional Park, which provides serviced and unserviced campsites, a diner, a good concrete boat launch with lots of dock space, and generous parking space for trailers. The lake is developed with summer cottages and cabins. It holds pike, walleye, and perch.

MINISTIKWAN LAKE (73K)

At 2,500 hectares, Ministikwan Lake is by far the largest in the Loon Lake area. It is located about 30 kilometres (19 miles) west of Loon Lake on gravel Grid Road 699. The lake is serviced by an outfitter, Johnson's Resort and Outfitters Ltd., which offers cottages, campsites, and outpost camping at Fowler Lake. (Fowler is 17 kilometres or 11 miles west of Loon Lake, and holds pike, walleye and perch.) Johnson's has boat and canoe rentals, marine and auto fuel, and filleting and freezing services, and rents moorage to anglers with their own boats. Ministikwan Lake holds pike, walleye, whitefish, and perch.

MOOSE MOUNTAIN LAKE (62E)

In spite of its name, Moose Mountain Lake is *not* located in Moose Mountain Provincial Park. This small, 554-hectare lake is located 24 kilometres (15 miles) north of the town of Stoughton, just off Highway 47. Privately run campgrounds are located at the lake, and there is a poor quality launch ramp. Moose Mountain Lake is a northern pike and yellow perch fishery.

NICKLE LAKE (62E)

Located 11 kilometres (7 miles) southeast of the town of Weyburn, Nickle Lake was formed by a dam on the Souris River, and is a popular local fishery featuring a regional park, a good launch ramp, and a healthy population of pike, perch and walleye. It offers a good winter ice fishery for perch.

NORTH SASKATCHEWAN RIVER (73F, 73C, 73B, 73G)

The North Saskatchewan River is one of three major river systems that dominates angling habitat in southern Saskatchewan.

This historic river rises on the eastern slope of the Rocky Mountains northwest of Edmonton, Alberta. It starts its journey as meltwater at the foot of Saskatchewan Glacier, in the valley between Mount Athabaska and Mount Saskatchewan. It then runs across the central part of Alberta and Saskatchewan, crossing mostly parkland and forested areas, until it meets up with the South Saskatchewan River just east of the city of Prince Albert. Here the two rivers join to form the Saskatchewan River, which ultimately flows into the north end of Lake Winnipeg. Here its waters mingle with that of Manitoba's big lake, and then flow northeastward as the Nelson River into Hudson Bay. On the way it picks up water from the Clearwater River, which has flowed west from northern Saskatchewan, only to travel all the way east again.

The North Saskatchewan River passes through Edmonton and Fort Pitt in Alberta, then on to the Battlefords in Saskatchewan and through Prince Albert to its junction with the South Saskatchewan at The Forks. From here, the river continues downstream as the Saskatchewan, passing by the town of Nipawin, through Tobin Lake, on into the Cumberland Delta into Cumberland Lake. After Cumberland House, the Saskatchewan flows eastward past The Pas, Manitoba, and on into Lake Winnipeg.

In Saskatchewan, the North Saskatchewan River is crossed along its length by numerous highways and back roads. Near the Alberta border, it is accessible from Highway 3 and from Highway 21. Further downstream, the river is paralleled by the Yellowhead, Highway 15, for more than 50 kilometres (31 miles) between Paynton and the bridge at the Battlefords. The Yellowhead crosses the river again just southeast of Borden, where the waters turn northeast toward Prince Albert. Highways 12 and 212 provide paved access to the river as it flows north, and it is accessible at several points through the town of Prince Albert. Anglers in Prince Albert can fish the North Saskatchewan from shore, and it provides them with angling adventures to match those of any body of water in North America.

East of Prince Albert, the river flows through a relatively roadless area to its junction with the south Saskatchewan. As the Saskatchewan River, it is crossed by Highway 6 north of Melfort, and it passes by the towns of Codette and Nipawin on its way into Tobin Lake. Here, the river, now in Saskatchewan's central angling zone, provides some of the most famous fishing in the province, and produces both huge pike and provincial record walleye on a regular basis. For more details on this extraordinary fishery, see Chapter 11.

OYAMA RESERVOIR (72I)

Oyama Reservoir is located 29 kilometres (18 miles) southeast of the city of Regina, just east of Kronau at Oyama Regional Park. A small, 28-hectare reservoir, it has a poor boat launch suitable for only very small craft, as befits a body of water this size. Over the years, Oyama has been stocked with rainbow trout and smallmouth bass. It currently holds fishable populations of small northern pike and yellow perch.

PASQUIA HILLS (63E)

To the south and east of Carrot River lies a largely roadless area called the Pasquia Hills. Within the region and accessible from Highway 9 which runs north from Hudson Bay to the Kelsey Trail (Highway 55) are a number of small streams stocked with brook trout. These include the Fir River, the Overflow River and the Pasquia River.

PECK LAKE (73F)

Peck Lake is accessible on the east side of Highway 21, 40 kilometres (25 miles) north of Paradise Hill, as is Little Fishing Lake on the west side of the highway. Both lakes have Saskatchewan Environment campsites on them, and both hold walleye, whitefish, and northern pike. Little Fishing Lake also has a population of yellow perch.

PIKE LAKE (72O)

Pike Lake, a small, 200-hectare lake, is located at Pike Lake Provincial Park, at the south end of Highway 60, about 50 kilometres (31 miles) southwest of Saskatoon. The lake is accessible by paved road, has a good launch ramp, and is home, as its name suggests, to a population of northern pike.

PINE CREE CREEK (72F)

Pine Cree Creek can be found about 13 kilometres (8 miles) east and north of the town of Eastend, where it crosses Grid Road 633. The area is serviced by a regional park that includes unserviced campsites in a beautiful natural setting. This small creek holds brook trout. Access is often through private land, and permission should be sought by anglers. However, the creek also flows through the campground, and there are small pools above and below the camping area.

QU'APPELLE RIVER SYSTEM (72I, 72J, 62K, 62L)

The Qu'Appelle River rises at the southeast corner of Lake Diefenbaker, at the Qu'Appelle Dam, and runs eastward through the province, flowing into the Assiniboine River in western Manitoba at the town of St. Lazare.

Along its length, the Qu'Appelle provides anglers with year-round access to some of southern Saskatchewan's best fishing, particularly at lakes that it feeds: Buffalo Pound, Pasqua Lake, Echo Lake, Mission Lake, Katepwa Lake, Crooked Lake, and Round Lake. The Qu'Appelle is home to burbot, walleye, perch, northern pike, and a very healthy population of carp. The river itself is often shallow, subject to both seasonal fluctuations in water level and fluctuations caused by human water management for agricultural and flood control purposes. While anglers do fish from its banks, it is not an easy river to access by boat except at the lakes along it. The Qu'Appelle is navigable by canoe, depending on water levels. Anglers are encouraged to explore this fishery at the five lakes, detailed descriptions of which follow.

BUFFALO POUND LAKE (72I) is the first impoundment of the Qu'Appelle River on its journey east from Lake Diefenbaker. Buffalo Pound is accessible from Highways 2, 202, and 301, north of Moose Jaw about 20 kilometres (12 miles). There is a full-service provincial park on the south side of the lake, which features a good launch ramp, and a stocked put-and-take trout pond. A narrow, shallow reservoir, about 20 kilometres (12 miles) end to end, Buffalo Pound is home to walleye, pike, whitefish, and yellow perch.

PASQUA LAKE (72I, 62L) is the most westerly of a group of four lakes (Pasqua, Echo, Mission, and Katepwa) located on either side of the town of Fort Qu'Appelle. Pasqua Lake is accessible from Highways 10, 35, and 210. Highway 210 crosses the bridge over the Qu'Appelle River between Pasqua and Echo Lakes. The lake is

SAB RA 21,160

Boy Scout Camp, Fort Qu'Appelle, 1911: These young fishermen are identified as Charlie Millagan, Bert Shaddich, George Sealey, and Baldy (Roy) Gore.

bounded by parkland and First Nations reserve land on its southern shore and is lined with cottages along its northern edge. The lake is about 2,000 hectares in size. Pasqua Lake has a good quality launch ramp adjacent to Echo Valley Provincial Park, a full-service park with facilities on both Pasqua and Echo lakes. The ramp can be difficult to use when water levels in the lakes are low. Pasqua Lake holds walleye, northern pike, perch, burbot, carp, and whitefish.

The far western basin of Pasqua Lake, between the narrows and the river mouth, is shallow and weedy in most years, but when higher water levels occur, walleye and pike fishing, particularly in spring, can be excellent.

The eastern end of Pasqua Lake is connected to Echo Lake by a short stretch of the Qu'Appelle River which passes under the Highway 210 bridge. This channel can be very shallow, and boaters moving between the two lakes should either run with motors trimmed up or use electric trolling motors. Shallow bars extend out into the mouths of both the entrance and exit to the river channel.

ECHO LAKE (62L) is the third lake moving east along the Qu'Appelle River. It is bounded by cottages on all sides, and a portion of the north shoreline is within a First Nations reserve.

Echo Lake is immediately adjacent to the town of Fort Qu'Appelle, which provides all services, including a hospital, Royal Canadian Mounted Police detachment, hotels, motels, restaurants, gas stations, and boat and auto dealerships. Fort Qu'Appelle is about an hour's drive from the capital city of Regina. The town is at the centre of four lakes—Pasqua and Echo to the west, Mission and Katepwa to the east. All four lakes are popular recreational areas, with numerous cottages, a provincial park, and lots of angling activity in the area. Fort Qu'Appelle hosts the fourth of five tournaments in the Saskatchewan Walleye Trail—the Qu'Appelle Valley Walleye Cup, held on the Labour Day weekend at the beginning of September each year.

The boat launch access to Echo Lake is at Echo Valley Provincial Park, at the far western end of the lake. It is an excellent launch. The major structural feature of

SAB RB 7351

B-Say-Tah Point at Echo Lake, ca. 1903 or 1904.

the lake—B-Say Tah point—lies halfway down the southern shore. It's a good spot for walleye first thing in the morning and as the sun is getting lower in the evening sky. The lake holds walleye, pike, perch, burbot, carp, and whitefish. At the eastern end of Echo Lake, right next to the town, the water becomes shallow and there are large weedbeds. This area is excellent for pike fishing in spring, and for fishing for carp.

MISSION LAKE (62L) is the first lake to the east of the town of Fort Qu'Appelle. It is accessible from Highways 10, 35, and 56. There is no navigable connection to it from Echo Lake as the river channel is blocked by a water control dam.

Much of the land that the town of Fort Qu'appelle is built on was reclaimed by landfill from a marshy wetland at the east end of Mission Lake. It was once a spawning ground for northern pike. Pike, walleye, perch, burbot, and carp are common in this lake. One of the most popular destinations in winter for ice anglers seeking perch, it holds large numbers of this fish, as do all four of the Qu'Appelle Lakes in this section of the river.

A number of shoreline points and shallow bays provide structure for anglers seeking walleye, as do drop off structures adjacent to shoreline flats on both the north and south sides of the lake. Northern pike and perch are found throughout the lake and are often caught incidentally by walleye anglers. The north side of Mission Lake is relatively undeveloped, except for a few cottages and the small village of Lebret. Much of the southern shoreline is cottage development. The boat launch on the north shore near the town of Lebret can be difficult to use in years of low water levels. Many anglers fishing Mission Lake will put in at the better boat launch at Katepwa Point Provincial Park on Katepwa Lake.

KATEPWA LAKE (62L), located immediately to the east of Mission Lake, is connected to it by a narrow channel that provides excellent passage for boaters. Gravel bars extend out into the channel at both ends, and boaters are advised to keep to the centre of the channel. In normal water years, the approach to each mouth of the river requires boaters to tilt their motors, but once into the channel, depths are sufficient for boats to run through with motors down. As one side of the river is marsh, and provides nesting habitat, boaters are encouraged to travel through the channel at no-wake speed.

At 1,600 hectares, Katepwa Lake is the second largest of this group of four lakes. It has the deepest water and the largest number of shoreline points providing interesting structure for anglers. The lake is nearly divided in two by long points that form a narrows. In winter the ice in this narrows is treacherously undependable, and ice anglers are advised to avoid it.

Anglers can access this lake from Highway 56, which runs along its north shore and around its eastern end. The boat launch at Katepwa Point Provincial Park, a day-use facility with no camping, provides good access to both Katepwa Lake and adjacent Mission Lake.

Katepwa Lake is known to produce more large walleye than the other three lakes, with fish up to 4.5 kilograms (10 pounds) taken each year.

CROOKED LAKE (62K) is 1,482 hectares in size and is about 60 kilometres (37 miles) east of Fort Qu'Appelle as the crow flies. If you were travelling the meandering Qu'Appelle River, the distance would at least double. The nearest towns of any size are Grenfell and Broadview, situated on the Trans-Canada to the south. Accessible by paved Highways 47 and 247, Crooked Lake is the site of Crooked Lake Provincial Park and is home to cottage development on its northern shoreline, with First Nations reserve land extending from west of Crooked Lake, along the Qu'Appelle River, to the far eastern end of Round Lake.

There is good boat launch access at the provincial park, and the lake holds a healthy population of carp, walleye, pike, perch, and burbot. Rock bass, working their way upriver from the Assiniboine, have been caught in this lake, and there are reports of the occasional catfish to liven up an angler's day.

ROUND LAKE (62K), the most easterly of the Qu'Appelle River chain of lakes, is 1,095 hectares in size and is accessible from Highway 247. This highway connects to the Trans-Canada by way of Highways 9, 47, and 201. The nearest town is Whitewood, located on the Trans-Canada about 25 kilometres (16 miles) south of the lake. There is a private campground on Round Lake. Accessible to boats by means of a poor quality launch ramp, Round Lake holds good populations of burbot, pike, walleye, perch, whitefish, and the occasional rock bass or catfish.

RAFFERTY RESERVOIR (62E)

Along with the Alameda Reservoir, the 51-kilometre-long (32-mile-long) Rafferty Reservoir was created when the waters of the Souris River were dammed just west of Estevan. The reservoir runs parallel to Highway 39. Primary access to the reservoir is on the grid road running south from Midale. Mainprize Regional Park, located on the shore of Rafferty, offers camping, a boat launch, store, cabins, and access to some of the best walleye fishing in southern Saskatchewan. As a new reservoir, Rafferty has experienced a rapid period of growth in the walleye population, and experienced anglers report catching and releasing a hundred fish in a day. Anglers should be cautioned that, as is usually the case with new reservoirs, mercury levels in fish are high, and consumption is not recommended. As well, anglers should follow careful catch-and-release practices and should assume that at least 5 percent of their catch will not survive handling.

REID LAKE (72F)

Reid Lake is located along Swift Current Creek, 65 kilometres (40 miles) southwest of the town of Swift Current. Take Highway 4 south to Highway 343, then access Reid Lake by way of Grid Roads 630 and 631. Reid Lake is over 1,400 hectares in size, has a good boat launch, and holds northern pike, walleye, and yellow perch.

RUSSELL CREEK (72G)

A prairie spring creek and a favourite of brook trout anglers, Russell Creek can be accessed south of the town of Neville, which is located on Highway 43. The highway runs parallel to the creek for some distance, and the creek is also crossed by Grid Road 628, south of Pambrun.

SANDS LAKE ((63D)

Sands Lake is a tiny, 9-hectare pond, located 15 kilometres (9 miles) north and east of the village of Mistatim on Highway 3. Accessible by trail, it is noteworthy in that it holds three trout species—brown, brook, and rainbow.

SOUTH SASKATCHEWAN RIVER (72J, 72K, 72O, 73B, 73H)

The South Saskatchewan River is one of a handful of river watersheds that play a major role in the landscape of the province and profoundly influence its angling resources. Because the river system is so large and so significant, it deserves considerable attention here.

The South Saskatchewan rises in southwestern Alberta, fed by the waters of the Old Man, the Bow, the Red Deer, and other rivers that take much of their water from the ice and snow of the Rocky Mountains. But the South Saskatchewan, like its sister branch to the north, is a shallow-running prairie river, filled with sandbars and cutting a deep valley across the open prairie.

The South Saskatchewan alternately narrows and widens as it follows its course eastward. As it passes under the bridge on Highway 4 at Saskatchewan Landing Provincial Park, it broadens considerably into southern Saskatchewan's largest lake, a man-made reservoir created by the building of the Qu'Appelle and Gardiner dams. Lake Diefenbaker is T-shaped, with the tail of the T pointing roughly southwest, and the top running northwest to southeast. After passing through Gardiner Dam, the river continues to flow north through the city of Saskatoon, then northeast, passing south of Prince Albert and meeting the North Saskatchewan River just east of that city. Both the river itself and Lake Diefenbaker provide exceptional angling opportunities.

Access points are many and varied. In its most western reaches, the river can be reached on Grid Road 635 at Estuary. Highway 21 bridges the river north of the town of Leader. There is a regional park situated where Grid 649 reaches the river, north of Lemsford. A grid road north of Lancer goes to the South Saskatchewan, and Highway 30, south of Eston, ends at the river and is the site of another regional park.

Highway 4 crosses the South Saskatchewan River due north of the city of Swift Current and just south of the town of Kyle. The junction of the river and the road is the entry point to Saskatchewan Landing Provincial Park. This full-service park with a good marina and launch ramp provides access to the western end of **LAKE DIEFENBAKER (72J, 72O)**. From here an angler with a good boat and a stout heart (Lake Diefenbaker can be more than a little difficult in a strong prairie wind) can travel as far as his gas tank and outboard will take him. Anglers can fish their choice of point as they work eastward, with favourite spots including the mouth of Swift Current Creek, Beaver Flats, and the Herbert Ferry area (the ferry no longer runs, but there are regional parks on both sides of the river). Saskatchewan Landing is home to the annual Walleye International Tournament, the third of five tournaments in the Saskatchewan Walleye Trail, held the final weekend of July each year. Highway 42 meets the South Saskatchewan River at Riverhurst, where a ferry crosses. Riverhurst hosts an annual walleye tournament on Father's Day each year. In recent years the area has attracted anglers seeking rainbow trout. In the late 1990s, a commercial fish farm on the reservoir near Riverhurst suffered a major release—more than 400,000 mature rainbows were released into the watershed. Needless to say, rainbow trout anglers have enjoyed a number of good years since then, both in open water and through the ice. Riverhurst is also home to Palliser Regional Park and the Rusty Coulee Marina, with good launching and docking facilities.

Highway 19 runs north from near the town of Central Butte, past the Qu'Appelle Dam, then through Douglas Provincial Park and the town of Elbow. Douglas Park is a full-service provincial park which has a launch ramp that is serviceable when water levels are sufficiently high. Check in advance with the park office. At Elbow, a protected deep-water harbour, excellent launch ramp, marina, store, and golf course provide anglers with excellent access to the midpoint of this T-shaped lake. The town of Elbow hosts the second of five tournaments in the Saskatchewan Walleye Trail, held each year on the last weekend of May. Anglers fish points and bars, the mouths of bays, and shorelines all the way to the Qu'Appelle Dam in the southeast and the Gardiner Dam and Coteau Bay in the northwest. Danielson Provincial Park provides access to the reservoir near Gardiner Dam. In the early season, flooded coulees to the south of Qu'Appelle Dam, the face of the dam itself, and Coteau Bay, to the southwest of Gardiner Dam, provide excellent spring walleye fishing. So do such inlets as Hitchcock Coulee, site of Hitchcock's Hideaway resort, and Sage Bay to the southwest along the river arm of the reservoir. Anglers fishing this large body of water should consult with local tackle shops, marinas, and provincial park staff for detailed information, as fishing conditions change significantly with seasons and with water levels in the reservoir. Outfitting services for the southwestern end of the reservoir near Saskatchewan Landing Provincial Park are also available from Thistlethwaite Outfitters of Stewart Valley.

Lake Diefenbaker is a large lake, open to prairie winds along its thousands of kilometres of shoreline. Anglers are wise to check weather conditions before heading out in a boat, carry all required safety equipment on board, and use available maps of the lake for navigation.

Lake Diefenbaker holds healthy populations of walleye, perch, pike, rainbow trout, burbot, and goldeye. There is even an occasional, though rare, lake trout to be caught in this big reservoir. All species can reach considerable size in this lake, with walleye over 4.5 kilograms (10 pounds), northern pike over 9 kilograms (20 pounds), and large rainbows caught every year.

Lake Diefenbaker boasts both the kept and the catch-and-release record rainbow trout for the province. The largest kept rainbow, weighing in at 12.435 kilograms (just over 27 pounds!) was taken by an angler fishing in the tailwaters of Gardiner Dam. The largest released rainbow weighed in at 5.85 kilograms (12 pounds, 14 ounces).

Anglers fishing this world-class reservoir should come equipped for jig fishing with both plastics and live bait; for fishing live-bait rigs and bottom bouncers for wall-

Fishing near the dam in Saskatoon, 1947.

eye; for trolling with crankbaits for walleye; and for trolling bright spoons and plugs for pike and rainbow trout. All species on Lake Diefenbaker can be taken through the ice in winter.

Live night crawlers, locally purchased leeches, and frozen minnows are the baits of choice for summer angling. Frozen minnows, live mealworms, and maggots are the most popular baits for ice-fishing these waters.

As it continues its journey northward to join the North Saskatchewan, the South Saskatchewan River passes through the town of Outlook at Highway 15, parallels Highway 219 as it passes Canadian Forces Base Dundurn, and continues on to the city of Saskatoon. The river is accessible to anglers from its banks at various points in Saskatoon. After leaving the City of Bridges, the river continues north past historic Batoche to meet the North Saskatchewan River about 15 kilometres (9 miles) east of the city of Prince Albert.

Throughout its length, the South Saskatchewan River is one of the richest fisheries in the province.

SOURIS RIVER (62E)

The Souris River runs across southeastern Saskatchewan through Estevan and Roche Percee, and near Oxbow, then continues south and east. It is accessible at a number of points where Highways 47, 39, and 9 and a number of grid roads cross over the river. Shallow for much of its length, the Souris is prone to winterkill. Access for launching boats is poor. The Souris holds northern pike, walleye, and yellow perch.

STEISTOL LAKE (63D)

Steistol Lake is in Greenwater Provincial Park, accessible by trail east of Highway 38. It holds good populations of rainbow trout, and is a favourite destination of fly fishers who like to get off the beaten track.

SUCKER CREEK (72F)

Sucker Creek is located 27 kilometres (17 miles) south of Maple Creek on Highway 21. There is a parking lot where the highway meets the creek. Sucker Creek holds brook and brown trout. See Chapter 5 for further details.

SWAN RIVER (63C)

The Swan River is one of the major drainages along the westerly side of the Porcupine Hills. It is accessible at a number of points, from crossings on Highway 8 north of Norquay or from a gravel trail that runs north from the end of Highway 8 to meet Highway 9 south of Hudson Bay. The trail crosses the Swan and several other tributary streams, has a side branch to McBride Lake, and has a campground and a couple of picnic sites along it. Swan River holds brook trout.

SWIFT CURRENT CREEK (72F)

Swift Current Creek rises near the eastern edge of the Cypress Hills, then flows northwest through Reid Lake, on through the town of Swift Current, and ultimately into the South Saskatchewan River where it has widened into the province's largest man-made reservoir, Lake Diefenbaker. Swift Current Creek is accessible at several points along its length. It is managed as a brook trout fishery in the Pine Cree Regional Park reach of the creek, located 54 kilometres (34 miles) south of the town of Tompkins on Grid Road 633. For more information, see Chapter 5.

TURTLE LAKE (73F)

Turtle Lake is located 8 kilometres (5 miles) north of Livelong. The lake is serviced by Turtle Lake Lodge outfitters, who provide cottages and campsites for rent, as well as auto and boat fuel, and boats and canoes for rent. The resort is an all-seasons operation which offers ice-fishing services in winter. Turtle Lake holds whitefish, pike, and walleye.

USINNESKAW LAKE (62M)

Five kilometres (3 miles) south of the town of Margo is 295-hectare Usinneskaw Lake. Accessible by gravel road, with a poor quality boat launch, this lake holds northern pike and walleye.

WAKAW LAKE (73A)

Wakaw Lake, located 63 kilometres (39 miles) south of Prince Albert and about 89 kilometres (55 miles) northeast of Saskatoon on Highway 41, has long been a cottage country haven for residents of Saskatoon. Situated just 2 kilometres (about 1 mile) east of the town of Wakaw, off Highway 2, Wakaw Lake is just over 1,000 hectares in size. The site of both a regional park and private campgrounds, it has one good launch ramp for boaters and holds populations of pike, walleye, and perch.

WHITEBEAR LAKE (62F)

Whitebear Lake is located 13 kilometres (8 miles) north of Carlyle on Highway 9, just on the southern edge of Moose Mountain Provincial Park. Both private and provincial park campsites are available near the lake. Boat launch access is poor. The lake contains a population of small walleye.

WHITESAND LAKE (62M)

Located 7 kilometres (4 miles) south of the town of Margo, 480-hectare Whitesand Lake is accessible by gravel road, has a poor quality boat launch, and contains northern pike and walleye.

PAY FOR PLAY FISHERIES

There are two "pay for play" commercial fishing ponds in southern Saskatchewan.

SILVER SPRINGS TROUT FARM is located just west of Condie Nature Reserve, northwest of Regina. It operates from May to the end of September each year, and provides several options to its customers. The rainbow trout fishery is typically a catch and keep fishery, with the average rainbow caught in the ponds being 30 to 40 centimetres (12 to 14 inches), while the occasional fish might be over 50 centimetres (20 inches). You'll pay an average of close to five dollars for each rainbow you catch and keep.

Silver Springs also offers a daily rate for fly fishers to come and practice their craft on a catch-and-release basis and maintains a perch pond which is operated exclusively as a catch-and-release fishery (barbless hooks only for catch-and-release fishing). Silver Springs offers group rates. For further information, contact 306-543-5575.

THE FORESTRY FARM POND is located at the Forestry Farm Park in Saskatoon in the northeast corner of the city. It is open from the first day of fishing season (this varies from year to year—anglers should check the Saskatchewan Environment Angler's Guide, published annually) until ice-up. Unlike many privately run ponds, this one requires everyone fishing to have a Saskatchewan fishing licence. The Farm Pond charges a two-dollar entry fee at the gate. Although anglers are allowed to keep up to two fish—for this privilege adults pay two dollars and children one dollar—catch-and-release is actively encouraged. The pond is stocked with rainbow trout. The average size of fish stocked in the pond is about 25 centimetres (10 inches). The average fish caught is 40 centimetres (14 inches long), but rainbows up to 8 pounds have been caught. The Forestry Farm Pond offers occasional educational programs, carried out by local angling groups such as the Fishing for Tomorrow Foundation, and the Kilpatrick Fly Fishers. The facility can be contacted for more detailed and up-to-date information at 306-975-3382.

The Saskatoon Wildlife Federation also operates a fishing pond in the Saskatoon area, located to the northeast of Saskatoon on Kinderdine Road. The pond operates from the opening date of fishing season until freeze-up in fall. Everyone fishing must have a valid Saskatchewan fishing licence. The fish is stocked with catchable rainbow trout. Catch-and-release is encouraged, but anglers are allowed to retain one fish. Barbless hooks are encouraged. For more up-to-date and detailed information, the Saskatoon Wildlife Federation can be contacted at 306-242-1666.

CHAPTER ELEVEN
WHERE TO FISH
IN CENTRAL SASKATCHEWAN

MELVILLE–NESS COLLECTION SAB S-MN-B 3677

Children fishing in Waskesiu River.

The central zone is bounded on the south by Highway 55 from the Alberta border through to Shellbrook, by Highways 55 and 3 through Prince Albert, by Highway 55 to its junction with Highway 9, and by Highway 9 to the Manitoba border. The north boundary runs along 57 degrees north latitude to 108 degrees of longitude. There it dips down to 56 degrees, 40 minutes north as far east as 106 degrees of longitude. At that point it dips again, to 56 degrees, 10 minutes north, all the way to the Manitoba border.

Anglers are encouraged to check their fishing location carefully against the zones, as regulations and opening and closing dates differ from zone to zone. When in doubt, check with your outfitter or with the nearest office of Saskatchewan Environment. Anglers should be aware that fishing in a National Park requires a special licence and that separate rules and regulations apply to angling in waters within National Parks.

Map 4. Saskatchewan's Central Fishing Zone

Saskatchewan's central zone extends from the forest fringe area of the province, where prairie and parkland turn to boreal forest, to the Canadian Shield. Here is some of the best drive-to and fly-to fishing to be found anywhere in Canada. Prince Albert National Park, Meadow Lake Provincial Park, La Ronge Provincial Park, the Churchill River system, lakes accessible along the Hanson Lake Road, and dozens of lakes that can be reached from Highway 102 are all within this zone. In addition to being an angler's paradise, this part of the province is also a primary destination for wilderness canoeists who can combine their favourite activity with excellent angling. The zone is well served by outfitters, who offer valuable and expert services to their clients.

Several highways provide ready access to anglers who wish to drive to their angling destinations in this zone. On the western side of the province, Highways 21, 26, and 4 run north from Highway 55 into and through Meadow Lake Provincial Park. Highway 903 runs north from Highway 55 to Canoe Lake and onwards. Highway 155 runs north from Highway 55, and branches off to Highways 955, 909, 918, 914, and 165, all of which provide access to the upper Churchill River watershed. Highways 924, 922, and 916 reach into the territory west and north of Prince Albert National Park.

Highway 2, paved until it passes the town of La Ronge and becomes Highway 102, is the main access route north from the city of Prince Albert to Prince Albert National Park, to Lac La Ronge, and to the central portion of the Churchill River. Highway 120 runs north from Highway 55 and connects to Highways 106 and 135. Highway 106, better known as the Hanson Lake Road, provides drive-in access to such destinations as Dechambault Lake, Jan Lake, and the eastern portion of the Churchill River's run through Saskatchewan.

These roads pass literally thousands of small lakes, creeks, major waterways, and watersheds. It would be impossible to list all of the water bodies in this part of the province in a book of this size. We will concentrate on only those areas with major fisheries, served by outfitters and accessible to anglers by road with normal vehicle equipment. The many smaller lakes we will leave to be discovered by those with a taste for maps, compasses, and adventure.

While the southern zone fishery is dominated by walleye, perch, stocked trout, pike, and carp, the central zone is home to walleye, large populations of trophy pike, and naturally reproducing populations of lake trout. Lac La Ronge and the Churchill River watershed, with its many tributaries, dominate this zone of the province.

A number of fishing outfitters operate in the central part of Saskatchewan. Some are listed here in individual lake and river descriptions. However, there are many more operating in the province, and the list of licenced operators is updated each year. To find out more about outfitters operating on the lake you wish to visit, contact Saskatchewan Environment in Regina (306-787-2080) or in Prince Albert (306-953-2322). A large number of outfitters are members of the Saskatchewan Outfitters Association, which can be reached in Prince Albert at 306-763-5434.

ALSTEAD LAKE (730)

Alstead Lake is located to the east of Lac Île-à–la-Crosse. It is accessible only by air and is serviced by Alstead Lake Wilderness Outfitters. They provide cabin accommodation on the lake, home-cooked meals, and boat and canoe rentals. Alstead Lake holds pike and walleye.

AMYOT LAKE (73N)

Amyot Lake is located to the west of Highway 155 and the southernmost bay of Lac Île-à-la-Crosse. The lake is not accessible by road or trail. It holds pike and walleye.

BESNARD LAKE (73O)

Besnard Lake is located at the north end of Road 910, which runs north from Highway 165. Two outfitters operate on Besnard Lake—Collins Camps and Outfitting, and Besnard Lake Lodge. Located 40 kilometres (25 miles) north on Highway 910, Collins Camps offers cabins, a store, campsites, fuel, boat rentals, and a launch ramp. They offer winter ice-fishing and snowmobiling on request. Besnard Lake Lodge, 33 kilometres (21 miles) north on Highway 910, provides cabins and campsites, fuel, and boat and canoe rentals. Besnard Lake holds burbot, pike, walleye, whitefish, and perch.

BIG SANDY LAKE (73I)

Big Sandy Lake is located just south of the junction of Highway 165 and the Hanson Lake Road (Highway 106). This 8,000-hectare lake has a private campground at the northwest corner of the lake, a poor launch ramp, and holds populations of pike, walleye, whitefish, and perch.

BIGSTONE LAKE (73P)

Bigstone Lake, located 5 kilometres (3 miles) west of the town of La Ronge, is accessible by gravel road. It has a poor launch ramp and holds pike, walleye, and whitefish.

BOW RIVER ((73I)

Bow River flows into the southern end of Lac La Ronge, crossing Highway 165 just east of Highway 2. It holds a population of northern pike and is one of the most southerly bodies of water in the region to support a population of Arctic grayling.

CAMP 10 LAKE (73I)

This small, 9-hectare lake is located at kilometre 2 of Highway 916, just west of Highway 2, outside Prince Albert National Park. The lake has a poor launch ramp and is stocked with rainbow trout.

CANDLE LAKE (73H)

Candle Lake, located 40 kilometres (25 miles) due north of Meath Park on Highway 120, is a large body of water, nearly 13,000 hectares. It is serviced by a provincial park located on both the east and west sides of the lake, featuring more than 300 campsites, a wheelchair-accessible trout pond, filleting stations, and four boat launches. Candle Lake provides good angling for pike, walleye, whitefish, and perch, as well as burbot. The park is accessible in winter for ice fishing.

SAB RA 16,663

Curley Hanson with a 110-pound sturgeon caught in Candle Lake in 1935. Today, sturgeon are under severe pressure all over the world. They are a threatened species in Saskatchewan, and a zero possession limit is in effect.

CANOE LAKE (73N)

Canoe Lake is located just to the south of the Churchill River, and is accessed by way of Highways 155 and 965, or by Highway 103. There are three settlements on the lake: Canoe Narrows (a First Nations reserve), Cole Bay, and Jans Bay. There is a privately operated campground near Cole Bay. The lake holds burbot, northern pike, walleye, and perch.

CHACHUKEW LAKE (63M)

Located just to the north of Pelican Narrows, Chachukew Lake is accessible by air or water. It holds burbot, pike, walleye, whitefish, and perch.

THE CHURCHILL RIVER WATERSHED (73N, 73O, 73P, 63M)

The Churchill River flows eastward from northwestern Saskatchewan all the way to Churchill, Manitoba, on Hudson's Bay. One of the dominant river systems in Saskatchewan, it is home to some of the north's best angling and has been the traditional river highway of the Cree people for thousands of years. The Churchill was the link between the east and the west for the fur trade—the famed "voyageur highway"—and saw some of the first contact between European and First Nations persons in this part of Canada. It is the site of the oldest permanent European building in Saskatchewan—the Anglican mission church at Stanley Mission—and includes one of the most beautiful provincial parks in Saskatchewan—Lac La Ronge Provincial Park.

The Churchill River drains a watershed of millions of square kilometres, reaching right across the edge of the Canadian Shield. The watershed is accessibly by road at eight points along its length.

In the far west, Highway 925 travels to Michel and Dillon on Peter Pond Lake. Highway 155 connects to Buffalo Narrows, and a short side trip on Highway 908 takes us to Île-à-la-Crosse. Highway 918 goes north to Patuanak, Highway 914 to Pinehouse Lake, Highway 102 to Missinipe, and a side trip on Highway 915 connects Highway 102 to Stanley Mission. Finally, Highway 135 travels north from the Hanson Lake Road to Sandy Bay.

Despite the relatively easy highway access, many reaches of the Churchill River itself look much as they did in the days of the voyageurs, and the fishing in parts of the river, and most of the watershed, is spectacular. As a river system, the Churchill is a chain of lakes with interconnecting channels. It is a canoeist's paradise, as well as a great place to fish. (For more detailed information on the Churchill River system, see *Canoeing the Churchill* by Greg Marchildon and Sid Robinson.)

While it would be impossible to identify all the good places to fish in this watershed, the following list—which is ordered not alphabetically but from west to east along the Churchill so that readers can more easily pinpoint these locations on the map—hits the high spots and identifies where outfitters offer angling services to visitors.

SAB RB 4752 (4)

Tourist anglers fishing in rapids on the Churchill River near McIntosh Lake, June 1959.

PETER POND LAKE (73N) is actually two large basins located on the province's western side, just southwest of Highway 155. The more northwesterly basin is called Big Peter Pond Lake, know locally in the Dene language as "big burbot lake." At more than 54,000 hectares, it is indeed a large body of water. It is accessible at Michel, at Dillon, and at Buffalo Narrows, which has an airport as well as road access. The lake holds northern pike and walleye, as does Little Peter Lake, which, at more than 18,000 hectares, is still a sizeable body of water.

NISKA LAKE (73N) is located to the south of Peter Pond Lake, connected by a long narrow channel which is crossed by Highway 925 on its way west to Dillon and Michel. The lake is about 4,500 hectares in size and holds both pike and walleye.

MICHAEL SNOOK

Pan-sized walleye from the Churchill River— perfect selective-harvest candidates for shore lunch.

KAZAN LAKE (73N) is connected to the southeast corner of Peter Pond Lake by the Kazan River. The lake is not accessible by road or trail and holds northern pike, burbot, and perch.

CHURCHILL LAKE (73N) is located to the north and east of Peter Pond Lake and is connected to it by a narrow channel called Kisis Channel. The town of Buffalo Narrows is located on the land between Peter Pond and Churchill lakes. Churchill Lake is a large lake (more than 54,000 hectares) and is accessible at Buffalo Narrows on Highway 155. The lake holds pike, walleye, whitefish, and perch.

LAC ÎLE-À-LA-CROSSE (73O) and the nearby town get their name from the games of lacrosse played on Big Island not far off shore. At its southern end, the lake is accessible from Highway 155 and at the townsite at the end of Highway 908. At its northern end, you can access the lake from the town of Patuanak at the end of Highway 918. Except for the townsites at either end, Lac Île-à-la-crosse is a wilderness lake, very long and narrow (seldom more than 3 or 4 kilometres—2 miles—across). It holds burbot, lake trout, pike, walleye, whitefish, and perch. Boats can be launched at either end of the lake at the townsites, which are also jumping off and ending points for canoeists.

SHAGWENAW LAKE (730) is the first lake downstream from Lac Île-à-la-Crosse. Accessible through the community of Patuanak at the north end of Highway 918, this lake is the first of a series of widenings in the Churchill as it turns eastward and heads downstream towards Manitoba. It is just under 17,000 hectares in size and holds burbot, lake trout, pike, walleye, whitefish, and perch.

DIPPER LAKE (730) is the second widening of the Churchill east of Lac Île-à-la-Crosse. Its 4,900 hectares hold lake trout, pike, and walleye.

PRIMEAU LAKE (730) is the third lake downstream from Patuanak. Like all of the lakes between Shagwenaw and Sandy Lake to the east, it is accessible only by water or air. Primeau Lake holds pike and walleye.

KNEE LAKE (730) is located about 47 kilometres (29 miles) east of Patuanak. One of the larger Churchill River lakes at more than 15,000 hectares, Knee Lake holds pike and walleye.

SANDY LAKE (730) is 22 kilometres (14 miles) north of the settlement of Pinehouse Lake on Highway 914—the Key Lake Road. The lake is to the west of the road. Churchill River Wilderness Camps, located on the south side of the lake, offers cabins, central dining, and one-day boat tours of the Churchill River. Their daily rate includes boat, motor, and gas. Sandy Lake holds pike, walleye, and whitefish.

GORDON LAKE (730) Cross over Highway 914 to the eastern side and you'll find 3,000-hectare Gordon Lake, which has a private campground and a good launch ramp. The lake holds lake trout, northern pike, and whitefish.

PINEHOUSE LAKE (730) is a sprawling, 35,000-hectare lake, found to the east of Highway 914 and accessible from the settlement of Pinehouse Lake. The lake is serviced by an outfitter—Kamkota Lodge—located 20 kilometres (12 miles) north of the town off the Key Lake Road. Kamkota offers cabins and campsites, fuel, boat rentals, and a boat launch. Pinehouse Lake holds burbot, pike, walleye, and whitefish.

SANDFLY LAKE (730) is located to the east of Pinehouse Lake and is accessible only by water or by air. This 9,000-hectare lake holds pike, walleye, whitefish, and perch.

BLACK BEAR ISLAND LAKE (73P) is located to the east of Sandfly Lake. It is noted both for its islands, which break the lake up into dozens of channels, and for its bear population, which is plentiful. Black Bear Island Lake Lodge is located on the lake, accessible only by water or air. The lodge has cabin accommodations, central dining, and offers ice fishing as well as summer angling. Black Bear Island Lake holds pike, walleye, and lake trout.

TROUT LAKE (73P) is located east of Black Bear Island Lake. Although the lake once held trout, as its name suggests, it no longer does. Trout Lake is serviced by Boreal Camp Services, a small camp situated on an island, which caters to one or two fishing parties at a time. It offers cabins equipped with propane appliances, central bath, boats, and motors. Trout Lake holds populations of pike and walleye.

OTTER LAKE (73P) is one of the more accessible stretches of the Churchill River, located where Highway 102 crosses the river. Saskatchewan Environment campgrounds are located at Devil Lake on the north side of the highway and Otter Rapids on the south side. Nearby Missinipe provides fuel and food services and is home to a public campground and to Thompson's Camps, one of the major outfitters on the Churchill. It offers all services needed by anglers, plus fly-outs to outpost camps, jet boat tours on the river, and houseboat tours. Otter Lake is a favourite jumping-off point for canoeists paddling downstream and a popular destination for anglers. Otter Lake holds populations of pike and walleye.

MOUNTAIN LAKE (73P) is located east of Otter Lake. At its southern end, you will find the community of Stanley Mission, another drive-in access point on the Churchill. Stanley Mission lies at the end of Highway 915, which runs east for 37 kilometres (23 miles) from Highway 102. The town has a good launch ramp at the river, a store and restaurant, a nursing station, and an RCMP detachment. At the northern end of Mountain Lake, between Robertson Falls and Twin Falls (both good fishing spots), is Beyond La Ronge Lodge. The lodge, which is accessible by river or by plane, offers cabin accommodations and full services to anglers, as well as an outpost camp on Robertson Lake. Mountain Lake holds good populations of pike and walleye.

NISTOWIAK LAKE (73P), located just to the east of the town of Stanley Mission, is home to picturesque Nistowiak Falls, which flows into the southern side of the lake, draining out of Lac La Ronge through Iskwatikan Lake. Near the base of the falls is Jim's Camp, which provides outfitter services to the lake. Jim's provides full services to anglers, including day trips to nearby lake trout waters. Nistowiak offers good angling for walleye, pike, whitefish, and perch.

ISKWATIKAN LAKE (73P) is located between Lac La Ronge and the Churchill River, at the head of Nistowiak Falls. Iskwatikan Lake Lodge is open from May until October and offers cabin accommodations, boat and canoe rentals, fuel, and filleting and freezing services. This 4,000-hectare lake holds walleye, pike, whitefish, and lake trout.

DRINKING LAKE (73P) is located to the east of Nistowiak Lake, just past Potter Rapids (formerly Drinking Falls). There are two outfitter camps on this relatively isolated stretch of the Churchill River. Angler Rapids Wilderness Lodge, located on the southerly shore of the rapids and open only in June and July, offers fully guided trips for pike and walleye. Churchill River Voyageur Lodge is located on the opposite shore. Open May to September, it offers boats, motors, guide services, filleting and freezing, shore lunches and cabin accommodations, as well as a central shower and barbecues. Pike fishing is good and walleye fishing is excellent in the area. Both lodges at Potter Rapids are accessible by air or by boat from Stanley Mission.

KEG LAKE (63M) is located one lake to the east of Drinking Lake. Accessible only by boat, canoe, or float plane, Keg offers excellent fishing for pike and walleye, and holds populations of burbot, whitefish, and perch.

TRADE LAKE (63M) is located east of Keg Lake and Frog Portage, the famous crossover point for the fur traders coming up the Sturgeon-Weir system. Accessible only by water or air, Trade Lake holds burbot, pike, walleye, whitefish, and perch.

USKIK LAKE (63M) is situated east of Trade Lake. Its 22,300 hectares hold northern pike, walleye, whitefish, and perch.

REINDEER RIVER (63M) connects Steephill Lake to the Churchill River. Accessible only by water or air, it holds lake trout, pike, walleye, and whitefish.

STEEPHILL LAKE (63M), located north of the Churchill River and connected to it by the Reindeer River, is serviced by a single outfitter—Steephill Rapids Camp. The camp books only one group at a time, providing cabin accommodations, boat, motor, and gas. Steephill Lake holds burbot, northern pike, walleye, whitefish, and perch.

PITA LAKE (63M) is about 28 kilometres (17 miles) west of the settlement of Sandy Bay. Accessible only by air or water, Pita Lake holds burbot, northern pike, walleye, whitefish, and perch.

REEDS LAKE (63M) is located 18 kilometres (11 miles) upriver from Sandy Bay, northwest on the Churchill River. Accessible by air or water, Reeds Lake holds burbot, northern pike, walleye, whitefish, and perch.

GUILLOUX LAKE (63M), located about 20 kilometres (12 miles) northwest of Sandy Bay, is connected to the north end of Pikoo Lake. It is accessible only by air or water, and holds pike, walleye, whitefish, and perch.

PIKOO LAKE (63M) is located 23 kilometres (14 miles) west of Sandy Bay and holds pike, walleye, whitefish, and perch.

SOKATISEWAN LAKE (63M), located at the north end of Highway 135, is home to Sandy Bay and Island Falls, two settlements at the eastern end of the Churchill River in Saskatchewan. The area is serviced by Slim's Cabins, which provides both cabin accommodations and campsites, fuel services, boat rentals, and launch ramp access to the Churchill River system. The lake holds pike, walleye, and whitefish.

WASAWAKASIK LAKE (63M), located northeast of Sandy Bay, holds burbot, northern pike, walleye, whitefish, and perch.

OKIPWATSIKEW LAKE (63M) lies between Sandy Bay and the Manitoba border. The lake is accessible by water or air. It holds northern pike, walleye, whitefish, and perch.

CLAM LAKE (73P)

Clam Lake is located east of Lac La Ronge between Nemeiben and Besnard lakes. Accessible only by air, it holds populations of burbot, pike, walleye, perch, and whitefish.

CLARK LAKE (73J)

Clark Lake is located just off Highway 922, approximately 80 kilometres (50 miles) north of Highway 55. There is a private campground on the lake and a good launch ramp. It holds populations of northern pike and whitefish.

COMPLEX LAKE (74B)

Complex Lake is located just north of the fifty-sixth parallel, west of Highway 914, and is accessible by air from Buffalo Narrows. Complex Lake Lodge offers cabins, hot showers, a well-equipped kitchen, boats, motors and fuel, as well as freezing services. Complex Lake holds lake trout, walleye, and northern pike.

CUMBERLAND LAKE (63E) (63L)

Cumberland Lake and the Cumberland Delta of the Saskatchewan River are accessible by way of Highway 123 north of Carrot River and east of Nipawin. The nearest outfitter to this 24,000-hectare lake is Cumberland House Outfitters, located 50 kilometres (31 miles) east of the settlement of Cumberland House on the Saskatchewan River. In addition to hunting and fishing packages, they offer an eco-tourism package that includes a Cree cultural tour of the delta. There is good launch ramp access to Cumberland Lake, accessible by paved road. The lake holds burbot, goldeye, northern pike, walleye, and whitefish.

CUP LAKE (74B)

Cup Lake is located 105 kilometres (65 miles) by air northeast of the town of Île-à-la-Crosse. It is also accessible from Highway 155. Cup Lake Adventures is the outfitter on the lake. They offer cabin accommodation, boat, motor, and gas. Cup Lake holds northern pike, lake trout, and walleye.

DELARONDE LAKE (73G)

A long, narrow body of water, 14,000-hectare Delaronde Lake can be accessed from Highways 55 and 922. Access to the southern end of the lake is 10 kilometres (6 miles) from the town of Big River. The lake is serviced by both a Saskatchewan Environment and a private campground. Boaters will find good launch ramp facilities on the lake, which holds good populations of pike, walleye, whitefish, perch, and burbot.

DICKENS LAKE (73P)

Located just east of Highway 102, about 15 kilometres (9 miles) north of Missinipe, Dickens Lake is accessible by gravel road and has a poor launch ramp. It holds lake trout, pike, and whitefish.

DORE LAKE (73J)

Dore Lake is located at the north end of Highway 924, accessible off Highway 55, northwest of the town of Big River. The village of Dore Lake is located at the end of the road at the south end of this 61,000-hectare lake. In addition to a Saskatchewan Environment campground, two outfitters service Dore Lake. Dore Lake Lodge is open from the beginning of May until the end of October and offers cabins, campsites, fuel, and boat rentals, as well as a boat launch. Michel Lodge offers beachfront cabins and a main lodge, boat rentals, fuel, and a boat launch. It is open for ice fishing as well as summer angling. Dore Lake holds northern pike, walleye, whitefish, perch, and burbot.

DOWNTON LAKE (73P)

Located 5 kilometres (3 miles) northwest of the town of La Ronge, Downton Lake is stocked with rainbow trout.

EAST TROUT LAKE (73I)

East Trout Lake is located 65 kilometres (40 miles) north of Candle Lake, off gravel Highway 913 on Highway 927. The lake is serviced by two outfitters. Bay Resort, located between East Trout and Nipikamew Lakes, offers campsites, cabins, central dining, fuel, boat and canoe rentals, and a boat launch. It offers ice fishing as well as summer angling opportunities. Pine Grove Resort, located near Clarence Steepbank Lakes Wilderness Park, provides cabins, camping, fuel, boat rentals, a boat launch, and freezing services. East Trout Lake holds lake trout, northern pike, walleye, and whitefish.

EGG LAKE (73P)

Egg Lake is located 10 kilometres (6 miles) west of La Ronge. This 10,000-hectare lake is not accessible by road. It holds northern pike, walleye, whitefish, and perch.

EMERALD POND (73I)

Named for the vivid colour of its water, tiny Emerald Pond (just one hectare in size) is located 40 kilometres (25 miles) north of Weyakwin, on the east side of Highway 2. It holds rainbow trout.

FELDSPAR LAKE (73P)

Feldspar Lake is located at kilometre 120 (mile 75) of Highway 102 north of Missinipe. It holds both cutthroat and rainbow trout.

GEORGE LAKE (74B)

Located east of Highway 914 and accessible only by air, George Lake is serviced by George Lake Camp Outfitting. Open May to October, the outfitter provides cabin accommodation, kitchen facilities, hot showers, boat, motor, and gas. George Lake holds lake trout and northern pike.

HANSON LAKE ROAD (63L)

The Hanson Lake Road (Highway 106) runs eastward from Narrow Hills Provincial Park to the Manitoba border. Along it you will find some of the most desirable fishing destinations in the province, almost all of them accessible by road. Lakes in the area that are neither accessible by road nor serviced by outfitters are not included in the following list, but information on them is available in other publications (see Appendix F).

AMISK LAKE (63L) is one of the largest lakes along the Hanson Lake Road. Just south of the town of Creighton and home to the settlement of Denare Beach, the lake is accessible by way of Highway 167, which runs south from Creighton. The lake is serviced by a Saskatchewan Environment campground and by two outfitters— Angell's Resort and Overland CrossCountry Lodge. Angell's Resort, located at Denare Beach, provides cabins, campsites, gas, diesel, and propane, is open year-round for ice fishing and summer angling, and provides boat and canoe rentals and a boat launch. Overland CrossCountry Lodge is located on the shore of Mosher Lake at Denare Beach. It offers cabins and campsites, boat and canoe rentals, is open for ice fishing as well as summer angling, and provides a boat launch. Amisk Lake holds burbot, pike, walleye, and whitefish.

ATHAPAPUSKOW LAKE (63L) straddles the Saskatchewan/Manitoba border east of Amisk Lake and south of Flin Flon, Manitoba. Pine Point Lodge offers outfitting services at the west end of the lake, 32 kilometres (20 miles) by air south of Creighton. It offers modern cabins, full packages including return airfare from Flin Flon, and access to four lakes in the area. Athapapuskow offers excellent fishing for lake trout, northern pike, and walleye.

DESCHAMBAULT LAKE (63L), at more than 54,000 hectares in size, is one of the largest lakes along the Hanson Lake Road. It is serviced by three private outfitters: Bloomfield's Resort, Deschambault Lake Resort, and Twin Bay Resort. Bloomfield's Resort is located just 1 kilometre (.6 miles) off the Hanson Lake Road at kilometre 195 (mile 121). It offers cabins and a motel, is open year-round for both summer angling and ice fishing, and provides gas, diesel, propane, boat and canoe rentals, filleting and freezing services, and boat launch access to the lake. Deschambault Lake Resort is located on Ballantyne Bay at kilometre 209 (mile 130) of the Hanson Lake Road. It offers lakefront cabins, camping, summer angling and winter ice fishing, fuel, diesel, propane, boat rentals, filleting and freezing services, as well as boat launch access to Deschambault. Twin Bay Resort is located at the north end of Highway 911, which runs north from Hanson Lake Road to the settlement of Deschambault Lake. Open year-round for both summer angling and ice fishing, it offers lakefront cabins, a coffee shop and café, fuel service, boat and canoe rentals, filleting and freezing services, and boat launch access to the lake. Deschambault holds populations of northern pike, walleye, whitefish, and burbot.

FLORENCE LAKE (63L/63K), located virtually on the Manitoba border, about 20 kilometres (12 miles) north of Creighton, is accessible only by air. Aerial Adventures Ltd., an outfitter based in Nipawin, offers cabin accommodation, boat, motor and gas. The lake holds walleye and northern pike. Lake trout fishing is available at nearby fly-out camps.

GILLINGHAM LAKE and **WINTERINGHAM LAKE (63L)** are two small lakes, each under 100 hectares in size, located on opposite sides of the Hanson Lake Road just west of Highway 135. Both have poor launch ramps. Both hold northern pike and perch.

GRANITE LAKE (63L) is just to the north of Highway 106, east of Highway 135. Accessible by road, it has both private and Saskatchewan Environment campgrounds, a good launch ramp, and holds burbot, pike, walleye, and whitefish.

HAMELL LAKE (63L) is accessible by trail on the north side of Hanson Lake Road just west of the turnoff to Creighton. It holds pike, walleye, and whitefish.

HANSON LAKE (63L), just over 4,000 hectares in size, is located approximately 10 kilometers (6 miles) south of the Hanson Lake Road. It is accessed by a gravel road located halfway between Highway 911 to Deschambault Lake and Highway 135 to Jan Lake. There is a private campground on the lake. Hanson Lake holds northern pike, walleye, and whitefish.

HOBBS LAKE (63L) is accessible only by air, and is serviced by Miskat Lake Outfitters, which offer cabin accommodation for six persons, and packages that include boat, motor, gas, and accommodation. Hobbs Lake holds pike, walleye, and whitefish.

JAN LAKE (63L), one of the Hanson Lake Road's most popular fishing destinations, is accessible from Highway 106 and Highway 135. It is serviced by four outfitters—F.A.T.S. Camp, Great North Lodge, Jan Lake Lodge and Three Lakes Camp. F.A.T.S. Camp is 6.4 kilometres (4 miles) north of Highway 106 on Highway 135, then west on the Jan Lake access road. It provides cabins, a motel, and campsites, as well as fuel, boat rental services, and a launch ramp. Great North Lodge is located 4.8 kilometres (about 3 miles) off Highway 135 on Doupe Bay. It offers cabins, boats, fuel, and campsites, as well as a launch ramp. Jan Lake Lodge is located 11 kilometres (7 miles) north of the junction of Highway 106 and Highway 135. A four-star-rated facility, it offers lakefront cabins and campsites, fuel services, boat rentals, filleting and freezing services, and a launch ramp, in a picturesque Precambrian Shield setting. Three Lakes Camp, located 11 kilometres (7 miles) north of Highway 106 on Highway 135, offers cabins, motel units, campsites, fuel and propane, boat rentals, and launch ramp. Jan Lake holds northern pike, walleye, and whitefish, and is a favourite destination for walleye anglers.

JOHNSON LAKE (63L) is found just south of the Hanson Lake Road, 30 kilometres (19 miles) to the north and west of Creighton. This 700-hectare lake holds pike and perch.

MCBRIDE LAKE (63L) is located east of Highway 135 just north of Highway 106. It holds pike, walleye, and whitefish.

MID LAKE (63L) is located just off the Hanson Lake Road 2 kilometres (a little over 1 mile) west of the Sturgeon-Weir River. This small, 8-hectare lake holds rainbow trout.

MIROND LAKE (63L) is another prime destination along the Hanson Lake Road. Located east of Highway 135, just north of Jan Lake, it is serviced by two outfitters—Newmart Fishing and Hunting Resort, and Silence of the North. Newmart is located 22 kilometres (14 miles) north of the Hanson Lake Road on Highway 135. They provide cabins, campsites, boat rentals, and a boat launch. Silence of the North is located 23 kilometres (14 miles) north of Hanson Lake Road on Highway 135. Open year-round, it offers log cabins on the lakefront as well as campsites, gas and diesel fuel services, boat and canoe rentals, a boat launch, ice fishing as well as summer angling, and a café specializing in home-cooked meals. Mirond Lake holds burbot, lake trout, northern pike, walleye, whitefish, and perch.

MOSHER LAKE (63L) is located 2 kilometres (a little over 1 mile) from Denare Beach and is home to Overland CrossCountry Lodge (see Amisk Lake). It holds burbot, pike, walleye, and whitefish.

PELICAN LAKE (63L) is accessible via Highway 135, which runs north from the Hanson Lake Road between Jan and Mirond lakes. The nearest outfitter is Thunderbird Camps at nearby Pelican Narrows, which also operates as a base camp for a number of fly-out wilderness destinations. Thunderbird Camps provides a cabin at each of its outpost lakes and offers boat rentals and filleting and freezing service. It outfits ice fishing as well as summer angling.

The **STURGEON-WEIR RIVER (63L)**, which connects the Churchill River to the Saskatchewan River system via Frog Portage at Trade Lake on the Churchill, is located just south of the Hanson Lake Road. Pawistik Lodge provides cabins, boats, motors, gas, and filleting and freezing services. The Sturgeon-Weir system offers excellent fishing for northern pike and walleye.

TULABI LAKE (63L) is located north of Highway 106, accessible by trail. It holds pike, walleye, and perch.

TYROLL LAKE (63L) is accessible by gravel road north of the Hanson Lake Road. It has a Saskatchewan Environment campground as well as a good launch ramp. It holds northern pike and perch.

HACKETT LAKE (73J)

Hackett Lake is located just off Highway 922, north of Highway 55, about 44 kilometres (27 miles) from Big River. There is a private campground on the lake, and a good boat launch. Hackett Lake, at just over 1,000 hectares, holds northern pike, walleye, and whitefish.

HIGHWAY 102 CORRIDOR (73P)

Between La Ronge and Missinipe, on either side of Highway 102, there are more than a dozen lakes of varying sizes, many accessible only by canoe and portage (the Lynx Lake loop, for instance). Several of these lakes (Althouse, Little Deer, Lynx, McKay, and Mullock) are accessible by gravel road. Most hold pike, walleye, or whitefish. A few, such as Bartlett, Haugen, and Hebden, hold lake trout. Several— Mekewap, Mullock, and Althouse—have been stocked with trout. Located in the beauty and wilderness of the Canadian shield, these small lakes are ideally suited to fishing from a canoe or to fly-fishing with a belly boat.

HOLT LAKE (74B)

Holt Lake is 112 kilometres (70 miles) by air northeast of Buffalo Narrows, just to the west of Highway 914. R & R Wilderness Lodge offers cabin accommodation, fly-outs to a number of outpost lakes, and packages that include boat, motor, gas, freezing service, and return airfare to Buffalo Narrows. Holt Lake holds northern pike and lake trout.

JUNCTION LAKE (73I)

At the junction of Highway 2 and Highway 165 is 8-hectare Junction Lake. It has a poor launch ramp and is stocked with both brook and brown trout.

KEELEY LAKE (73K)

Keeley Lake, a little over 9,000 hectares in size, is located due north of the town of Meadow Lake, 16 kilometres (10 miles) east of gravel Road 903 on Road 904. There is a private campground at the south end of the lake on Road 903, operated by Keeley Lake Lodge. The lodge offers cabins as well as campsites, a licenced dining room and lounge, fuel, and boat and canoe rentals, and is open year-round to provide services to ice anglers as well as summer fishermen. Keeley holds good

Lac La Ronge: Four men show off their two-to-three foot specimens of lake trout (1950s). Below, fishing from boats, July 1950.

populations of northern pike, walleye, and whitefish. Other small lakes within a few kilometres of Keeley offer trout fishing as well as pike and walleye fishing.

LAC LA PLONGE (730)

Lac la Plonge is east of the town of Beauval on Highway 165. At nearly 20,000 hectares, it is one of the larger lakes in this area and is home to Angler's Trail Resort. The resort provides cabins, camping, fuel, boat and canoe rentals, a boat launch, and services for both summer angling and ice fishing. Lac la Plonge holds burbot, lake trout, pike, whitefish, and perch.

LAC LA RONGE (73)

Lac La Ronge is one of the primary angling destinations in northern Saskatchewan. Accessible by paved road (Highway 2), the town of La Ronge offers full services, including restaurants, hotels, tackle shops, hardware stores, grocery stores, marina services, guide and outfit-ter services, a float plane base, hospital, and RCMP detachment. Nut Point is a Saskatchewan Environ-ment campground located on the

SAB RB 5098 (10)

SAB RA 13,445

Above, right: Dr. D. Robb, Regina, displays a 19-pound lake trout, June 1957. Inset: Gust Hangsleben, East Grand Forks, Minnesota, holds a 28½-pound lake trout caught in Hunter Bay, 1962. Today, most northern outfitters impose a catch-and-release policy on large lake trout, and reduced limits are in effect on Lac La Ronge.

lake just outside the town. Lac La Ronge Provincial Park extends north and east of the town and encompasses all of the lake within its boundaries. Much of the park is a wilderness environment.

A number of outfitters operate on Lac La Ronge. B & L Cabins is located on English Bay, 19 kilometres (12 miles) north of town on Highway 102. It offers modern cabins, boats and motors, gas, filleting and freezing services, and launch ramp access to the lake. Camp Kinisoo is one of several camps on Hunter Bay, a one-hour boat ride or half-hour flight across the lake from La Ronge. It offers boat rentals, cabin accommodations, fuel, and filleting and freezing services. Cornhusker Fishing Camp, also on Hunter Bay, offers full services to anglers, including round-trip transport from La Ronge. Rusty's Lodge, also on Hunter Bay, provides accommodation, boats, fuel, filleting and freezing service, and guide services if requested, and has a tackleshop and grocery store on site. Pickerel Bay Cabins is located an hour and a quarter boat ride across the lake from La Ronge. It offers logs cabins, central bath, central dining, and full services to anglers. Vanco 4 Seasons Resort is 19 kilometres (12 miles) north of La Ronge. Open year-round, it provides cabins and camping, boat and canoe rental, fuel, and filleting and freezing services. Wadin Bay Resort, located 27 kilometres (17 miles) north of La Ronge on Highway 102, provides accommodation in log cabins, fuel, boat rentals, freezing services, and guided fishing trips.

Lac La Ronge is a large lake—over 126,000 hectares in size. The southern part of the lake is mostly open water and can become quite rough in windy conditions. The northern half of the lake is dotted with islands and reefs—not all of them marked on maps. Anglers visiting the lake with their own boats should be cautious until they get to know the waters. Excellent maps are available of the lake and surrounding area.

La Ronge, with its active float plane base, is a jumping-off point for anglers flying in to more remote lakes and outpost camps across northern Saskatchewan. While gravel roads can take anglers much further north in the province, the paved highway ends a short distance north of La Ronge.

Lac La Ronge holds pike, walleye, lake trout, burbot, and whitefish. Special limits apply to lake trout, and a special endorsement (free of charge) in addition to a regular angling licence is required for fishing on the lake. Further information is available through Saskatchewan Environment.

LITTLE AMYOT LAKE (730)

Little Amyot Lake is located to the west of Beauval, just off Highway 155. There is a regional park on the lake, a private campground, and a good boat launch. The lake holds pike and walleye.

LITTLE BEAR LAKE (731)

Little Bear Lake is located off Highway 106 (the Hanson Lake Road), just north of Narrow Hills Provincial Park. Little Bear Lake Resort, located at the southeastern end of the lake, is open year-round and has an air strip. They offer a central lodge, cabins, campsites, central dining, fuel, boat and canoe rental, a boat launch, and services to ice fishermen as well as summer anglers. Little Bear Lake holds lake trout, northern pike, walleye, whitefish, and yellow perch.

LUSSIER LAKE (73P)

Lussier Lake is located at kilometre 77 (mile 48) of Highway 102, just south of Missinipe. It is accessible by gravel road, has a poor launch ramp, and holds brook trout.

MAISTRE LAKE (73I)

Located directly opposite Whelan Bay on Whiteswan Lake, Maistre Lake is a small, 6-hectare lake, accessible by trail from the southwest side of Whiteswan. It is stocked with brook trout.

MANAWAN LAKE (63M)

Manawan Lake is on the upper Sturgeon-Weir river system, which connects the Churchill to the Saskatchewan River system by way of Frog Portage. Manawan Lake is accessible by air or water. It holds burbot, pike, walleye, whitefish, and perch.

MAWDSLEY LAKE (74B)

Mawdsley Lake is accessible by driving north from Pinehouse Lake on Highway 914 and then boating in from kilometre 160 (mile 99). Mawdsley Lake Fishing Lodge Inc. offers lodge accommodation, central kitchen and bath, packages that include the boat trip in, boat, motor and gas, and freezing services. Mawdsley Lake holds northern pike, lake trout, and Arctic grayling.

MCINTOSH LAKE (73P)

McIntosh Lake is located just to the north of the Churchill River system and is not accessible by road. At 7,500 hectares, it is one of the larger lakes in the area and holds burbot, lake trout, northern pike, walleye, and whitefish.

MCLENNAN LAKE (73P)

McLennan Lake is located along Highway 102, just east of the village of McLennan Lake. It has a Saskatchewan Environment campground and a poor launch ramp. It holds burbot, lake trout, northern pike, and whitefish.

MEADOW LAKE PROVINCIAL PARK (73K)

Meadow Lake Provincial Park is located north of Highway 55 and runs from Cold Lake on the Alberta border on the west to gravel Highway 903 in the east. The park can be accessed by way of Highways 21, 26, and 4 and by Highway 234, which runs through the heart of the park.

This large natural environment park, nearly 160,000 hectares in size, provides nearly a thousand campsites in fourteen separate campgrounds. While there are nearly two dozen fishable bodies of water in the park, the following are among the most popular, accessible and fishable lakes.

COLD LAKE, at the western edge of the park, can be reached on gravel Highway 919, off Highway 21. Its 9,000 hectares hold lake trout, northern pike, walleye, and whitefish. There is a poor quality boat launch and Saskatchewan Environment camping nearby.

FLOTTEN LAKE, located 30 kilometres (19 miles) north of the town of Dorintosh, is known for its excellent walleye fishing. A classic northern lake featuring rock reefs, points, and other structural elements familiar to walleye anglers everywhere, Flotten Lake is serviced by Flotten Lake Resort, which provides both campsites and cabins, as well as boat rental, fuel, and filleting and freezing services. In addition to walleye, the lake holds northern pike, whitefish, and perch.

GREIG LAKE is located 12 kilometres (7 miles) north of the town of Dorintosh, off Highways 4 and 224. There is a Saskatchewan Environment campground at the lake, with a good launch ramp. The lake holds pike, walleye, whitefish, and burbot.

LAC DES ILES is located about 10 kilometres (6 miles) north of the town of Goodsoil, off Highway 26. At 4,600 hectares, it is a perfect setting for anglers seeking pike, walleye, whitefish, and perch. In addition to Saskatchewan Environment camp-grounds, the lake is serviced by Big Island Cove Resort, which offers year-round services to anglers, hunters, and ice anglers. The resort features lakefront cabins, boat rentals, fuel, and freezing services. Lac Des Iles is also home to Northern Cross Resort Limited, which offers cabins, seasonal campsites, boat rentals, and fuel.

MISTOHAY LAKE is located 12 kilometres (7 miles) north of the town of Goodsoil, just off Highway 224. There is a Saskatchewan Environment campground and a poor quality launch ramp. The lake holds populations of pike, walleye, and white-fish.

MUSTUS LAKES (first, second and third) are located along Highway 224, within 20 kilometres (12 miles) of the town of Dorintosh. First and Second Mustus Lakes have poor quality launch ramps. All three lakes hold pike, walleye, and whitefish.

PIERCE LAKE is located 18 kilometres (11 miles) off Highways 21 and 919. It is serv-iced by a Saskatchewan Environment campground and by Pierce Lake Lodge. The lake has a good launch ramp, and holds lake trout, northern pike, walleye, and whitefish.

WATERHEN LAKE is located east of Highway 904 at the eastern edge of Meadow Lake Provincial Park. At over 7,300 hectares, it is one of the larger lakes in the park. In addition to Saskatchewan Environment campgrounds, the lake is home to Tawaw Cabins, with year-round cabins, campsites, boat and motor rentals, fuel, and freez-ing services. Waterhen Lake holds pike, walleye, and whitefish.

MEYOMOOT RIVER (73I)

The Meyomoot River flows into the southern end of Lac La Ronge and crosses Highway 165 east of Highway 2. The river holds a population of brook trout.

MONTREAL LAKE (73I)

Montreal Lake is located between Highways 2 and 969. Montreal Lake First Nations Reserve is located at the southern end of the lake, and the village of Timber Bay is located about 20 kilometres (12 miles) up the east side of the lake. Montreal Lake is also accessible on a good road that runs east from Weyakwin on Highway 2. Montreal Lake is large—nearly 42,000 hectares—and holds good populations of burbot, northern pike, walleye, whitefish, and perch.

MONTREAL RIVER (73I)

The Montreal River flows from Montreal Lake through Sikachu, Egg, and Bigstone lakes into Lac La Ronge. There are access points where the river crosses Highway 2, Highway 165, and where the river enters Lac La Ronge. The river holds pike, walleye, and whitefish. Anglers should take note that the river is closed to fishing year-round from the centerline of the Highway 2 bridge at La Ronge to Lac La Ronge. A portion of the lake at the river mouth is closed as well.

NAGLE LAKE (74A)

Nagle Lake is located 69 kilometres (43 miles) north of Missinipe (Otter Lake) by air. Nagle Lake Outfitters offers cabin accommodation and packages that include boat, motor, gas, filleting and freezing services, as well as return airfare from Otter Lake. Nagle Lake holds walleye, lake trout, and northern pike.

NAMEW LAKE (63L)

Namew Lake is located on the Sturgeon-Weir River system right at the Manitoba border. The lake is accessible from the Manitoba side by way of a gravel road that runs in from Manitoba Highway 10 to Sturgeon Landing. Namew Lake is serviced by Sturgeon Landing Outfitters, which offers cabins and camping from May to October. Fuel, boat rentals, and filleting and freezing services are available. Namew Lake holds burbot, lake trout, northern pike, walleye, and whitefish.

NARROW HILLS PROVINCIAL PARK (73H)

Narrow Hills Provincial Park, set in the Cub Hills, is home to a number of stocked trout streams and smaller ponds and lakes. A number of streams are identified in Chapter 5, but in addition, a number of lakes are worth mentioning here.

The park is accessible either via Highway 106 north of Smeaton or via Highway 120 north of Meath Park. It features more than 1,780 camping sites in four separate campgrounds and provides the opportunity to fish twenty-five bodies of water in the area. These are stocked with rainbow trout, Arctic grayling, kokanee salmon, brown trout, brook trout, and splake, as well as walleye, pike, whitefish, and perch. Two outfitters operate in the park. Caribou Creek Lodge on Upper Fishing Lake is open for twelve months of the year for ice fishing as well as open-water angling. Pine Ridge Resort is located on Lower Fishing Lake. The following lakes and streams are all within the boundaries of Narrow Hills Provincial Park.

BALDY LAKE (73I) is a small (25-hectare) lake located at kilometre 80 (mile 50) of Highway 106. It is accessible by gravel road, has a Saskatchewan Environment campground, and a decent launch ramp, and holds populations of pike and walleye.

BEAN LAKE (73I) is a 135-hectare lake located due south of the south end of Little Bear Lake. It is accessible only by trail, and holds pike and walleye.

BURTLEIN LAKE (73I) is located just off Highway 106 at kilometre 98 (mile 61). It is accessible by trail only, is only 14 hectares in size, and holds splake and tiger trout.

DIAMOND LAKE (73I) is a tiny four-hectare lake located by footpath off Highway 913 near the western edge of the park. It holds populations of brook trout and splake.

FAIRY GLEN LAKE (73I) is accessible off Highway 912 in Narrow Hills Park. It has a poor boat launch and holds pike and walleye.

FOX LAKE (73I) is a small lake, 32 hectares in size, accessible by foot only, located north of Highway 913. It holds pike and whitefish.

GLACIER CREEK (73I) is found between Fairy Glen Lake and Lost Echo Creek. It holds brook trout.

HEART LAKE (73I) is a 174-hectare lake accessible from the northeast end of Little Bear Lake. It holds pike and whitefish.

JADE LAKE (73I) is just to the west of Diamond Lake, accessible only by foot trail off Highway 913. This 12-hectare lake holds rainbow trout, tiger trout, and splake.

LOST ECHO LAKE (73I) is in the park, located south of Highway 913 and east of Highway 912. It is accessible by trail only and holds pike, walleye, and whitefish.

LOWER FISHING LAKE (73I) is a 300-hectare lake located just east of Highway 106 near Highway 920. It features a Saskatchewan Environment campground, is accessible by gravel road, and has a good launch ramp. It holds pike, walleye, whitefish, and perch.

MCDOUGAL CREEK (73I) runs along the eastern edge of Narrow Hills Park. It is accessible from Highway 106 and via a number of trails. There is a Saskatchewan Environment campground on McDougal Creek, which holds a population of brook trout. (See also Chapter 5.)

NIPAWIN LAKE (73I) is a tiny, 5-hectare lake located near Highway 920. It is accessible by trail and holds brook trout.

SAPPHIRE LAKE (73I) is located by trail off Highway 913, between Summit Lake and Piprell Lake. This tiny, 3-hectare lake holds a population of splake.

SEELEY LAKE (73I) is located at kilometre 100 (mile 62) on Highway 106 through Narrow Hills Park, near the park's northern boundary. It is 72 hectares in size, is adjacent to a paved road, has a good boat launch, and holds brook trout and rainbow trout.

SHANNON LAKE (73I) is a 10-hectare lake located at kilometre 69 (mile 43) of Highway 106. It is accessible by paved road, has good boat launch access, and holds brown trout.

SUMMIT LAKE (73I) is located on the south side of Highway 913 in the centre of Narrow Hills Park. It holds northern pike, walleye, and whitefish.

UPPER FISHING LAKE (73I) is located just to the west of Highway 106 and is serviced by Caribou Creek Lodge. Upper Fishing Lake holds pike, walleye, and whitefish.

NEMIEBEN LAKE (73P)

Aside from Lac La Ronge, Nemieben Lake is one of the principal destinations for anglers in the La Ronge area. Located 25 kilometres (16 miles) north of La Ronge on Highway 102, it offers camping at a Saskatchewan Environment campground and is serviced by Lindwood Lodge. The lodge offers cabin accommodation, central bath, fuel, boat rentals, filleting and freezing services, and launch ramp access to the lake. Nemieben Lake holds lake trout, northern pike, walleye, and whitefish.

NIPIKAMEW LAKE (73I)

Nipikamew Lake is located just east of East Trout Lake, accessible via Highways 913 and 927. Nipikamew is serviced by outfitter Bay Resort, located between this lake and East Trout (see East Trout Lake), and by Katche Kamp Outfitters, who provide camping and cabin accommodation, boat rentals, fuel, boat launch, and filleting and freezing services. The lake holds populations of pike, walleye and whitefish.

PAULL RIVER (74A)

Paull River is located 112 kilometres (70 miles) by air north of La Ronge. Paull River Wilderness Camp offers cabin accommodation, and boat and canoe rental. The camp offers winter ice-fishing packages and snowmobile excursions from La Ronge to camp. The Paull River area holds excellent populations of lake trout, walleye, and northern pike.

PIPRELL LAKE (73I)

Piprell Lake is located just to the south of Highway 913, 65 kilometres (40 miles) northeast of Candle Lake. There is a private campground on the lake and a boat launch. The lake is stocked with browns, rainbows, splake, and tiger trout. The largest brown trout caught and kept in Saskatchewan, 8.06 kilos (17 pounds, 13 ounces), came from Piprell Lake in 1987.

POINTER LAKE (63M)

Located about 65 kilometres (40 miles) by air east of Missinipe, Pointer Lake is serviced by Pointer Lake Lodge. The lodge offers packages that include boat, motor, gas, and cabin accommodation. Pointer Lake offers pike and lake trout fishing.

PRINCE ALBERT NATIONAL PARK (73J, 73G)

Prince Albert National Park is Saskatchewan's only national park. Special regulations for fishing apply here, and a national parks fishing licence is required to fish in national park lakes. A number of water bodies exist within the boundaries of the park. Some are accessible by road, others by canoe or by hiking trail. Some lakes, such as Waskesiu, are developed; others are quite remote backcountry places. The following lakes are all located within the park boundaries.

CREAN LAKE (73J), located in the north-central area of Prince Albert National Park, has a campground at the southwest corner of the lake. The lake holds populations of lake trout, northern pike, walleye, and whitefish.

HALKETT LAKE (73G), found in the southeast corner of the park, is a 1,000-hectare lake accessible from Secondary Road 952. There is a camping area on the northern side of the lake, which holds lake trout, northern pike, and walleye.

SAB RA 13,988

KINGSMERE LAKE (73J) is home to Grey Owl's cabin. Accessible by hiking trail or canoe, it holds pike, lake trout, walleye, and whitefish.
LAVILEE LAKE (73J) is located in the northwest corner of the park. This 2,400-hectare lake holds northern pike, walleye, and whitefish.
THE HEART LAKES (73G) are located between Waskesiu Lake and Crean Lake. Accessible from the end of Highway 952 on the north side of Waskesiu Lake, the lakes hold a population of northern pike and walleye.
TIBISKA LAKE (73J) is found in the northeast part of the park. It holds northern pike and walleye.
WABENO LAKE (73J), located on the northern edge of the park, holds northern pike and walleye.
WASKESIU LAKE (73J) is the main developed lake in the park, with marina services, a store, cabins, and access by paved road. Waskesiu hosts populations of northern pike, walleye, and whitefish.
WASSEGAM LAKE (73J) is found in the north-central part of the park. It holds lake trout, northern pike, and walleye.

In this photograph taken in August 1958, H.J. Thorimbert holds a lake trout weighing 51 pounds, 10 ounces. Taken from Kingsmere Lake, Prince Albert National Park, this was the largest trout caught in Saskatchewan waters that year. Lake trout are scarce in Prince Albert National Park today, and anglers should release any they happen to catch.

SASKATCHEWAN RIVER (63E)

After leaving the E.B. Campbell Dam at Tobin Lake, the Saskatchewan River continues eastward towards Manitoba, splitting into the old channel, which is paralleled by Highway 123 all the way to Pemmican Portage, and the channel which flows into and through the Cumberland Delta and into Cumberland Lake. Along its length, the river is an excellent fishery for pike, walleye, whitefish, perch, and goldeye. (See also Cumberland Lake).

SETTEE LAKE (73P)

Settee Lake is 115 kilometres (71 miles) by air northeast of La Ronge. It is serviced by Josdal Camps, which provides base camp and outpost (Thoreson Lake, Kakabigish Lake, Forbes Lake) cabins and packages including accommodation, boat, motor, and gas, and freezing service. Fishing for pike, lake trout, and walleye is available on these lakes.

SHADD LAKE (73P)

Located to the north of the Churchill River, Shadd Lake is about 70 kilometres (43 miles) north of La Ronge by air. It is serviced by Shadd Lake Cabins, an outfitter that offers packages including cabin accommodation, boat, motor, and gas, as well as filleting and freezing services. Shadd Lake holds populations of walleye and pike.

SLED LAKE (73J)

Sled Lake is a 3,600-hectare lake situated just off Highway 924, north of Highway 55. The village of Sled Lake is located at the southeast corner of the lake. Mercer Outfitting operates a six-room lodge, offers boat and canoe rentals, is open in winter for ice fishing, and provides a boat launch. Sled Lake holds populations of northern pike, walleye, and whitefish.

SMOOTHSTONE LAKE (73J)

Smoothstone Lake is located north of Highway 916, east of Dore Lake. This 29,000-hectare body of water is serviced by a Saskatchewan Environment campground and by Smoothstone Lake Lodge. The lodge offers hunting and fishing, cabin accommodation, a central dining room, fuel, boat rental, a boat launch, and is open for ice fishing. Smoothstone Lake holds populations of northern pike, walleye, and whitefish.

SMOOTHSTONE RIVER (73O)

The Smoothstone River is found south of Pinehouse Lake. It is crossed by Highway 165, providing access to the river's pike and walleye population.

STEEPBANK LAKE (73I)

Steepbank Lake is in the Clarence-Steepbank Lakes Provincial Wilderness Park, which is located off Highways 913 and 927, northwest of Narrow Hills Provincial Park. The lake is accessible by trail only and holds populations of northern pike and walleye.

THOMPSON LAKE (73P)

Thompson Lake is located 96 kilometres (60 miles) north of La Ronge by air. Thompson Lake Lodge, the outfitter on the lake, is a family-run operation that offers cabin accommodation, boat, motor, and gas. In addition to fishing and hunting packages, they offer canoeing and hiking opportunities in this very isolated and scenic area. Thompson Lake holds walleye, northern pike, and lake trout.

TOBIN LAKE (63E)

Tobin Lake is one of Saskatchewan's premier pike and walleye fisheries. The lake was formed by the construction of the E.B. Campbell Dam on the Saskatchewan River (formerly called the Squaw Rapids Dam). The reservoir actually runs between the Codette Dam and the E.B. Campbell, with both a riverine section (accessible directly from the town of Nipawin) and the lake proper (accessed via the river or from Highway 35 on the north shore of the lake, and by Highway 255 and the village of Tobin Lake on the south shore).

Tobin Lake and the Saskatchewan River between Tobin Lake and Codette Lake (a few kilometres upstream) are host to an annual pike festival (a summer-long event), the Premier's Cup Walleye Tournament (in mid-August), and the Vanity Cup (in early October), the province's richest tournament with a $50,000 first prize. This body of water produces numerous northern pike over 9 kilograms (20 pounds) and walleye over 4.5 kilograms (10 pounds) each year. It currently holds the provincial record walleye—an 8.2-kilogram (18-pound) monster, caught and released in 1997. In fact, provincial record fish were caught in Tobin Lake for several years running in the mid to late 1990s.

With its fame spreading, the lake has seen significant fishing pressure, particularly in fall, for much of the last decade. Slot size limits for both walleye and pike were put in place to protect these species from overharvesting. The size of slots does change from time to time, so visiting anglers are advised to check on the latest regulations.

Tobin Lake is serviced by a number of outfitters. Trail's End Outfitters of Nipawin specializes in spring and fall black bear hunts, but offers walleye and pike fishing as well. MacSwaney's Cabins operates year-round in Nipawin Regional Park at the town of Nipawin, and offers both accommodations and services. Pruden's Point Resort, located on the north shore of the lake, offers cabin accommodations and boat rentals and is open for the winter ice-fishing season. Scot's Landing, located on the opposite shore of the river from the town of Nipawin, offers accommodation, boat rental, and boat launch and docking; they also will arrange for guides. Silver Tip Outfitting, located at the end of Highway 255 at the village of Tobin Lake, offers cabins, boat rentals, and guide services and is open from May 1 to March 31 to include the ice-fishing season. Twin Marine, located on the waterfront in Nipawin Regional Park, offers boat and houseboat rentals, an excellent boat launch, store, and marina, and a licenced restaurant. White Rock Outfitters, located at Nipawin Regional Park, offers boat rentals, a confectionary store, live bait, and guide service. Saskatchewan River Hunting Camps operates on the north side of Tobin Lake and offers snowmobiling, hunting, and fishing packages. Tobin Lake Resort, located 34 kilometres (21 miles) northeast of Nipawin on the south shore of the lake, offers camping and cabins, boat and canoe rentals, and fuel, and is open for ice fishing as well as summer angling.

In addition, the town of Nipawin provides motel and hotel services, restaurants, boat dealerships, marine and auto gas, shopping, and medical services.

Besides excellent populations of walleye and pike, Tobin Lake holds goldeye, whitefish, and perch, and the occasional sturgeon (no open season exists for sturgeon on these waters).

TORCH RIVER (73H)

The Torch River is accessible from Candle Lake—it runs out of the southeast corner of the lake. It holds populations of pike, walleye, perch, and burbot. The Torch River is serviced by Torch Camp Outfitters, located 55 kilometres (34 miles) north of Carrot River on the Torch River. They offer accommodation, hunting and fishing packages, and guide services.

TRIVEET LAKE (73P)

Triveet Lake is located 15 kilometres (9 miles) west of Nemieben Lake and is not accessible by road. It is serviced by Triveet Lake Lodge, located on the west shore of the lake, a 25-minute flight from La Ronge. The lodge provides cabin accommodations and a central bathing facility. The cabins are available for winter use by ice anglers. Triveet Lake holds burbot, northern pike, walleye, and whitefish.

WAPAWEKKA LAKE (73I)

Wapawekka Lake, over 24,000 hectares in size, is located at the end of Highway 912, southeast of Lac La Ronge. The lake is serviced by Northern Echo Lodge, a fly-in facility that offers cabin accommodation, boats, fuel, and filleting and freezing service. There is a poor launch ramp at the western end of the lake where it meets the road. Wapawekka Lake holds pike, walleye, and whitefish.

WASKWEI LAKE (63M)

Waskwei Lake is located 30 kilometres (19 miles) east of Pelican Narrows. The lake is serviced by Northern Nights Outfitters Ltd., offering lodge accommodations and packages which include boat, motor, and gas. The outfitter offers winter packages as well. Waskwei Lake holds northern pike and walleye.

WEYAKWIN LAKE (73J, 73I)

Weyakwin Lake is located in the Thunder Hills between Highways 2 and 916, just north of Prince Albert National Park in the heart of the boreal forest. There is a Saskatchewan Environment campground at the south end of the lake at the end of a 14-kilometre (9-mile) gravel road running in from Highway 2. There is a poor launch ramp. This 8,000-hectare lake holds northern pike, walleye, whitefish, and perch.

WHITESWAN LAKES (73I)

Whiteswan Lakes are situated off Highway 913, north of Highway 120, and serviced by White Swan Lake Resort, an outfitter located on Whelan Bay, 38 kilometres (24 miles) north of Candle Lake. The resort is open year-round for the ice fishing and snowmobiling season and offers cabin accommodations and campsites, fuel, boat and canoe rentals, filleting and freezing servicees, and central dining. Whiteswan Lakes hold lake trout and northern pike.

WOOD LAKE (63M)

Part of the upper Sturgeon-Weir River system, Wood Lake is about 30 kilometres (19 miles) long, is accessible by water or air, and holds burbot, pike, walleye, whitefish, and perch.

CHAPTER TWELVE
WHERE TO FISH
IN NORTHERN SASKATCHEWAN

COURTESY OF SYLVIA FEDORUK

Former Saskatchewan Lieutenant Governor Sylvia Fedoruk
fishing at Costigan Lake in northern Saskatchewan, July
1951. Today's conservation regulations restrict anglers to
possession of only one lake trout over 65 centimetres
(25½ inches).

T he Northern Zone is bounded on the north by the Northwest Territories' border, and on the south by the 57th degree of latitude from the Alberta border eastward to 108 degrees of longitude. There it dips to 56 degrees, 40 minutes north, as far east as 106 degrees of longitude. At that point it further dips to 56 degrees, 10 minutes of latitude and remains there to the Manitoba border. Because of the definition of this boundary, anglers visiting this part of Saskatchewan to fish should check with the nearest Saskatchewan Environment office regarding the exact location of the zone boundary.

The northern zone extends from boreal forest through to the sparsely forested lands at the northernmost points of the province. There are several roads into the far

Map 5. Saskatchewan's Northern Fishing Zone

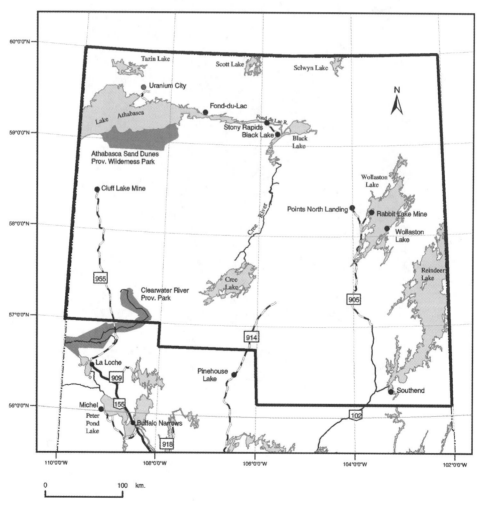

north in Saskatchewan. In the west, the Semchuk Trail (Highway 955) runs all the way to the Cluff Lake Mine, well north of the fifty-eighth parallel. In the centre of the province, the road to the Key Lake Mine (Highway 914) reaches past the fifty-seventh parallel. And in the east, Highway 102 continues north from La Ronge to Reindeer Lake, Wollaston Lake, and Points North Landing, again, north of the fifty-eighth parallel. These roads travel through some of the most beautiful and isolated land in the province, and those wishing to drive their more remote sections should be well prepared for wilderness travel and for survival in the event of mishap.

This is the land of trophy lake trout and northern pike, of Arctic grayling, of waters managed for premier quality fishing. The isolation of waters in the far north reduces the fishing pressure on them significantly, but the maintenance of a world-class fishery in northern Saskatchewan is also due to the catch-and-release ethic promoted by both regulators and lodge operators. Provincial fisheries regulations designate most northern lakes as "CR"—catch-and-release—lakes with varying degrees of reduced possession limits. CR1 is the least restrictive and CR3 the most restrictive of these designations. Visiting anglers should check the most recent Anglers' Guide to determine the designation at the lake they will be fishing, as well as the specific species limits that apply. Most of the far northern lodges have implemented a "catch-and-release only" policy for all trophy fish. Anglers visiting these lodges are permitted to keep a few smaller fish for shore lunch, but must return all trophies to the water. A quick photo and and a few simple measurements are all that are needed to have a superb replica mount made. For many anglers, a good photo is souvenir enough. The reward for honouring this catch-and-release ethic is the opportunity to catch the fish of a lifetime—northern pike and lake trout exceeding 30 pounds.

These northern waters provide anglers the opportunity to fish for one of the most beautiful, and rarest, of freshwater sport fish—the Arctic grayling. These silver gray beauties with the extraordinary dorsal fin are found only in the coldest, clearest, cleanest water around. The largest grayling caught and kept in the province weighed in at 1.96 kilograms (4 pounds, 5 ounces), and was caught in the Fond du Lac River. The largest released specimen measured 53 centimetres (just under 21 inches) taken from Highrock Lake.

Most anglers fishing the far northern waters of Saskatchewan will fly into a remote lodge accessible only by small aircraft. Most fly-in lodges offer not only premium fishing at their base camps, but also have fly-out outpost fishing camps for even more remote angling experiences. Many northern lodges have airstrips at or near the lodge or offer float plane access to private pilots.

Air services are available from La Ronge, Buffalo Narrows, Missinipe, Points North Landing, Beauval, Île-à-la-Crosse, or direct from Saskatoon. Anglers visiting remote northern lodges will make arrangements through lodge owners for their flights to and from the north.

The waters described in this chapter are primarily those serviced by northern outfitters. Northern Saskatchewan is home to many fishing outfitters. Some are mentioned here, but not all. Information about licenced outfitters is readily available from Saskatchewan Environment, at its Regina office (306-787-2080) or through its Prince

August, 1957: Norman Jeppeson of Uranium City (right) and Alan Hill display part of their catch of lake trout from Beaver Lodge Lake, situated just north of Lake Athabasca. Beaver Lodge Mountain is in the background.

SAB RB 6797 (2)

Albert office (306-953-2322). In addition, outfitter information is available from the Saskatchewan Outfitters Association in Prince Albert (306-763-5434).

ATHABASKA LAKE (74N/74O)

Athabaska Lake, one of the largest inland lakes in Canada and the largest body of water in Saskatchewan, is home to some of the largest lake trout in the world. The provincial record released fish, measuring 132 centimetres (52 inches) was caught here in 2000. This huge lake is serviced by several outfitters.

In the east arm of the lake is Athabaska Camps Inc., which offers angling on Athabaska, and outposts on Richards, Fontaine, Engler, and Alces lakes. Full American Plan packages include return airfare from Saskatoon.

Lakers Unlimited Inc. has two locations—Johnston Island Lodge and Spring Bay Lodge, both on the north shore of Lake Athabaska. Full service packages include return transportation from Edmonton.

Luffy's Lodge is located on Mahood Island, 30 kilometres (19 miles) southwest of Uranium City, on the north shore of the lake. The lodge is owned by James and Luffy Augier, who showcase their native Cree culture through their services as outfitters.

In addition to trophy lake trout, Athabaska and area waters offer excellent fishing for northern pike, walleye, and grayling.

BEAVER LODGE LAKE (74N)

Beaver Lodge Lake is located on the north side of Athabasca Lake, adjacent to the settlement of Uranium City. The lake holds populations of lake trout and northern pike.

BEET LAKE (74P)

Beet Lake is located just east of Highway 955 (the Semchuk Trail), 158 kilometres (98 miles) north of La Loche. Anglers take the Semchuk Trail to the Patterson Lake sign, where transport into the lake is arranged with Forrest Lake Outfitters, who service Beet Lake and an outpost camp on Forbes Lake.

The outfitter operates from May to September and offers cabin accommodations, central bath and dining, and filleting and freezing services. Beet and neighbouring lakes offer angling for walleye, northern pike, lake trout, and Arctic grayling.

BLACK LAKE (74P)

Black Lake is located to the east of Lake Athabaska on the Fond du Lac River. It is the site of Camp Grayling, an outfitter located near Elizabeth Falls, 24 kilometres (15 miles) by gravel road from the airstrip at the village of Stony Rapids. In addition to base camp on Black Lake, Camp Grayling offers fly-outs to Riou, Dodge, and Selwyn lakes. Black Lake offers walleye, northern pike, lake trout, grayling, and whitefish.

Norm Ferrier (right), Saskatoon, and C.A.L. Hogg fish for Arctic grayling at Fond du Lac River (June 1949).

SAB RA 11,638 (3)

Local guide fillets fish at Cree Lake, 1955.

BURBIDGE LAKE (74A)

Burbidge Lake is 184 kilometres (114 miles) by float plane north of La Ronge. Burbidge Lake Lodge services this remote wilderness lake, and offers day-use outpost lakes as well. The lodge provides packages that include cabin accommodations, central dining and bath, boat, motor and fuel, and freezing services. Burbidge Lake holds lake trout, northern pike, and whitefish.

COSTIGAN LAKE

Costigan Lake is located to the east of Highway 914, the Key Lake Mine road, southeast of Cree Lake and north of Mawdsley Lake. It holds populations of northern pike, lake trout, and walleye.

CREE LAKE (74G)

Cree Lake is located northwest of the Key Lake Mine and is accessed by float plane from a base at kilometre 176 (mile 109) of Highway 914—the Key Lake Road. It is also accessed by air from La Ronge, 300 kilometres (186 miles) to the southeast. Several outfitters provide service to anglers on Cree Lake.

Boreal Camp Services operates from June to October. The lodge is located on a sand cliff overlooking the lake, and operates on a trophy catch-and-release basis. Cree Lake Lodge is at the north end of the lake on the tip of Rushmer Peninsula.

Open from June to October, Cree Lake Lodge offers cabin service, home-cooked meals, and guide services. All-inclusive packages provide return airfare from La Ronge. Crystal Lodge is located on Ipatinow Island in the middle of Cree Lake. It offers cabin accommodations, boat, motor and gas, and guide service.

Cree Lake holds populations of trophy northern pike, lake trout, Arctic grayling, and walleye.

CUELENAERE LAKE (64D)

Cuelenaere Lake is located 128 kilometres (80 miles) by air northeast of Otter Lake. Cuelenaere Lake Lodge, located on an island in the Buss Lakes chain, provides cabin accommodation and meals, boat, motor, gas, guide services and return air transport. Cuelenaere Lake holds northern pike and lake trout.

DAVIN LAKE (64D)

Accessible by air or by road, Davin Lake is located on Highway 905 about 75 kilometres (47 miles) north of Highway 102. Davin Lake Lodge provides cabin accommodations, central dining and bath, boat, motor, and gas, and fish processing. Fly-out trips are available to Wathaman Lake. Davin holds lake trout, northern pike, and walleye.

FOSTER LAKES (LOWER) (74A)

Lower Foster Lake is 155 kilometres (96 miles) by air north of La Ronge. Beaver Lodge Fly-Inn Company, the outfitter on the lake, offers both a main lodge and cabins. This lodge has a unique history: the main lodge was built by Jacques Cousteau and his filming team when they were making a documentary about beavers in northern Saskatchewan. The lodge offers full American Plan services including return airfare from La Ronge. The lake offers trophy lake trout and northern pike fishing.

GOW LAKE (74A)

Gow Lake is 166 kilometres (103 miles) by air north of La Ronge, or 100 kilometres (62 miles) north from Otter Rapids. Located in the heart of the Precambrian Shield, the lake is serviced by Northern Reflection Lodge, which also offers fly-outs to an outpost lake. Accommodation at Gow Lake is a log cabin, with central dining and bath provided. Gow Lake holds walleye, northern pike, and lake trout.

HASBALA LAKE (64M)

Hasbala Lake is located just inside Saskatchewan at the border with Manitoba, Nunavut, and the Northwest Territories, 224 kilometres (139 miles) by air north of Wollaston Lake. Hasbala Lake Lodge operates from June to September and offers cabin accommodation, home-cooked meals, and guide service to small groups of up to eight anglers. Packages include return airfare from Points North Landing. The lodge operates with a catch-and-release policy.

Hasbala Lake is in subarctic terrain and offers trophy fishing for grayling, northern pike, and lake trout.

HATCHET LAKE (64L)

Hatchet Lake is a fly-in lake located northeast of Wollaston Lake about 128 kilometres (80 miles) south of the Northwest Territories border. Hatchet Lake Lodge, located on an island in the lake, has a 5,000-foot airstrip within 3.2 kilometres (2 miles) of camp. The lodge offers modern cabins, central dining, and full American Plan packages. Hatchet Lake offers world-class fishing for lake trout, northern pike, grayling, and walleye.

HAWKROCK RIVER (74I/74P)

The Hawkrock River is located just south of the Fond du Lac River in far northern Saskatchewan. Hawkrock Wilderness Adventures offers trophy-class fishing as well as hunting trips. Located just east of Black Lake, the lodge offers full American Plan packages. The lodge offers angling for walleye, northern pike, grayling, and lake trout.

JOHNSON RIVER (64E)

Johnson River is located east of Reindeer Lake at kilometre 142 (mile 88) of Highway 905, approximately 150 kilometres (93 miles) north of Highway 102. Located on the Johnson River, Johnson River Camps offers access to five surrounding lakes and provides modern cabins with central bath. Angling opportunities are for walleye, northern pike, and lake trout.

MISAW LAKE (64M)

Misaw Lake is remote—208 kilometres (129 miles) northeast of Wollaston Lake and just a few kilometres south of the Northwest Territories border—and accessible only by air. Misaw Lake Lodge offers fishing on multiple waters, including the Schwant River system. The lodge, which operates on a catch-and-release basis, opened a new outpost camp on Patterson Lake in 2002 and provides package deals that include return airfare from Winnipeg. Misaw Lake and neighbouring waters hold trophy grayling, lake trout, and northern pike.

OLIVER LAKE (64D)

Oliver Lake is accessible by air from Otter Rapids (Missinipe), located on Highway 102. Thompson's Camps Inc. offers light housekeeping cabins or American Plan packages from June to September. Flyouts to Horvath, Nokomis, Ghana, and Pritchard lakes are also available. Oliver Lake, which is located due west of Reindeer Lake, holds lake trout, northern pike, walleye and Arctic grayling.

ONEMAN LAKE (74A)

Oneman Lake is located 103 kilometres (64 miles) by air north of Otter Rapids and 162 kilometres (101 miles) north of La Ronge. Grey Owl Camp provides outfitter services to groups of up to ten persons at a time. The lodge has a catch-and-release policy for all trophy fish. Oneman Lake holds lake trout and northern pike.

PHELPS LAKE (64M)

Located in the far northeastern corner of Saskatchewan, Phelps Lake is accessible only by float plane. Wolf Bay Lodge/Phelps Lake Camp Inc. offers full services on Phelps Lake and fly-outs to Sava Lake. The lodge operates on a trophy catch-and-release policy. The area offers northern pike, lake trout, grayling, and walleye fishing.

PIPESTONE LAKE (74G)

Pipestone Lake, located north of Cree Lake, is accessible by a float plane flight of one hour and twenty minutes from La Ronge. Pipestone Lake Fishing Lodge operates on the lake, with fly-out fishing on Mayson and Granbois lakes. Modern cabins, boats, motors, and gas are available at the lodge. Pipestone Lake and neighbouring lakes offer lake trout, walleye, and northern pike fishing.

REINDEER LAKE (64D)

One of the largest lakes in Saskatchewan, Reindeer Lake is accessible by way of Highway 102 through Southend, or by float plane out of La Ronge or Otter Rapids. The lake is serviced by several outfitters.

Lawrence Bay Lodge is located 56 kilometres (35 miles) northeast of Southend by air or water. In addition to fishing on Reindeer, it offers two outpost camps on Pagato Lake and Kamatsi Lake. Packages offered include air service from Southend.

Lindbergh's Reindeer Lake Lodge, located halfway up the west side of Reindeer Lake, is the most northerly and most isolated lodge on the lake. It offers fly-outs to Reilly Lake and McKenzie Lake. The lodge package includes direct flights from Winnipeg.

Nordic Lodge is located in a sheltered bay at the south end of Reindeer Lake, accessible from kilometre 216 (mile 134) of Highway 102. Packages include accommodation, boat, motor, gas, and fish processing.

Reindeer Lake Trout Camp is located 24 kilometres (15 miles) north of Southend on Reindeer Lake. Its base camp accommodates up to sixty persons. The lodge also offers fly-outs to Kyaska Lake, Harriot Lake, and Gladman Lake.

Reindeer Lake offers angling for lake trout, northern pike, walleye, and Arctic grayling.

SCOTT LAKE (74O)

Scott Lake is on the Northwest Territories border, due north of Stony Rapids. Scott Lake Lodge operates on the lake, the most northerly outfitter in Saskatchewan. In addition to base camp on Scott Lake, the lodge has an outpost camp at Wignes Lake. All-inclusive packages include return airfare from Saskatoon. Scott Lake holds trophy northern pike, lake trout, and grayling.

SELWYN LAKE (74P)

Selwyn Lake is located right on the Northwest Territories border, due north of Points North Landing. Selwyn Lake Lodge, which services the lake, offers fly-outs to locations in the Northwest Territories. (They also offers wilderness location fly-ins in the Churchill River area out of La Ronge.) In addition to angling services,

Selwyn Lake Lodge offers exploring, sightseeing, canoeing, trapline expeditions, wildlife safaris, barren grounds and Arctic tundra charters, and dogsledding and snowmobile tours. The lodge is open year-round and operates on a trophy catch-and-release basis. Selwyn Lake and neighbouring waters hold trophy northern pike, lake trout, and grayling.

TAZIN LAKE (74N)

Tazin Lake is located in the far northwest corner of Saskatchewan, north of Lake Athabaska. Cheemo Lodge, the outfitter on the lake, is accessible by air from Uranium City, Fort McMurray, Alberta, or Fort Smith, Northwest Territories. Cheemo Lodge also has access by short trail to Tsalwor Lake and Thluicho Lake. Tazin Lake offers trophy lake trout and northern pike fishing.

THERIAU LAKE (74I)

Therieau Lake, 400 kilometres (249 miles) by air north of La Ronge, is located in the Athabaska sand basin region of northern Saskatchewan. Theriau Lake Lodge offers full services, including a main lodge, central dining, shore lunch, and side trips to the Waterfound River and Ward Creek. Theriau Lake holds northern pike and lake trout. The Waterfound River holds pike, grayling and trout. Ward Creek holds walleye and pike.

UBIQUITY LAKE (74G)

Located southeast of Cree Lake, Ubiquity Lake is 173 kilometres (108 miles) by air north of Buffalo Narrows. It is accessible only by float plane. Ubiquity Lake Outfitters provides service to the lake and also operates an outpost camp at Carpenter Lake. The outfitter provides cabin accommodation, central bath and dining, and access to four lakes in the area. Packages are available that include return airfare from Buffalo Narrows. Ubiquity Lake and the surrounding area offers excellent fishing for northern pike, lake trout, and walleye.

WAPATA LAKE (74I)

Wapata Lake is located 480 kilometres (298 miles) by air north of La Ronge. It is serviced by Cree River Lodge, located on the shore of the Cree River, south of Black Lake. The lodge can be accessed by air from nearby Stony Rapids. The outfitter has a central lodge and cabins and offers central dining and American Plan packages. There is excellent fishing in the area for walleye, northern pike, lake trout, and grayling.

WATERBURY LAKE (74I)

Waterbury Lake, located a scant 160 kilometres (99 miles) south of the Northwest Territories border, is accessible by air, with an airstrip less than 1 kilometre (less than 1 mile) away. Waterbury Lake Lodge offers all-inclusive packages which include flights from Saskatoon, home-cooked meals, guide service, and shore lunch. The lodge, which offers cabin accommodation and central dining, operates on a trophy catch-and-release basis. Waterbury Lake holds walleye, lake trout, northern pike, and Arctic grayling.

Fishing at Trout Narrows on Wollaston Lake, June 1948.

WHEELER RIVER (64E)

Wheeler River is located 220 kilometres (137 miles) north of Otter Lake (Missinipe) by air. Wheeler River Lodge is located on the river system, with access to a number of local lakes. It offers lodge accommodations and a package deal that includes return airfare from Otter Lake. The Wheeler River area offers walleye, whitefish, Arctic grayling, northern pike, and lake trout fishing.

WOLLASTON LAKE (64E/64L)

Wollaston Lake is one of northern Saskatchewan's largest lakes and a premiere fishing destination. It can be accessed at two points from Highway 905. The first is at kilometre 190 (mile 118) and the other at kilometre 220 (mile 137), north from the junction of Highway 102. It is also accessible by air from La Ronge, from Otter Rapids, or from Points North Landing which is located at the northern end of Highway 905.

Several outfitters provide services on Wollaston Lake. D and D Camps is located at kilometre 190 of Highway 905, at the southern end of the lake. It offers log cabin accommodations along with boat, motor, fuel, and filleting and freezing services. Local guides are available.

Minor Bay Lodge is located at kilometre 220 of Highway 905. In addition to Wollaston, it offers fly-out fishing at McDonald, Simpson, and Spence lakes. There is both a main lodge and modern cabins at base camp, with non-modern cabins at outposts.

Wollaston Lake Lodge is located within 30 kilometres (19 miles) of Points North Landing. Air charter service is provided from Winnipeg. It is located at the mouth of the Umpherville River in a sheltered bay and offers fly-outs as well as fishing on Wollaston. All angling at Wollaston Lake Lodge is catch-and-release.

Wollaston Lake offers northern pike, walleye, grayling, and lake trout fishing. These waters are known for producing trophy northerns. And some of the best grayling fishing in northern Saskatchewan is found on the Geikie River, which flows into the south end of Wollaston Lake.

WOLVERMAN LAKES (74P)

The Wolverman Lakes, located due north of Clearwater River Provincial Park, are 190 kilometres (118 miles) north of Buffalo Narrows and accessible only by air. Wolverman Wilderness Outfitters services the area, operating modern tent camps. They offer all-inclusive packages that include guides, with return air transport to either La Loche or Fort McMurray, Alberta. Area waters hold northern pike, walleye, lake trout, and Arctic grayling.

CHAPTER THIRTEEN
FISHERIES MANAGEMENT AND CONSERVATION

SAB RA 11,408

Ken Rommings, a Conservation Officer, checks a fisherman's license on the shore of the South Saskatchewan River in Saskatoon, 1957.

Saskatchewan enjoys an extraordinary fishery. It is diverse, it is plentiful, and in many parts of the province, it is not heavily pressured. Where significant fishing pressure does exist, it occurs in close association with population density, on the one hand, and with easily accessible, popular fishing destinations, on the other.

The most popular fishing lakes in southern Saskatchewan are the four lakes along the Qu'Appelle River adjacent to the town of Fort Qu'Appelle. Pasqua and Echo Lakes to the west of town and Mission and Katepwa Lakes to the east are favoured destinations not only for anglers from the neighbouring towns and cottage developments, but also for the capital city of Regina and its surrounding population. These lakes also enjoy significant visitation levels from American anglers travelling into Saskatchewan from nearby border states.

These lakes are popular for a number of reasons. They are reasonably rich fisheries with a strong forage base, a large population of perch that serve as prey species to larger walleye and northern pike that are found in all four lakes. The lakes also support a good population of tullibee, carp, sucker, and drum, and there are reports of rock bass being taken from Katepwa, the most easterly of the lakes.

The four lakes are virtually ringed with cottage development and are easily accessible on paved roads. The town of Fort Qu'Appelle can provide all the services—accommodation, food, tackle, bait, marine dealers, medical care—that visiting anglers might possibly need.

The Qu'Appelle lakes, as they are commonly known, receive fishing pressure year-round—they are very popular destinations for ice anglers from December through to the end of March. Some of the best walleye and pike angling to be had in these lakes is through the ice.

In addition to fishing pressures, these lakes are also facing environmental pressure on the quality of the water within them. Human habitation around the lakes is significant—cottage developments, year-round residents, and the town of Fort Qu'Appelle, as well as several First Nations Reserves, ring the lakes. The surrounding watershed drains from farmland into the Qu'Appelle Valley, increasing the nutrient load in the lakes each year. A major algae bloom occurs on these lakes as soon as the combination of air and water temperature, along with a few days of calm weather, occurs. Such blooms are common from early summer through to September. In addition, the four lakes constitute the first major catch basins along the Qu'Appelle River downstream of Regina and a large agricultural area along the river.

At the time this book was written, no special regulations applied to the fishery in the four popular Qu'Appelle Lakes. Anglers who fish these lakes continue to report good harvest levels, and good results for the level of angler effort required. However, they are typical of waterbodies that are worthy of monitoring, for, as we have seen with others, the decline of a fishery can be sudden, and dramatic. The story of one such fishery's dramatic decline follows.

The town of Nipawin lies at the centre of one of the finest pike and walleye fisheries in North America. The Saskatchewan River, in particular the stretch that runs through Codette Lake, past the town of Nipawin and on into Tobin Lake, is remarkable for the number of large fish it produces. In the river section, the provincial record wall-eye was caught four years in a row. The most recent record, taken in 1997, weighed in at just over 18 pounds—8.2 kilograms—and was caught just a few minutes boat ride on the river from the town of Nipawin itself. Tobin Lake is an exceptional northern pike fishery, with big fish over twenty pounds taken annually during the Nipawin Pike Festival.

Twenty years ago, this fishery was virtually unknown outside of a small population of local anglers and a few regular visitors. It owes its existence to the building of the hydroelectric power dam that created Tobin Lake—the E.B. Campbell Dam. In the late 1980s, however, everything changed. A walleye tournament, the Premier's Cup, was held on the river, and anglers from across western Canada and many of the U.S. border states discovered an exceptional fishery for the first time. Big walleye—over 10 pounds—were plentiful, and those in the mid-size ranges, 4 to 6 pounds, were relatively easy to catch in good numbers. The fishery had not been pressured and was producing remarkable numbers of fish. The pike fishery was equally strong.

As a result of the attention brought to these waters by events such as the Premier's Cup and by coverage on several television fishing programs, a new tourism boom began for the town of Nipawin, as anglers from all over flocked to the area. Fishing pressure increased quickly, and far too many fish were being filleted and taken home for food, especially those female walleye in the prime of their breeding years—fish in the 2 to 4-kilogram (4 to 8-pound) range. A few anglers from both the local and visiting population began to express concerns about the fishing pressure, but the fishing was so good that no one really paid much attention.

Then, seemingly overnight, a dramatic change took place in the fishery. Anglers, especially those fishing the Premier's Cup tournament event, reported that they were able to catch lots of small fish—mostly under 40 centimetres (about 16 inches)—some large trophy walleye, but very few fish in between. This trend continued, and caused sufficient concern that a consultative group—consisting of representatives of the town, local outfitters, anglers, and the Saskatchewan Environment Department—met to discuss a strategy.

The problem was this: if the observations of anglers were true—and they appeared to be—then what was missing from the walleye population was precisely that part most needed for continuing the health of the population—prime breeding fish. After considerable consultation, a solution was decided upon. Protective slot limits were put in place—no fish between 55 centimetres and 70 centimetres (22 to 28 inches) could be retained by any angler at any time, including during tournament events. The upper end of the slot limit has since been extended to 80 centimetres (31.5 inches), in order to protect more of the trophy-sized fish. A similar slot limit for northern pike—no fish between 75 and 105 centimetres may be retained—was put in place to protect the future of the pike fishery.

Since these limits were imposed in the mid-1990s, some improvements in the quality of angling have been reported. More medium-sized walleye are being caught and released by anglers. And the extraordinary trophy fishery in the Nipawin reach of the

Saskatchewan River continues to be one of the best in North America.

This is the story of a once highly successful fishery that was saved barely in time. It took the cooperative efforts of anglers, outfitters, townspeople, politicians, and government biologists and officials to make it happen. It is an object lesson in just how quickly an excellent fishery can be put at risk, and the kind of effort it takes to restore the damage once it has been done.

In order to protect the walleye fishery in the entire province, the regulation limiting anglers to one walleye in possession over 55 centimetres in length has been extended to all waters in Saskatchewan. Similar restrictions have been placed on other vulnerable species. Anglers fishing in Saskatchewan waters may have in possession only one pike over 75 centimetres, one lake trout over 65 centimetres, and one grayling over 35 centimetres.

Conservation and management of the fishery in Saskatchewan is, as it must be everywhere, a shared responsibility, entirely dependent for its success on the cooperation of many parties. It involves at least two, and often three, levels of government, private businesses in the form of outfitters, tourist operators, and commercial fishers, volunteer angler groups and clubs, individual anglers, and the general public.

SAB RA 2708

Catches such as this, from a single afternoon's fishing on Last Mountain Lake during the "good ol' days" (c. 1910), far exceed modern fishing limits.

Saskatchewan Environment, through its Fish and Wildlife Branch, is primarily responsible for putting in place and enforcing the rules and regulations that are designed to manage and protect the fishery. Theirs is the task of issuing licences, setting regular and special limits, drafting rules and regulations governing behaviour, setting opening and closing dates, and enforcing the rules, as well as protecting habitat. The federal government's Department of Fisheries and Oceans (DFO) is primarily concerned with the protection of habitat.

In addition to government agencies, there are several volunteer organizations that are involved in conservation activities in Saskatchewan on a province-wide basis.

The Fishing for Tomorrow Foundation, based in Saskatoon, is dedicated to the promotion of the fishery and to raising money for conservation and educational activities. Its volunteer members carry out a major fish rescue operation each fall when irrigation canals are drained for the winter, and thousands of fish are trapped. Fishing for Tomorrow volunteers net the trapped fish and return them to the adjacent waters of Blackstrap Lake.

The Saskatchewan Wildlife Federation is the largest outdoor sporting organization in the province, oriented primarily to fishing and hunting activities, with local chapters around the province and a paid professional staff based in Moose Jaw. The Federation raises money to purchase habitat, is involved in conservation education, and is a lobby group on behalf of outdoor sportspersons, representing their interests to the provincial government.

The Kilpatrick and Flatland Flyfishers are two clubs, the first based in Saskatoon, the second in Regina, that together form the Saskatchewan Fly Fishers. In addition to bringing new fly fishers into the sport each year and holding club events for their members, these organizations actively participate in fish conservation activities in the province, cooperating with government and other volunteer-based groups.

The Saskatchewan Walleye Trail collects fees from each angler's registration for each tournament, placing it in a fund for the purpose of promotion of the fishery, conservation, and education.

Once upon a time, fisheries biologists and government officials made policy decisions and set out rules and regulations quite independently of the groups and individuals who had a stake in the resource being managed. That style of resource management has long since fallen into disrepute. In managing the fishery, Saskatchewan Environment has adopted what they refer to as an ecosystem management approach. Overall goals are to maintain or restore ecosystem health, including fish and wildlife resources and habitat; to monitor ecosystem health, including the condition of fish and wildlife resources and habitat; and to allocate use of resources in a manner that is ecologically, economically, and socially sustainable—simple words, but a very tall order.

The management principles that support these goals include taking a long-term rather than short-term view on any issue; concentrating on the health and integrity of ecosystems; taking into account sound science, First Nations traditions, and local knowledge as a basis for decision-making; involving those who will be affected by decisions in the making of them; adapting management decisions by learning from

Conservation Officer Bob Albus, North Battleford, checks a commercial fisherman on Murray Lake, 1954.

experience; and making an effort to look at the larger picture when dealing with specific issues. This approach to resource management takes into account that the ecosystems in which we all live have value in and of themselves, but are unavoidably linked to social, economic, spiritual, and political forces in the human community.

Managing a resource like the Saskatchewan fishery is a complex undertaking. Fish, like all wild flora and fauna, are seen as a public resource and thus are ultimately the responsibility of the Crown. A source of subsistence for some, a commercial livelihood for others, and a recreational resource for many, fish also have their own intrinsic value. Current government policy includes setting objectives that aim at optimum, rather than maximum, use of the resource. The policy gives priority to native species of fish, and at the same time promises to conserve non-native species, provided they do not negatively impact native species or habitat. This is an important consideration, given that all trout species except lake trout and all the carp and all the bass in the province are exotics. They may have been here for a long time, but they don't come from here. Whenever fish species are moved around—into or out of the province, or from location to location within it—there are ecological, genetic, economic, and social impacts to be considered.

Contemporary fisheries management is a balancing act. Recreational anglers have their concerns and interests. So do commercial fishers, and so, too, do First Nations. Those interests may not always be in harmony. In addition, environmental conditions affecting the health of a fishery will always affect management decisions. Saskatchewan fish and wildlife management policy states clearly that conservation is the first priority. Once conservation goals are achieved, First Nations people who are legally entitled to subsistence use have first access to any resource surplus. After conservation and subsistence requirements are met, then the public has priority access to fish and wildlife in the province.

The art of managing a fishery resource in the modern context of multiple uses and multiple users is one in which ensuring collaboration and cooperation amongst all stakeholders, while making use of the best science possible, is critical to the health of that resource. It is not a simple task and it is a task made harder when the money needed to support both management programs and scientific research is less than sufficient to the task. In recent years, governments across Canada have reduced their spending in order to lower their debt, decrease tax levels to citizens, and balance their budgets on an annual basis. Fisheries, wildlife, and natural resources management departments have not fared all that well as these cuts have been made. All too often the casualty has been good field work and good scientific research. These two activities are time-consuming and expensive. Yet the information they yield is crucial to wise and informed decision-making by resource managers.

In their place, fisheries managers have taken to using other means to obtain data on such things as fishing pressure on particular bodies of water. For example, on Lac La Ronge and Jan Lake, both popular drive-to fisheries in the north-central part of Saskatchewan, anglers must have "endorsements" in addition to their regular fishing licence in order to fish on these lakes. These endorsements provide Saskatchewan Environment with a means of identifying the levels of angler activity. They cost the recreational angler nothing and are a relatively low-cost source of data to the department. In addition, some of the anglers who hold these endorsements will be sent questionnaires to provide further information about fishing activity on a particular body of water.

Participants in fishing tournament are asked to provide data on the number and species of fish that they catch. So are tournament organizers. In some cases, this kind of data gathering replaces the field work that only a few years back would have taken the form of a creel census or harvest survey and regular test nettings of selected water bodies. Whether they are as effective a means of measuring fishing pressure and population health is open to question. Whether numbers and tick marks on a sheet of paper can ever replace first-hand observations by a biological scientist working in the field or direct observation of angler activities and activity levels is debatable.

However, a policy to involve local communities and stakeholder groups in decisions about the resource is of great value, in that it encourages the angling public to

Terry Smith, a visiting angler from the United Kingdom releases a large carp into Last Mountain Lake.

participate in the management of the fishery and to develop a sense of "ownership." This is a good thing, both for the fishery and for the anglers who make use of it.

CATCH-AND-RELEASE

One of the revolutionary ideas affecting the conservation of the fishery is the concept of catch-and-release fishing. While it was popularized in the last decade of the twentieth century, it isn't that new. One of its early proponents was Lee Wulff, renowned fly fisher, who pronounced to the world a half-century ago that his beloved Atlantic salmon were far too valuable to catch only once!

Catch-and-release represents a fundamental change in attitude: instead of catching and keeping a limit, we think of limiting what we catch. The effects of this new attitude are widespread and profound, not only for the individual angler, but also for fisheries managers, tackle manufacturers, outfitters and lodge owners, angling educators, television producers, and hosts of television fishing shows—in short, almost everyone involved in the angling community.

A study released early in 2002 by University of Calgary ecology professor John Post stated flatly that, in areas of dense population—such as British Columbia's lower mainland, southern Ontario, and the greater Calgary area—fisheries are in danger of collapsing under the pressure put upon them by anglers. We are loving our favourite fishing holes to death.

In some areas of truly high fishing pressure, for instance, those near major population centres, the only antidote, according to Post, may be to actually limit the number of anglers who have access to a fishable body of water. But in areas where fishing pressure is more moderate—and that would certainly apply to most places in Saskatchewan—what has to change is the idea that we should catch as many fish as we can or should keep our limit of whatever we do catch.

And that is at the heart of the catch-and-release philosophy. When catch-and-release was first being promoted, it was put forward as an absolute—keep nothing, put everything back. This would certainly have the effect of reducing the harvest of fish from any given body of water, but it probably places an unrealistic expectation on the angling community. Besides, fish taste good and are healthy food, and part of the fun of fishing is taking a few home for supper. The key to catch-and-release is moderation, governed by a good measure of common sense.

It was the editors of *In-Fisherman* magazine who first used the term "selective harvest" to describe the practice of keeping a few fish for the pan and releasing the rest—and it's an excellent description of good conservation behaviour. If an angler is out for walleye, the odds are good that he will catch a mixed bag of fish—many will be smaller fish, some will be larger, and a very few will be large trophy specimens. This simply reflects the normal distribution of the age and size ranges of any given fish population. An angler applying the principles of catch-and-release and selective harvest will keep a few of the smaller fish for the frying pan—those large enough to fillet and eat, but not large enough to be prime breeding stock. All of those mid-size fish that are returned in good condition to the water are the future of the fishery—they are at the peak of their sexual maturity. A 3- to 5-pound female walleye in good condition will release literally hundreds of thousands of eggs to be fertilized. Given the low survival rate of eggs and fry in the wild—about 1 percent will make it through—the more eggs laid, the bigger the population of catchable fish to come in a few years time. By sacrificing our appetite for a few more fish in the bag today, we guarantee the fishery of the future.

The principle of catch-and-release can be applied to all species, almost all of the time. But there are exceptions, and catch-and-release doesn't work very well if the fish we release don't survive. Careful handling of fish is essential to successful catch-and-release fishing, and handling starts earlier than you might think.

Except when fishing in deep water, fight a fish quickly, and retrieve and release it quickly. Don't play a fish to exhaustion—the odds are it won't survive release. If you are retrieving fish from deep water, bring them up slowly to avoid damage due to sudden pressure changes. All freshwater fish caught in Saskatchewan have an "air bladder"—a part of their anatomy that allows them to adjust their buoyancy in the water. Some species, such as northern pike and lake trout, can literally "burp" their air bladders, so a rapid rise to the surface from deep water does not create a problem for them. However, in walleye and perch, this bladder adjusts very slowly to differences in atmospheric pressure. These fish suffer fatal injury if they are caught in deep water and reeled to the surface. Pulling them quickly from anything deeper than 6 metres (about 20 feet) can result in the air bladder overinflating—in some cases, to the point where it will distend and protrude through the mouth of a perch—most likely killing the fish. So, unless you plan to take them home for supper, common sense dictates that you avoid catching walleye or perch from deep water .

Once a fish is caught and brought to the net, the less it is handled, the more likely it is to survive. If you plan to release the fish you catch, use barbless hooks (or make your hooks barbless by crimping down the barb with a pair of pliers) to make the release easier. On catch-and-release designated waters in Saskatchewan, barbless hooks are mandatory. If possible, release a fish while it is still in the water. Carry a pair of long needle-nose pliers or surgical pliers or clamps called haemostats for the purpose of popping the hook out. And if you must hold the fish up for a photo, make sure you support it under the heaviest part of its belly and its tail, take the photo quickly, and get the fish back into the water as quickly as possible. Aim to take less than sixty seconds.

Sometimes the hook won't come out of a fish easily; sometimes the fish is tangled in fishing line. If you must handle the fish to release it, wear light cotton gloves that are wetted thoroughly. Hold the fish as gently as possible—squeezing it will bruise the skin and may cause internal injuries. If you are going to use a net, first be sure that it is relatively shallow so that the fish cannot become entangled; second, be sure that is has a rubber-coated mesh so the netting does not damage the skin of the fish. Large fish are best handled using a fish cradle, rather than a net. Never lift a fish by the gill cover, never touch its eyes, and keep your hands away from its gills if you want it to survive.

If a fish has taken a hook too deeply for it to be removed without causing further injury, cut your line off as close to the hook as possible, and release the fish. Don't throw the fish back into the lake. Hold it upright in the water until it is able to swim off on its own. If a fish is bleeding, turns belly up when you release it, or is unable to swim away on its own in a reasonable amount of time, then count that fish towards your limit.

If you're having a great day of fishing, catching and releasing plenty of fish, assume that a percentage of what you catch—say, 5 percent—will be injured and not survive release. Once that 5 percent, plus whatever you have kept already, adds up to your daily limit for that species, stop fishing or change target species. Put down your live-bait rigging rod for walleye, and go trolling a spoon or plug for northern pike instead. You get to fish; the fish get to rest.

A half-century ago in northern Ontario, when I was learning to untangle bird's-nests of fishing line after every bad cast, when a 25-horsepower motor was a huge outboard, when casting a Len Thompson spoon from a shoreline point into a spring school of "pickerel" was as sophisticated as fishing got, our attitudes towards the fishery were very different. Little thought was given to the quality of the water in which we fished. One of the few people I ever heard voice concerns about the health of the fishery was my own father. He would tell me how concerned he was that what we were putting into the waters of our home lake would eventually affect the fish we loved to catch, and all the other life around the lake as well. He said the possession limits were too high and that we should keep fewer fish, or they'd be gone someday.

Most of us gave little thought to the number of fish we harvested. There were plenty of them. It was a measure of your skill as an angler that you could go out and catch your limit any time you wanted. No one released fish. What was caught was kept. The lake, a six-hour drive into northern Ontario from the U.S. border, was a magnet for Americans looking for the ultimate Canadian fishing trip. Fishing pressure was unrelenting. A commercial fishery was maintained on the lake, as well as a First Nations subsistence fishery.

By the time I left home in the late 1960s, the lake was noticeably in decline. It was harder to catch fish. Limits were rare. The fish you did catch were smaller. A particular subspecies of walleye which I had caught regularly as a child—the blue walleye—had disappeared. Some of the more popular spots for spring fishing were now devoid of fish. The huge schools of spawning walleye that I could watch from the beach in front of our family home had disappeared from our bay. All the anglers fishing that lake had, effectively, mined the fish from the lake. Now, nearly four decades later and after major reductions in possession limits and the use of slot limits, there are signs that the fishery may be recovering. It's an object lesson worth contemplating.

Closer to home, Lac La Ronge was, in the not-too-distant past, a premier destination for those seeking to fish for lake trout. It was relatively easy to get there—a long but reasonably comfortable drive—and the fishing was great. Not only was the lake trout fishing good, but there were plenty of walleye and northern pike in the lake as well. Fishing-based tourism was a significant part of the local economy. So was a commercial fishery, and a First Nations subsistence fishery. It was another case of a lake that we were, collectively, loving to death.

By the early 1990s, it was apparent that the lake trout fishery in particular was not in good shape. Local anglers spoke openly about the difficulty of catching lake trout even in the fall, when they were up in shallow water for the spawn, and usually easy to catch. Before long, commercial quotas on the lake were significantly reduced. New recreational angler limits were put in place—two lake trout in possession and a maximum harvest of four lake trout per angler per year. Anglers on Lac La Ronge must carry both a fishing licence and an endorsement (free) to lawfully fish on the lake. The endorsement gives Saskatchewan Environment officials a means to monitor fishing traffic on the lake. While the walleye and pike fishery on the lake remains a reasonably good one, and reason enough to take the drive north, the reduced limits on Lac La Ronge lake trout will likely be there for some time to come. Lake trout are a slow growing, cold water fish. It will take time for the population to recover.

The Saskatchewan fishery is a great gift. With a few exceptions, it is only moderately pressured, and largely in good health. If we care for it, if we are modest in the demands we place upon it, if we harvest it selectively and practise catch-and-release, if we learn from past mistakes, and if we are prepared to make some tough decisions that may, in the short term, be unpopular and require sacrifice, then it is possible that this wonderful fishery will still be a source of joy and wonder in the days of our great-great-grandchildren.

CHAPTER FOURTEEN
PARTING WORDS

MICHAEL SNOOK

Sunset on Last Mountain Lake.

The publication of this book marks the fiftieth year I've held a fishing rod in my hands. The first time remains etched indelibly in my memory. My father and his best fishing buddy, both of whom have long since taken up catch-and-release fishing in the next world, decided to take me out for a day of fishing on Callander Bay, in the southeast corner of Lake Nipissing in northern Ontario. I was five years old, the year was 1953, and the world was a dramatically different place. Metal boats were rare. Where we fished, wooden boats made by Giesler or Nipissing Boat Works were the rule. A fifteen-horse motor was a monster, used mostly by the rich for waterskiing. Fishing boats traveled a few miles an hour—slower if rowed—and no one minded. Good fishing was not far from the dock. Depth finders, underwater cameras, and graphite rods were not yet twinkles in the eyes of their inventors. Even spinning reels were relatively rare in our part of the world.

Fishing tackle was simple. A hook, tied to the end of a line. A sinker, made of lead, a couple of feet up the line from the hook. A live minnow on the hook. Drop your line straight over the side. Hold the minnow just off the bottom. Wait for a bite. It was the bite part that was tricky, and for a five-year-old, a mysterious puzzle yet to be solved.

We fished with ancient Pfleuger level-wind reels (if I had them today, they would be collector's items, but they've disappeared into the trash bin of the past, along with my grandfather's movie posters, my original Boy Scout uniform with the pointy RCMP-style hat, first dates, and my family's first black-and-white television set). They were rigged with Dacron line. Ed (my dad) and his friend Bev had the latest in fibreglass rods. As the kid in the boat, I got the hand-me-down metal rod, complete with wire guides and heavy thread wraps that were starting to fray a bit, like both men's tempers whenever I got my line tangled up in that Pfleuger into the infamous bird's-nest—which was often.

When we left the dock in Callander, the day was full of promise. We rode a gentle swell as the five-horse Evinrude pushed a sixteen-foot wooden, slightly waterlogged cedar-strip boat out onto the bay, and towards its mouth on the main lake. It was warm and hazy, late June; we had a full bucket of bait, and a full day of fishing ahead of us. As a young boy I was eager about nearly everything and particularly about fishing. If my dad and his friends loved it so much, it must be something special. I was so excited I could hardly sit still.

That's probably why, as we got further from shore, Dad, in a tone of voice that would allow no dissent, ordered me to sit in the bottom of the boat. I'd be safer there, he said.

If any of you are old enough to remember wooden fishing boats, you will know that there were floorboards to cover the ribs that held the bottom of the boat together. These floorboards—wooden strips nailed together in a square lattice pattern—were meant to keep the boaters' feet dry and clean, because the only way to truly empty the flotsam from the bottom of such a craft was to haul it up on dry land, give it a good flooding with a hose, then turn it over to drain. It was hard work for two men, heaving a heavy wooden boat over like that, and it didn't happen even once from the day the boat returned to the water in spring until it was put up on dry land in fall.

In the meantime, what fell between the floorboards stayed where it dropped—for the duration. It mixed with lake water, spilled soft drinks, and coffee, simmered in long days in the sun, and made a soup the likes of which has seldom been seen by mortal eyes. No living thing could survive in it for long. Minnows from the bucket, should they slip out of a young and inexperienced hand, would never be seen again. Their essence would add to the rich tang of that soup which, by the heat of midday, had even the most seasoned anglers standing up and hoping for a breeze.

I believe my father knew this. I do not believe he thought of it when he ordered me down to the floor of that boat. I think it just slipped his mind at the time.

At first, sitting down there wasn't so bad. The day was fine, the air was cool, I could fish from the bottom as easily as from the wooden seats—the view wasn't quite as good and I couldn't quite see the horizon line, but the sky was blue and all was well with the world. I was finally fishing.

It was one of those days that come into the life of every angler—a slow, meandering kind of day, during which Ed and Bev stopped and fished, talked about why they weren't biting and how the fishing had been so much better when they had been kids, and then they'd fire up the five-horse and we'd move off to another spot, a better spot to be sure. On days like this, my father would sing to the fish, off-key and a bit yodelly, enticing them to bite. On this particular day, the fish were tone deaf.

It was a slow enough day that Dad and Bev had time to teach me a few things—the right way to put a live minnow on a hook, through the nose, they said, so it would keep flipping and stay alive longer. They showed me how to properly tie a hook to the end of the line and how to squeeze a sinker onto the line in just the right spot. And they tried to teach me what a bite from a walleye (pickerel, as they called them then), would feel like, but the fish would not cooperate.

As the day progressed, and the sun warmed the air, the soup in the bottom of the boat began to come alive, to show its true power. At first the smell was faint, still masked by the sharp odour of gasoline fumes from the old outboard. But as it collected the heat of the early summer, that bilge began to fester and reek. I could escape, just, by arching my back as far as it could go, raising my nose to the heavens, and breathing in the air that the breeze was blowing over the high sides of the boat. Soon, even that respite was gone. I stood, and was promptly ordered down by adults who knew that it was not safe to stand up in a boat, even in a relatively calm sea.

Around midday, lunch was served, from black and battered tin lunch boxes—salmon sandwiches, with lots of mayonnaise. I didn't eat much. The men, preoccupied with the listless fish, didn't notice. They did notice that the wind was picking up, and that the waters around them were no longer calm, as they had been when we left. The wind was westerly, a rising wind on Lake Nipissing, and one sure to bring whitecaps before the day was over. Before long, the boat, which was anchored and swinging with the stiffening wind, was lurching from side to side, its motion not quite predictable. Its effect on my stomach was more so.

As the wind rose, Ed and Bev began to be concerned about our safety, the boat began to heave, and before long, so did I, right over the side. It was an embarrassing, inauspicious way to end one's first fishing adventure, but between my heaves and those of the boat, we were soon on our way back to the dock.

I caught no fish that day. Neither did the men. My seasickness refused to go away, lingering for another twenty-four hours. For a time, I could look at nothing that moved without feeling a little unsure of myself, a little queasy, a bit unbalanced. But it passed.

My mother, who pretty much refused to go out in such fishing boats because they "didn't smell quite right," was of the opinion that my father had made a mistake in making me sit down there, in the bottom of the boat, with the rotting minnows and the spilled coffee and the gasoline fumes, mixed with the bilge-water under those wooden floorboards. She was equally convinced that the experience would sour me forever on fishing, that I'd never want to venture out in boats again, and that I'd probably end up taking up some other hobby—like quilting—rather than bait another hook.

About the first point, she was dead right. About the second, her usually infallible judgment failed her. I couldn't wait to get out again. Dad was, understandably, a bit more reluctant, but that too, passed.

In the fifty years since, I have never once been seasick. I've fished on the Pacific in two-metre rolling swells off the north coast of the Queen Charlottes, waiting for a coho or sockeye to chomp on the cut bait riding the tidal current below. I've sat on Saskatchewan's Last Mountain Lake and been battered by two-metre-high whitecaps in a strong northwesterly prairie breeze. I've watched more than a few anglers around me turn green in such conditions, without a single queasy moment of my own. If I should ever find myself sitting, once again, in the bottom of a wooden boat, with latticed floorboards over bilge like thick gray paint and a smell I cannot describe, I make no promises.

After an uncertain beginning, I fished uncounted numbers of days with my father, my brother, and friends. I skipped a few years during my university days, but came back to it when my own family was young. I taught my daughters to bait hooks with nightcrawlers and leeches and watched them catch walleye on some of Saskatchewan's best waters, yet the fishing bug did not bite them.

During the last few years of his life, Dad could only get out fishing if I or my brother happened to be around to take him out. It was not often enough. And after he was gone, whenever I was in the neighbourhood, I would stop in and try to catch a few walleye with my brother, a feed for the family.

I am convinced that the fishing gene runs in families, like red hair, or crooked bottom teeth. Perhaps, like these things sometimes do, it skips a generation. And so, when grandchildren reach an age where holding a fishing rod in hand should be second nature, I'll take them out in a boat, too. I'll show them how to bait a hook, how to tell when a walleye is biting. I'll sing the fish in if it's a slow day. But I promise, I will not make them sit in the bottom of the boat.

APPENDIX A
TRAVEL CONTACTS

TOURISM SASKATCHEWAN

Phone:	1-877-237-2273 (ask for operator 21AN)
On the web:	www.sasktourism.com
e-mail	travel.info@sasktourism.com

Tourism Saskatchewan operates seasonal information booths on the Trans-Canada (Highway 1) at the Manitoba border east of Fleming and at the Alberta border west of Maple Creek. On the Yellowhead (Highway 16), information booths are found near the Manitoba border at Langenburg, and at the Alberta border at Lloydminster. Visitors driving north from the United States will find an information booth at North Portal on Highway 39.

As well, Tourism Saskatchewan has year-round information offices in each of Saskatchewan's thirteen cities. Amongst the materials available from Tourism Saskatchewan are an annual *Vacation Guide; Accommodation, Resort and Campground Guide; Fishing and Hunting Guide; Golf Tour Guide; Events Guide*, and official road maps of the province.

SASKATCHEWAN ENVIRONMENT DEPARTMENT

Phone:	53 offices—see the annual *Anglers' Guide*
Phone:	Turn In Poachers (TIP) Line: 1-800-667-7561
On the web:	www.serm.gov.sk.ca

This provincial government department is responsible for management of wildlife and fisheries resources in Saskatchewan, as well as provincial parks, provincial historic sites, and environmental protection. They publish an annual *Anglers' Guide*, and an annual *Hunting and Trapping Guide*. Both publications contain up-to-date information on limits, closures, regulations affecting specific areas, and other useful information. The department employs a sport-fishing specialist, based in Regina, who can be contacted at 1-306-787-2877.

SASKATCHEWAN OUTFITTERS

The Saskatchewan Outfitters Association represents a significant number of outfitters and camp operators in Saskatchewan. Many are listed in Tourism Saskatchewan's annual *Fishing and Hunting Guide*, but for the latest information, the Association can be contacted directly at:

Saskatchewan Outfitters Association	Phone:	1-306-763-5434
3700-2nd Avenue West	Fax:	1-306-922-6044
Prince Albert, Saskatchewan, S6W 1A2	e-mail:	soa@sk.sympatico.ca

Saskatchewan Environment maintains a database of currently licenced outfitters in the province, whether they are members of the Outfitters Association or not. For further information on licenced outfitters, please contact Saskatchewan Environment in Regina (306-787-2080) or in Prince Albert (306-953-2322).

INFORMATION SERVICES CORPORATION

A great source for maps and aerial photographs of the province.

260 - 10 Research Drive, Regina, Saskatchewan, S4S 7J7

Phone:	1-306-787-2799

APPENDIX B
CLUBS, ASSOCIATIONS, TOURNAMENTS

There are a number of outdoor associations and clubs, as well as conservation organizations and tournament fishing organizations in Saskatchewan of interest to resident and visiting anglers alike.

SASKATCHEWAN WILDLIFE FEDERATION

The SWF is a non-profit, charitable organization. A membership organization of anglers and hunters, the largest of its kind in Saskatchewan, with more than 25,000 members and chapters throughout the province, the Federation is involved in: member support activities such as skills training; lobbying on behalf of anglers and hunters with the provincial government; and raising funds for conservation purposes, particularly the preservation of habitat.

Saskatchewan Wildlife Federation
444 River Street
Moose Jaw, Saskatchewan, S6H 6J6

Phone: 1-306-692-8812
Fax: 1-306-692-4370
On the web: www.swf.sk.ca
eimail: info@swf.sk.ca

FLATLAND FLY FISHERS

The Flatlanders are a non-profit fly-fishing association, established in 1985 and based in Regina. Their activities include: the promotion of fly-fishing as a recreational sporting activity; member support through education, skills training and fishing excursions; conservation activities; and lobbying on behalf of their members to influence government policy regarding fishery management and habitat conservation in Saskatchewan. The Flatland Fly Fishers are affiliated with the Saskatchewan Fly Fishers Assocation and with the Federation of Fly Fishers.

Flatland Fly Fishers
Box 732
Regina, Saskatchewan S4P 3A8

On the web: www.flatlandflyfishers.com
e-mail: flyfisher@flatlandflyfishers.com

KILPATRICK FLYFISHERS

The Kilpatrick Flyfishers, a volunteer-based fly-fishing club located in Saskatoon, was established in 1985 for the purpose of practicing and promoting the sport of fly-fishing, and to further fish conservation, propogation, and research.

Kilpatrick Flyfishers
Box 9132
Saskatoon, Saskatchewan, S7K 7E8
On the web: www.kilpatrickflyfishers.com

NORTHERN WATERS FLYFISHERS

Northern Waters Flyfishers is a volunteer organization based in Prince Albert. The club's objectives are to promote the sport of fly-fishing and to promote the conservation of the fishery.

Northern Waters Flyfishers
c/o 3344 Dent Crescent
Prince Albert, Sasakatchewan, S6V 7H1

On the web: www.nwf.ca
e-mail: glendig@sk.sympatico.ca

SASKATCHEWAN FLYFISHERS

Saskatchewan Flyfishers is an umbrella organization representing the interests of the three fly-fishing clubs in the province.

Saskatchewan Flyfishers
214 3rd Street East
Saskatoon, Saskatchewan, S7H 1C3

FISHING FOR TOMORROW FOUNDATION

Fishing for Tomorrow is a volunteer organization of anglers based in Saskatoon who are working for conservation of the fishery and fish habitat. Their activities include: consulting with and lobbying government on behalf of the recreational fishery; fundraising activities; educational activities; and a fish rescue operation, recovering fish trapped in a major irrigation channel by lowering water levels each fall.

Fishing for Tomorrow Foundation
c/o Michael J. Costello
1116 9th Street East
Saskatoon, Saskatchewan, S7H 0N5
Phone: 1-306-343-8707

SASKATCHEWAN WALLEYE TRAIL

The Saskatchewan Walleye Trail organizes a series of five walleye tournaments held at locations across southern Saskatchewan. The events take place at Elbow Harbour on Lake Diefenbaker in May; on Last Mountain Lake at Regina Beach in June; at Saskatchewan Landing Provincial Park on Lake Diefenbaker in July; on the Qu'Appelle Lakes at Fort Qu'Appelle on the Labour Day weekend at the beginning of September; and at Rowan's Ravine Provincial Park on Last Mountain Lake in September. In addition to organizing tournaments, the Walleye Trail promotes tournament fishing and supports conservation activities related to the fishery.

Saskatchewan Walleye Trail
Box 20066
Regina, Saskatchewan, S4P 4J2
Phone: 1-306-924-2339
On the web: www.walleyenow.com

APPENDIX C
NORTHERN FLY-IN FISHING GEAR

Flying in to a remote northern location to fish is one of the great treats this world has to offer the avid angler. The fishing is usually great, the landscape inspiring, the hospitality excellent. The shopping is none of these things. While many remote camps will have a few items on hand for the forgetful angler, and most will have fishing licences to sell, none are equipped with full-service tackle shops and general stores.

The following list is offered as a useful start to your personal planning—use it as a checklist or the start to your own list when preparing for a northern trip.

PERSONAL ITEMS

* fishing license
* one complete outfit to wear fishing
* one complete change of clothing to wear fishing

> NOTE: long sleeved shirts and long pants are recommended. Cotton is okay for hot summer days, but nylon or other synthetics are better—cooler in the hot sun, more likely to offer a UV filter against sunburn, and much quicker drying

* one outfit of clothing to wear in the evening
* one warm sweater or fleece
* one windproof jacket or light parka
* one waterproof/windproof rainsuit
* one pair runners or hiking boots
* several pairs of socks
* your favourite hat
* toiletries and shaving kit
* personal medications
* sunglasses and spares
* prescription glasses and spares, if you have them
* sunscreen, bug repellant
* first aid kit to suit your needs
* check to see what the outfitter offers in the way of bedding—you may have to bring your own, or it may be provided. Outpost camps usually mean that you're bringing along at least your own sleeping bag. Check with your outfitter.

FOOD ITEMS

Some lodges offer American Plan packages, where all food is provided for you except for your personal choices of cold beverages. However, other lodges may offer housekeeping cabin facilities, in which case you will likely be responsible for your own breakfasts and lunches, your guide will prepare shore lunch, and all snacks and beverages will be your responsibility. Check with your outfitter and get the details. Some remote lodges are on rivers or lakes where the water can be safely consumed without any treatment. Others are not. Again, check before you go. In the case of outpost camps, you will likely be responsible for all your food needs, including staples like sugar, coffee, tea, etc. Once again, be sure to check with your outfitter, and get detailed information.

The following list assumes an American Plan situation, where you are not responsible for meals, but will want to bring along other snack and personal choice items.

* snacks for use in the boat while fishing (chocolate bars, gorp, etc.)

* soft drinks, bottled water (if necessary), other refreshments of your choice

* if you have special dietary needs, you may have to bring such items yourself

TACKLE

The following list is based on the species most commonly fished for in northern Saskatchewan: walleye, pike, grayling, and lake trout.

* a medium-light spinning rod, 6- to 7-foot, spinning reel to match, 6- to 10-pound-test monofilament or FireLine—for walleye and spinfishing for grayling

* a medium-heavy spinning rod, 6- to 7-foot, spinning reel to match, 12- to 17-pound-test monofilament or FireLine—for spinfishing for pike or lake trout

* a medium-heavy casting rod, 6- to 7-foot, baitcasting reel to match, 12- to 17-pound-test monofilament or FireLine—for trolling for larger pike and lake trout

> NOTE: the choice of pound test fishing line is always a personal matter. Some anglers won't fish for big pike and lake trout with anything less than 20-pound-test line. In some waters, where fish in the 30- or 40-pound range are possible on any fishing day, heavier line is a must. Some anglers are prepared to take the extra time to fight a fish, and risk losing it, to get the fun of fishing with light tackle. Others are not. Check with your outfitter for recommendations, and make the choice that suits you best.

* jigs, from ¼ ounce up to ½ ounce for walleye, from ⅛ ounce up to ¼ ounce for grayling, from ½ ounce to 1 ounce or greater for lake trout. Several colours, several sizes, several styles. Don't bring just one of any colour or size, since jigs are notorious for snagging up on rocks, and you're going to lose some of them.

* plastic tails for jigs, sized from 1 inch for grayling, to 3 or even 4 inches for large trout or pike. Varying colours, including white, black, silver or clear, yellow, orange, and bi-colours. Scented plastics, such as Berkley's Power Bait, are ideal.

* casting and trolling spoons and spinners, ranging from the smallest available (1 inch or shorter) for grayling, to 3 inches or longer for pike and lake trout

* crankbaits—floating, sinking, suspending—in several sizes from small to medium for walleye, to 7 inches or larger for lake trout and northern pike. Colours ranging from black-and-white, to perch-coloured, to silvered, to photorealistic finishes. Once again, don't bring just one of any particular lure that you like—if it turns out to be the hot one, and you lose it, you won't be able to replace it. Check with your outfitter for lure recommendations on specific waters.

* spare hooks, swivels, snaps, leaders, sinkers

* spare spools of line to replace what you bring on your fishing reel, or spare spools already loaded with line if you have them

* pliers or haemostats for removing hooks from fish

* fishing gloves for handling and releasing large fish

* landing net, unless provided by your outfitter

* portable sonar/depth finder
* portable GPS, especially if you are going without a guide
* basic repair tools for your fishing reels (the right screwdrivers really help)
* emergency rod tip replacement kit
* pocket knife and filleting knife, sharpener, and hook sharpener or hook file
* check to see if your outfitter has a supply of frozen/salted minnows. If not, bring lots with you.
* a cooler, if you plan to bring home some fish
* no-scent soap for cleaning your hands, particularly if you smoke, are running or fueling the outboard, handle pike with your bare hands, or are doing the cooking
* scent attractants for application to lures and baits (mostly they help to camouflage your scent, which may spook fish)
* specialty tackle for fishing for deep lake trout (heavy in-line sinkers, steel line, Pink Lady divers, etc.)

PRACTICAL GEAR AND SURVIVAL GEAR

* binoculars, camera, film, spare batteries
* map of the area you're fishing (1:50,000 scale topographic) and a good compass
* waterproof matches, fire-starting materials
* a good, sturdy belt-knife
* a signaling mirror (also useful for shaving in outpost camps)
* flashlight and spare batteries

NOTE: This list is a guide only. Depending on the services provided by the outfitter and whether you are in a base camp situation or in an outpost camp, you may need more or less equipment to make yourself and your fishing companions safe and comfortable. Always check with the outfitter before you leave home, so that you are equipped appropriately for the trip you're taking.

APPENDIX D
GEAR LISTS

There is no end to the gear anglers can purchase in support of their favourite recreational activity. The options available in type, size, colour, weight, and style are almost endless. But there are basic tools of the trade that work for each species. The following species by species list is not exhaustive. No two anglers will take the same gear on the same day, and even the best of fishing buddies can spend an entire day on the water debating the merits of one piece of gear over another. These lists won't please everyone, and they're not intended to be "compleat"—just a good start. For trout species, under most conditions, fishing with a fly rod is both more fun and more productive. Fly-fishing is not covered in this appendix—for notes on fly-fishing gear, see Chapter 5.

BROOK TROUT, PERCH, GRAYLING
* light or ultralight spinning rod, 5- to 5½-foot, reel to match, 4- to 6-pound-test monofilament
* small spoons or spinners, the smallest size available, in a variety of colours and metallic finishes
* small jigs, ⅛ or 1/16 ounce, various colours
* small plastic grubs or twister tails, 1 inch, variety of colours
* casting bubble and flies
* live bait (where permitted)—night crawlers or leeches, live mealworms, grasshoppers
* slip bobbers and bobber stops
* split-shot sinkers
* small No. 4, No. 6, No. 8 hooks
* small needle-nose pliers or haemostats for removing hooks
* small landing net

BROWN TROUT
The brown trout is a hard fish to catch with anything but a fly rod, especially in Saskatchewan, where they are found primarily in smaller creek and stream waters, not in larger open lakes. However, browns are sometimes taken with spinning tackle.
* medium-light spinning rod, 6- to 7-foot, reel to match, 6- to 10-pound-test monofilament
* small spinners or spoons
* live bait (where permitted)—night crawlers and leeches are best
* split-shot sinkers
* small No. 4, No. 6, No. 8 hooks
* small needle-nose pliers or haemostats for removing hooks
* small landing net

BURBOT

Burbot are most commonly caught through the ice with standard ice-fishing gear (jigs or swimming jigs tipped with mealworms or minnows), but can also be taken during the open-water season. Since they prey on the same forage base as walleye, pike, or perch, many of the same lures and baits are effective, fished near or on bottom.

* medium-light to medium spinning rod, 6- to 7-foot, spinning reel to match, 6- to 12-pound-test monofilament or FireLine
* live-bait rigs, tipped with leeches, worms, or frozen minnows
* jigs, 1/8 ounce to 3/8 ounce
* small spoons (DarDevle, Len Thompson, Williams, etc.)
* needle-nose pliers or haemostats for hook removal
* medium to large landing net

CARP

* medium to medium-heavy spinning rod, 10- to 13-foot, bait-runner spinning reel to match (e.g. Mitchell Full Runner Electronic), 12- to 17-pound-test monofilament line or FireLine
* forked rod holders, with strike alarm
* pre-tied whisker or boilie rigs, and components for tying new ones in the field
* sweet, softened field corn, large quantities for chumming
* chumming slingshot
* needle-nose pliers or haemostat for hook removal
* large, long-handled landing net

RAINBOW TROUT

* light or medium-light spinning rod, 6- to 7-foot, reel to match, 4- to 8-pound-test monofilament
* small spoons or spinners, bright and metallic colours are best
* small crankbaits—sinking, floating, suspending
* casting bubbles and flies
* live bait (where permitted)—nightcrawlers or leeches, live mealworms, grasshoppers
* slip bobbers and bobber stops
* split-shot sinkers
* No. 4, No. 6, No. 8 hooks
* small needle-nose pliers or haemostats for removing hooks
* small to medium-sized landing net

LAKE TROUT

* medium to medium-heavy spinning rod, 6- to 7-foot, reel to match, 10- to 17-pound-test monofilament or FireLine for deep jigging or light trolling
* medium to medium-heavy casting rod, 6- to 7-foot, reel to match, 12- to 20-pound-test monofilament or FireLine for heavier trolling, deep water trolling with weight
* medium to large spoons (DarDevle, Len Thompson, Williams) and spinners (Mepps)—bright colours and metallic finishes
* medium to large crankbaits—colours to imitate local forage base
* heavy jigs—1/2 ounce to 1 1/2 ounce, various colours

* large plastic worms and grubs—3 inch or larger
* needle-nose pliers or haemostats for removing hooks
* medium to large landing net

WALLEYE

* medium-light to medium-heavy spinning rods, 6- to 7-foot, shorter for jigging, longer for live-bait rigging, reels to match, 6- to 12-pound-test monofilament or FireLine
* medium-light to medium-heavy casting rods, 6- to 7-foot, for trolling crankbaits and bottom bouncers, 12- to 15-pound-test monofilament or FireLine
* jigs, various styles, weights from ⅛ to ⅝ ounce, various colours, stinger hooks
* casting and swimming jigs, various weights, colours, and styles
* plastic grubs and twister tails, 2-inch, 3-inch, various colours and styles
* medium-sized crankbaits—sinking, floating, suspending, in colours to match local forage
* live bait where permitted—night crawlers, leeches, frozen or preserved minnows
* live-bait snells—various lengths, double and single hooks, hooks sized from No. 2 to No. 8
* spinnerbait snells, various lengths, double and single hooks, hooks sized from No. 2 to No. 6
* bottom bouncers—weights from ¼ ounce to 2 ounces
* slip sinkers, weights from ¼ ounce to 1½ ounces
* slip bobbers of various sizes and shapes and bobbers stops
* split-shot sinkers
* live-bait hooks, No. 2 to No. 8
* needle-nose pliers or haemostats for hook removal

LARGEMOUTH BASS

* medium to medium-heavy spinning rod, 6- to 7-foot, reel to match, 8- to 12-pound-test monofilament or FireLine
* medium to medium-heavy casting rod, 6- to 7-foot, reel to match, 12- to 17-pound-test monofilament or FireLine
* jigs, ¼ ounce to ¾ ounce, various colours and styles, including weedless
* spinnerbaits, buzzbaits, large in-line spinners
* medium-sized crankbaits—floating, suspending, sinking
* jerkbaits
* plastic worms, frogs, lizards, grubs, and other bait imitations
* live bait—nightcrawlers are particularly good
* egg sinkers
* long-shanked hooks—No. 2 to 2/0
* needle-nose pliers or haemostats for removing hooks
* medium-sized landing net

NORTHERN PIKE

* medium to medium-heavy spinning rod, 6- to 7-foot, reel to match, 10- to 17-pound-test monofilament or FireLine
* medium to medium-heavy casting rod, 6- to 7-foot, reel to match, 12- to 17-pound-test monofilament or FireLine

* medium to large spoons (DarDevle, Len Thompson), in-line spinners (Mepps) in bright colours and metallic finishes
* medium to large crankbaits—floating, suspending—in colours to match local forage
* large preserved or frozen minnows
* jigs—½ to ¾ ounce
* large plastic grubs, twister tails
* long-shanked bait hooks, No. 2 to 2/0
* large slip bobbers and bobber stops
* needle-nose pliers or haemostats for hook removal
* large landing net

GENERAL AND PERSONAL EQUIPMENT
* cotton or specialized gloves for handling fish for release
* line clippers, small scissors, or pocket knife
* spare fishing line
* rod tip repair kit
* snaps, swivels, steel leaders
* beads, blades, floating and spinning beads and clevises for making live-bait rigs
* no-scent soap and small towel for cleaning hands
* scent attractants for application to lures and bait
* sunscreen, hat
* good polarized sunglasses
* bug repellant

APPENDIX E
TACKLE SHOPS AND OTHER SOURCES

Privately owned tackle shops are often your best source of information, both general and specific, about fishing conditions, hot locations, and the best choice of tackle and lures for the region in which the shop is located. Local boat dealers carry the supplies boating anglers need, offer repair services, and may also carry fishing tackle and licenses.

In smaller communities, fishing tackle can often be found at the local gas station, at the local Co-op, at the hardware store, convenience store, or general store. Fishing tackle departments are found at most Canadian Tire Stores and Walmart Stores throughout Saskatchewan.

— BEAUVAL —

BEAUVAL MARINE AND SMALL ENGINE REPAIR
Beauval Forks
Beauval, Saskatchewan
Phone: 1-306-288-4433

— FORT QU'APPELLE —

KEVIN'S MARINE
Highway 35
Fort Qu'Appelle, Saskatchewan
Phone: 1-306-332-5888

MARINE SERVICES LTD.
Fort Qu'Appelle, Saskatchewan
Phone: 1-306-332-5747

— LA RONGE —

AIR RONGE CO-OP GAS BAR AND CONVENIENCE STORE
Air Ronge, La Ronge, Saskatchewan
Phone:1-306-425-1252

DRIFTS AND WAVES LEISURE INC.
Air Ronge, La Ronge, Saskatchewan
Phone: 1-306-425-5500

GENE'S SPORTS CENTER
719 La Ronge Avenue
La Ronge, Saskatchewan, S0J 1L0
Phone: 1-306-425-3040

—LLOYDMINSTER —

BORDER CITY RV CENTER LTD.
Lloydminster, Alberta
Phone: 1-306-875-0345

— MOOSE JAW —

DJ'S RV CENTER
Highway 1 East
Moose Jaw, Saskatchewan
Phone: 1-306-694-6048

ROD AND GUN SPORTING GOODS
305 Fairford St. West
Moose Jaw, Saskatchewan, S6H 1V8
Phone: 1-306-694-4200

— NORTH BATTLEFORD —

GRONDIN RV LTD.
Highway 4 North
North Battleford, Saskatchewan
Phone: 1-306-446-8325

SILVESTER RV CENTER
2701 99th St.
North Battleford, Saskatchewan
Phone: 1-306-445-2079

—PREECEVILLE—

MATT'S OUTDOOR SUPPLIES LTD.
28 1st Avenue N.E.
Preeceville, Saskatchewan
Phone: 1-306-547-3128

— PRINCE ALBERT —

JACK PINE MARINE
Highway 2 South
Prince Albert, Saskatchewan
Phone: 1-306-764-3646

MADRAGA SPEED 'N SPORT
4189 2nd Avenue West
Prince Albert, Saskatchewan
Phone: 1-306-764-4044

— REGINA —

ALSPORT SALES LTD.
1900 1st Avenue
Regina, Saskatchewan
Phone: 1-306-525-0189

CMS HOOK 'N' HUNT
909 8th Avenue
Regina, Saskatchewan, S4N 6S3
Phone: 1-306-352-2500

GREAT NORTHERN ROD AND REEL
1755 Park Street
Regina, Saskatchewan, S4N 2G3
Phone: 1-306-359-7378

JAGWIRE SALES AND SERVICE
1001B Osler St.
Regina, Saskatchewan
Phone: 1-306-757-3909

PERFORMANCE MARINE AND LEISURE CENTRE
3310 Pasqua Street
Regina, Saskatchewan
Phone: 1-306-586-2628

POKEY'S TACKLE SHOP
1001 Osler Street
Regina, Saskatchewan, S4R 8N5
Phone: 1-306-359-1910

PRECISION PROPELLOR REPAIR
526 10th Ave.
Regina, Saskatchewan
Phone: 1-306-585-2628

REGINA MARINE
Highway 1 East
Regina, Saskatchewan
Phone: 1-306-775-1006

— SASKATOON —

BORDER CITY RV/BAYLINER BOATS
4120 Thatcher Ave.
Saskatoon, Saskatchewan, S7R 1A2
Phone: 1-306-955-7283

BOOMTOWN OUTFITTERS
210 20th St. West
Saskatoon, Saskatchewan, S7M 0W9
Phone: 1-306-242-0882

EB'S SAIL AND SPORTS
1640 Saskatchewan Ave.
Saskatoon, Saskatchewan, S7K 1P6
Phone: 1-306-652-0385

EVANOL RECREATIONAL PRODUCTS
2334 Hanselman Avenue
Saskatoon, Saskatchewan, S7L 5Z3
Phone: 1-306-664-3984

NORTHERN FLY FISHERMAN
1 Stephenson Crescent
Saskatoon, Saskatchewan, S7H 3L6
Phone: 1-306-665-0076

SASKATOON CO-OPERATIVE ASSOCIATION LTD.
Ave. C and Circle Drive West
Saskatoon, Saskatchewan
Phone: 1-306-933-3830

THE FISHIN' HOLE
805 Circle Drive East
Saskatoon, Saskatchewan, S7K 3S4
Phone: 1-306-665-7223

WHOLESALE SPORTS OUTDOOR OUTFITTERS
2731 Faithfull Avenue
Saskatoon, Saskatchewan, S7K 7C3
Phone: 1-306-931-4475

— SWIFT CURRENT —

BENDER'S GUNS AND ARCHERY
414 North Railway St. East
Swift Current, Saskatchewan
Phone: 1-306-773-8683

ELMWOOD GROCERY
936 Chaplin St. East
Swift Current, Saskatchewan, S9H 1J7
Phone: 1-306-773-6225

— YORKTON —

BUCKHORN SPORTS
129 Myrtle Ave.
Yorkton, Saskatchewan, S3N 1P9
Phone: 1-306-782-3629

APPENDIX F
FURTHER READING AND REFERENCES

BOOKS AND OTHER PUBLICATIONS

(except fly-fishing—see below)

Beard, Henry, and Roy McKie. *Fishing: An Angler's Dictionary*. Workman Publishing, 1983.

Brooks, Joe. *Complete Guide to Fishing Across North America*. Outdoor Life, Harper and Row, 1970.

Carpenter, David. *Fishing in Western Canada, A Freshwater Guide*. revised and updated. Greystone Books, 2000.

Clancy, Michael, and Anna Clancy. *Discover Saskatchewan: A User's Guide to Regional Parks*. Canadian Plains Research Center, 1999.

Critical Concepts: Walleye Fundamentals. In-Fisherman, 1998.

Critical Concepts: Walleye Location. In-Fisherman, 1999.

Critical Concepts: Walleye Presentation Perspectives—Classic Systems. In-Fisherman, 1999.

Critical Concepts: Walleye Presentation Perspectives—Beyond Basic Systems. In-Fisherman, 2000.

Gooding, Frederick W. *Lake, River and Sea-Run Fishes of Canada*. Harbour Publishing, 1997.

Gruenwald, Tom. *Hooked on Ice Fishing*. Krause Publications, 1999.

Gulig, Anthony G., "Sizing Up the Catch." *Saskatchewan History*. Vol. 47, No. 2, Fall 1995: 3–10.

Howarth, A. Jan. *The Canadian Fish Cookbook*. Douglas and McIntyre, 1983.

Kavajecz, Keith. *Walleye River Strategies*. In-Fisherman Inc., 1990.

Lindner, Al, Fred Buller, Doug Stange, Dave Csanda, Ron Lindner, Bob Ripley, and Jan Eggers. *Pike, An In-Fisherman Handbook of Strategies*. Al Lindner Outdoors Inc., 1983.

Lindner, Al, Dave Csanda, Tony Dean, Ron Lindner, Bob Ripley and Doug Stange. *Walleye Wisdom, an In-Fisherman Handbook of Strategies*. Al Lindner Outdoors Inc., 1983.

Macpherson, Andrew. *The Canadian Ice Angler's Guide*. Lone Pine Publishing, 1985.

Maher, Tom. "The Saskatchewan Commercial Fishery." Unpublished paper presented to the Standing Committee on Fisheries and Oceans, November, 1992.

Marchildon, Greg, and Sid Robinson. *Canoeing the Churchill: A Practical Guide to the Historic Voyageur Highway*. Canadian Plains Research Center, 2002.

Marshall, T. Lawrence, and Ronald P. Johnson. "History and Results of Fish Introductions in Saskatchewan, 1900–1969." Unpublished paper prepared for Fisheries and Wildlife Branch, Saskatchewan, 1971.

McLane, A.J. *McLane's New Standard Fishing Encyclopaedia and International Angling Guide*. Holt, Rinehart and Winston, 1974.

Murray, Bobby, Al Lindner, Chet Meyers, Ron Lindner, and Billy Murray. *Bass, An In-Fisherman Handbook of Strategies*. Al Lindner Outdoors Inc., 1984.

Roach, Gary, Randy Amenrud and Bob Jensen. *Pro-Mo's Secrets to Finding and Catching Walleyes*. Pro-Mo's Secrets, 1989.

Roach, Gary, Randy Amenrud, and Bob Jensen. *Pro-Mo's Secrets to Jigging for Walleyes*, 1989.

Roach, Gary, Randy Amenrud, and Bob Jensen. *Pro-Mo's Secrets to Live Bait Fishing for Walleyes*, 1990.

Scott, W.B., and E.J. Crossman. *Freshwater Fishes of Canada*. Canadian Government Publishing Centre, 1990.

Schultz, Ken. *Ken Schultz's Fishing Encyclopedia, Worldwide Angling Guide*. IDG Books Worldwide, 2000.

Schwanky, T.J. *Walleye Across the West.* T.J. Schwanky, Box 1330, Cochrane, AB, Canada, T0L 0W0, 1955.

The Hunting and Fishing Library. Multiple volumes. Cy DeCosse Inc., 1987.

Wooding, Frederick H. *The Book of Canadian Fishes.* McGraw-Hill Ryerson Limited, 1959.

FLY-FISHING

Cordes, Ron, and Randall Kaufmann. *Lake Fishing with a Fly.* Frank Amato Publications, 1984.

Fling, Paul N., and Donald L. Puterbaugh. *Expert Fly Tying.* Sterling Publishing Co., 1986.

———*Fly Tying.* Forum House Publishing, 1982.

Hackle, Sparse Grey. *Fishless Days, Angling Nights.* Simon and Schuster, 1971.

Hafele, Rick, and Dave Hughes. *The Complete Book of Western Hatches.* Frank Amato Publications, 1982.

Haig-Brown, Roderick. *A Fisherman's Spring.* Totem Books, 1975.

———*A Fisherman's Summer.* Totem Books, 1975.

———*A Primer of Fly Fishing.* Douglas and McIntyre, 1964.

———*A River Never Sleeps.* Totem Books, 1981.

———*Return to the River.* Douglas and McIntyre, 1997.

———*The Western Angler.* Totem Books, 1981.

Hellekson, Terry. *Popular Fly Patterns.* Peregrine Smith Books, 1984.

Kreh, Lefty. *Advanced Fly Fishing Techniques.* Dell Publishing, 1992.

Kaufman, Randall. *American Nymph Fly Tying Manual.* Frank Amato Publications, 1986.

Leonard, J. Edson. *The Essential Fly Tier.* Prentice-Hall Inc., 1976.

McNally, Tom. *Fly Fishing.* Outdoor Life Books, Harper and Row, 1978.

Oko, Andrew. *Country Pleasures: The Angling Art of Jack Cowin.* Fifth House, 1984.

Reynolds, Barry, Brad Befus and John Berryman. *Carp on the Fly, A Flyfishing Guide.* Johnson Books, Spring Creek Press, 1997.

Schwiebert, Ernie. *Matching the Hatch.* Stoeger Publishing Company, 1981.

———*Trout Strategies.* E.P. Dutton Inc., 1978.

———*Trout Tackle One and Trout Tackle Two.* E.P. Dutton Inc., 1984.

Shaw, Jack. *Fly Fish the Trout Lakes.* Mitchell Press Ltd., 1980.

Stewart, Dick. *Universal Fly Tying Guide.* Greene Press, 1979.

MAGAZINES

The following magazines are readily available at news-stands and fishing tackle shops. This is by no means a complete list, nor is it an endorsement of any particular magazine, merely a starting point for those looking for current information on angling topics, presented by professional magazine writers. Both Canadian and American publications are listed.

Outdoor Canada

Western Sportsman/Canada's Outdoor Sportsman

In-Fisherman

Walleye Insider

Fly Fisherman

Sports Afield

Outdoor Life

THE WORLDWIDE WEB

There are literally thousands of websites dedicated to fishing. Go to your favourite browser and enter any fishing related word, from "fishing" or "fly-fishing," to specific species like "walleye" or "carp," and you'll find a wealth of sites to check out. Because many sites are unstable, here today and gone tomorrow, like a migrating school of big water walleye, websites are not listed in this book. They're easy enough to find.

As well, the quality of websites varies greatly from site to site. Information published by websites that are associated with recognized publications, magazines, government agencies, tourism agencies, or sporting organizations, generally provide accurate, useful, dependable information.

Search and enjoy.

CONSERVATION SUBJECTS

de Villiers, Marq. *Water.* Stoddart, 2000.

Leopold, Aldo. *A Sand County Almanac.* Oxford University Press, 1949.

Protecting Canada's Endangered Spaces: an Owner's Manual. Monte Hummel, General Editor. Key Porter Books, 1995.

Abbey, Edward. *Desert Solitaire, A Season in the Wilderness.* Simon and Schuster, 1968.

MAPS AND GUIDES

Where to Fish in Southern and Central Saskatchewan. Fishing for Tomorrow Foundation, 2000.

Trout Streams of the Cub Hills. Saskatchewan Environment and Resource Management, Fish and Wildlife Branch, 1999.

Trout Streams in Southwest Saskatchewan. Saskatchewan Environment and Resource Management.

Saskatchewan 2002 Fishing and Hunting Map, supplement to the *2002 Fishing and Hunting Guide,* Tourism Saskatchewan, 2002.

Saskatchewan Anglers' Guide, published annually, Saskatchewan Environment and Resource Management.

Saskatchewan Hunting and Fishing Guide, Tourism Saskatchewan, published annually.

Maps of the National Topographic System of Canada, Index 2 (covers Saskatchewan), Canada Map Office, 615 Booth Street, Ottawa, Ontario, Canada, K1A 0E9.

Saskatchewan Information Services Corporation (maps): 306-787-2799

Saskatchewan Accommodation, Resort and Campground Guide. Tourism Saskatchewan, published annually.

Saskatchewan Vacation Guide, Tourism Saskatchewan, published annually.

GLOSSARY OF TERMS

Experienced anglers will recognize most if not all of the terms used in this book. For those who are less familiar with the sometimes arcane language of recreational angling, the following glossary is offered.

American Plan: descriptive term for services offered by an outfitter. American plan usually means that meals, bedding, boat, motor, gas, and guide are included in the package price. Definitions vary. Check with your outfitter.

Backing (also backing line): a length of line, usually braided, that connects the near end of your fly line to your fly reel. Fly lines are generally short (around a hundred feet long) and backing is needed to make your fly line long enough to handle larger fish, or fighting fish in current.

Bait (live and artificial): usually something edible (or that appears to be edible) placed on a hook or lure as an enticement for fish to strike. In Saskatchewan, live night crawlers, live leeches (ribbon leeches caught within the province) and frozen minnows are common baits for most fish. (Live minnows, as well as leeches imported from outside Saskatchewan, are not legal for use in this province). In place of live bait, anglers commonly use plastic imitations, often scented, such as Berkley Power Bait. Plastic baits come in many shapes and sizes, from grubs to minnows to imitation worms and crayfish. Colours range widely.

Baitcasting (as in baitcasting reel, baitcaster, baitcasting rod): refers to a style of fishing reel, one in which the line spool is at ninety degrees to the direction of line travel, and the reel resembles a small, lightweight winch. Baitcasting reels ("baitcasters") allow for very accurate casting once the angler has learned to control the line spool with his thumb. This takes some practice. Baitcasting reels (also called level-wind reels) are designed to handle larger lure weights and heavier pound-test lines. They are ideal for trolling large spoons and crankbaits.

Bait hook: a hook used to hold bait. Some have barbs on the hook shank. Most have barbs at the point (though these may be flattened with a pair of needle-nose pliers for barbless fishing). Sizes and shapes range from small, short-shanked hooks used to hold leeches, to longer shanked models often used for threading on a minnow. Bait hooks for small trout or for finesse fishing for walleye, can be as small as No. 8 or No. 10. Hooks for larger pike, lake trout, or largemouth bass can be as large as 2/0.

Bait runner: term for a spinning reel, such as those made by Mitchell and Shimano, which allows the spool to run freely, with no friction from the drag mechanism. Drag is reset when the reel handle is turned. Particularly useful in bank fishing for carp.

Barbless hook: a fish hook made without barbs on the shank or point, or on which the barbs have been flattened.

Bell and bank sinkers: bell- and pyramid-shaped lead weights, with a wire eye embedded in the top or narrow end for attachment to a fishing line. Used where heavy weights are required.

Bird's-nest: the tangled mess of line that appears on baitcasting reels when the angler loses control of the cast and the spool overruns. You'll recognize it the moment it happens to you.

Blade (blade rig): a small, teardrop-shaped piece of thin, light metal, used as part of a live-bait trolling rig. Some blades are painted in various colours; others are polished silver-, gold-, brass- or copper-coloured.

Boilie: a bait for carp, a small ball, about two and a half centimetres (one inch) across, made of boiled dough, with scent and flavour, as well as colour, added.

Bobber: a small float designed to ride on the surface of the water, with fishing line attached to it. When a fish bites, the bobber is pulled beneath the surface, signaling a strike to the angler. Bobbers can be made from hard plastics, plastic foam, balsa wood and other materials, and they come in various shapes and sizes for various kinds of fishing applications. Bobbers can be attached to the fishing line in two ways: a *clip-on bobber* uses a small, spring-loaded clip to attach to the line in a fixed position; a *slip bobber* has a hole through its centre, and is threaded onto the line. The position of the bobber on the line is set using a bobber stop.

Bobber stop: a small latex rubber bead, or a pre-tied knot, designed to be slipped onto the main fishing line, and used in conjunction with a glass or plastic bead, to position a slip sinker on the line. Bobber stops are adjustable so that the amount of line that hangs from the bobber can be lengthened or shortened.

Bottom bouncer: a form of sinker—sometimes called an "Arkansas Bottom Bouncer" or just plain "bouncer"—such as Northland Fishing Tackles Rock Runner bottom bouncers and slip bouncers. A lead weight is formed in the middle of a thin piece of wire about a foot long. At the top of the wire, a loop, or a bend and loop are formed for attaching the bouncer to the main line. A live-bait rig, usually using blades, is attached to trail behind the bottom bouncer as the whole rig is trolled. Bottom bouncers are useful when the bottom is brushy or weedy, and likely to snag rigs. The bottom bouncer holds the bait rig up off the bottom.

Braided line: a soft, limp fishing line made from braided fibers. Older braided lines were made from Dacron. Newer super lines are made from synthetic fibres such as Micro Dyneema.

Buzzbait: a flashy, splashy, noisy, surface lure, an in-line spinnerbait with large, shiny wings or propellers that imitate an injured fish flopping across the surface. They are great lures for bass and pike.

Casting: the act of propelling line and lure using a fishing rod as a spring-loaded lever. In the case of spinning or casting reels, the line is pulled off the fishing reel by the weight of the lure used. In the case of fly casting, it is the weight of the line itself that is used to cast the lure, since tiny flies are essentially weightless.

Casting rod: a fishing rod designed for use with baitcasting reels.

Catch-and-release: conservation-oriented fishing, in which all or the vast majority of fish are released unharmed after being caught. Catch-and-release requires that fish be handled quickly and gently to avoid injury. Even catch-and-release anglers should limit their catch on any given day, since it is inevitable that some released fish will be injured and die.

Chumming: the practice of pre-baiting an area to attract fish. In carp fishing, for example, it is common to spread sweetened field corn over a small area of lake bottom to attract carp to the area for a few days before fishing.

Clevis: a tiny, horseshoe-shaped piece of metal used to thread blades onto fishing line.

Crankbaits: lures designed to look like minnows or small fish, often made from plastic, sometimes balsa wood, and painted in many colours. Some are finished with photorealistic images. Crankbaits are cast, then retrieved or "cranked" back to the boat or to shore. These baits are made in floating, sinking, and neutrally buoyant models, and range in size from an inch long to a foot or more in the case of large muskie and pike lures such as the handmade Suick.

Creel: a canvas, nylon, or wicker bag or basket used to carry fish, often lined with wet grass or moss to keep fish cool.

Dapping: a fly-fishing technique used when brush and trees are too close and thick for casting. An angler pulls a couple of metres of line off the reel, extends his or her arm and fishing rod as far as possible, and drops the fly on the surface. Dry flies may then be allowed to drift with the current, or the rod may be repeatedly lifted and lowered to "dap" the fly onto the surface of the water.

Downrigger: device attached to the side of a boat for fishing in deep water. Consists of a spool of wire and an arm that reaches over the side of the boat. A heavy weight called a downrigger ball is attached to the wire. Fishing line is clipped to the wire, and the weight lowered to the desired depth. When fish bite, the angler sets the hook, pulls the line free of the clip on the wire line, and retrieves the fish.

Drag: the braking system built into fishing reels such that, when a fish is caught and attempts to swim away, resistance is put on the line spool to help the angler "fight" the fish and keep control of its movements. Drag mechanisms are basically slip clutches that permit the line spool to spin slowly, allowing the fish to take line, but against a controlled resistance.

Drift sock: sometimes called a "boat brake," this is a conical sack, open at both ends like a funnel, tied to the side of a boat with rope, and thrown overboard. As water fills the funnel, it slows the drift of a boat on a windy day, permitting anglers to slow the presentation of bait to fish. Especially useful for walleye anglers fishing big, open lakes.

Dry fly: a fly-fishing lure designed to float on the surface, imitating insects that are found there during "hatches" (mayflies, chironomids, etc.) or that fall into the water and float (ants, hoppers, etc.). Flies are often treated with a "floatant" that keeps them from becoming waterlogged.

Finesse fishing: a term used to describe the presentation of bait to particularly nervous and uncooperative fish, especially walleye. Usually involves the use of the lightest line and sinker combination possible, small, light wire hooks tied on long snells (up to 3 metres or 10 feet in some cases), and live bait such as leeches or night crawlers.

Float tube (belly boat): an inner tube stuffed into a nylon doughnut or horseshoe-shaped tube, with a harness in the middle in which the angler sits, suspended at the surface of the water. It is most often used by fly fishers, and is an ideal substitute for canoes or boats on small water. The angler propels the belly boat by kicking with diver's swim fins and moving the whole apparatus backwards through the water. Awkward to get into and move about in on land, the belly boat is an elegant fishing platform on the water.

Fly hooks: hooks in sizes, shapes, and weights specifically designed for tying artificial flies. Some fly patterns, such as nymphs, call for long, slender-bodied imitations, using long-shanked hooks that are heavy enough to sink on their own. Dry flies require lighter-weight hooks. Tiny patterns such as midges require very small, light wire hooks with extra short shanks. Most fly-tying recipes will specify the type of hook needed for the pattern being tied.

Fly line: a coated fishing line, in floating, sinking, or sinking-tip configurations, made most commonly as weight-forward, double-taper or shooting tapers, used to transport the leader and fly to the fish. Fly anglers cast the weight of their fly lines, not their tiny lures. Lines are weighted (1-weight being ultralight for fishing for small fish in small waters with ultralight tackle, 12-weight being more suited to fishing tarpon in salt water).

Fly rod: a fishing rod designed to cast fly lines. Rods are marked to indicate the line weight for which they are best suited.

Fluorocarbon lines: fishing lines made from fluorocarbon synthetics. They are noted for being ultra-clear in the water.

Hatch: an event where large numbers of a single species of insect "hatch," or emerge, at the same time and place. It is a time when a fly fisher who can "match the hatch" can enjoy considerable fishing success.

Jerk bait: a type of crankbait (or plug), usually made of wood, that has no action of its own when retrieved with a steady retrieve. Jerk baits are retrieved with a sequence of sharp jerks of the rod tip, while the angler reels in line. They are fished on and just below the surface, and imitate a wounded or disabled fish—easy prey for a healthy bass or pike.

Jig: a weighted fish hook. Traditional jigs had a round ball of lead moulded onto the hook. Contemporary jigs come in all sizes, colours, and shapes. The weight takes the hook and bait (either live or artificial) to the bottom, where it can be jigged up and down to attract fish. Jigs can also be cast and retrieved, or dragged along the bottom from a slowly drifting boat. They can also be "ripped"—pulled rapidly from the bottom or through weeds.

Jigging: fishing with a jig.

Leader: a length of line, or wire, with one end tied to the end of the fishing line and the other attached to the lure. Fly-fishing leaders are usually monofilament and used because their light weight and transparency is less visible to easily spooked fish. The length and weight of a fly leader depends on the species fished for. Steel leaders are used at the end of monofilament or super lines when fishing for pike or lake trout, which have the ability to sever most synthetic lines.

Ledgering: a European technique for fishing from the shore, or bank, especially useful in carp fishing. See detailed description in Chapter 4.

Live-bait rigging: a technique for presenting live bait to fish, commonly used in walleye fishing. The live-bait rig is a length of monofilament, dressed with one or more hooks, optional coloured beads, coloured spinning blades, etc.

Livewell: an aerated tank built into many modern fishing boats. Acts as a holding tank to keep fish alive. Recirculating water pumps and air bubblers keep fish healthy for extended periods of time.

Lure: an artificial bait used to entice fish to strike. Spoons, spinners, crankbaits, stick-baits, jigs, and flies are all types of lure used to attract and catch fish. Lure designs are usually based on the principle of "matching the hatch"—the better the lure's shape, size, colour, and movement in the water mimics the available natural forage for a particular species of fish, the more likely it is to catch fish.

Monofilament line: the most commonly used fishing line, made from plastics, most often clear or translucent, sometimes coloured. Monofilament lines designed for casting and baitfishing applications (Berkley Trilene XL) are thin, soft, and flexible, but are easily abraded by rocks or other underwater obstacles. Abrasion-resistant lines that are tougher and used for larger fish or for trolling larger baits are generally stiffer and a bit more difficult to cast (Berkley Trilene XT).

Nymph: a tied fly which imitates the aquatic stage of an insect's life cycle. They are used by fly anglers to fish deep when no insects are on the surface of a pond or stream. Fly-fishing with a nymph is referred to as "nymphing."

Pickerel rig: a time-tested method for stillfishing for walleye (misnamed pickerel in many parts of Canada, including Saskatchewan). It consists of a length of stout monofilament with a swivel at the top for attaching to the main fishing line. Two light wire arms are fastened to the mono. Hooks with short snells are attached to the wire arms. At the bottom of the monofilament is a snap for attaching a bell or bank sinker. The two arms suspend bait at the bottom. These rigs are particularly useful for shore-bound anglers.

Pike rig: like a pickerel rig, but with heavier monofilament, heavier wire arms, and larger hooks.

Pink Lady: a weighted disc, clipped to the end of a fishing line, used to get lures and baits to deep water (25 metres, 80 feet, or more) to catch lake trout during the summer.

Plug: a minnow-imitating lure, usually floating, often made of wood, that is retrieved on or near the surface. Plugs are particularly useful for fishing for bass and pike.

Presentation: the manner in which bait or lures are put in front of the fish. Trolling, jigging, drifting, casting, and stillfishing are all presentation techniques. There are several elements to presentation for anglers to consider—the speed at which a bait is presented, the size and type of bait or lure presented, the colour of lure presented, the depth at which lure or bait is presented, and the "action" or type of movement imparted to a bait or lure (still, swimming, stop-and-go, erratic, etc.). The choice of presentation of a lure or bait is dependent on the species and fishing conditions.

Sinker: a small weight, commonly made of lead, attached to a fishing line a short distance up the line from the bait or lure.

Slip sinker: a weight that attaches to the fishing line in such a manner that it can slip up and down the fishing line.

Slot size limits: a fisheries management tool for controlling the harvest of fish. Anglers are prohibited from keeping fish that fall within certain specified lengths. Often used to protect breeding-sized fish from overharvest.

Snap: a small, safety-pin-like clasp, tied to the end of the fishing line, used to attach lures and leaders.

Snap swivel: a snap with a swiveling eye attached for tying to the fishing line, so that as a lure twists in the water, it does not twist the fishing line.

Snell: a length of line tied to a hook or combination of hooks, beads, blades, etc., that is a pre-tied leader. The other end of a snell attaches to the main fishing line. Snelled hooks are hooks with a short length of leader already attached to them.

Spinner: a lure with a rotating blade, used in both casting and trolling lures. Fish are attracted to the vibration and flash of the spinning blade.

Split shot: a small, round, lead sinker, about the size of a BB, nearly split in half with a cut on one side. By pinching the split side closed around the fishing line, the sinker can be attached a short distance above the hook.

Spoon: a lure made from shaped metal—brass or steel are common—in various shapes, sizes, and colours. Spoons are designed to be trolled behind a moving boat, or cast using either spinning or baitcasting rods and reels. Spoons are very effective lures for northern pike and for lake trout. They imitate—particularly when one side of the lure is left as bright, polished metal, and unpainted—baitfish swimming through the water. Their flash is highly visible to species which depend on sight for finding their prey.

Stillfishing: a presentation technique in which live bait is suspended near bottom, and left to hang there, rather than being trolled, or cast, or moved about. It is useful for fishing in open water for schooled fish once their location is known, and in ice fishing.

Super lines: a generic term for modern fishing lines, such as Berkley FireLine, or Spiderwire, made from synthetic materials such as Dyneema. Known for a very high strength to diameter ratio, and characterized by the fact that they stretch very little.

Tippet: a piece of line, usually monofilament, tied between the end of a fly line and the fly itself. Usually tapering, with the thickest diameter at the fly line and the thinnest diameter at the fly, it is rated for pound-test strength at the tip.

Tip-up: gadget used for "hands-free" ice fishing. A spool of line is attached to a balanced or spring-loaded arm. Line and bait are lowered into the water. When a fish bites, the arm springs free, or "tips up."

Treble hook: a three-tined hook joined to a single shank, like a miniature grappling iron. Common on minnow baits such as Rapala or Berkley Frenzy lures.

Trolling: fishing by dragging a lure behind a moving boat. The speed of movement, size, and colour of lure, as well as the depth at which the lure is trolled, are dependent on the species sought.

Waders: waterproof boots and "pants," made from rubber, plastic, waterproofed nylon or neoprene, allowing an angler to fish while wading in water. This is a common accessory for fly fishers.

Wet fly: a fly pattern designed to be fished "sunk," or below the surface of the water. Patterns are tied to resemble insect nymphs and larvae. Wet flies tied to resemble minnows or small bait fish are called "streamer flies."

Whisker rig: a particular way of tying on a hook used in carp fishing. See detailed description in Chapter 4. Also called a "hair rig."

Whirling disease: an infectious disease affecting particularly rainbow trout that causes skeletal/muscle damage such that the fish "whirls" rather than swimming in the normal manner. It is especially problematic for hatchery-raised rainbows.

INDEX

bold page numbers indicate photographs or maps

Admiral Reservoir, 135
Alameda Reservoir, 135
alarms, 45
Alstead Lake, 161–62
aluminium boats, 66
Amisk Lake, 170
amur, white, 18
Amyot Lake, 162
anchors, 66
Angler/Young Angler Walleye
    Championship, 112
Armit River, 136
Assiniboine River, 136
associations, 216–17
Athabaska Lake, 190
Athapapuskow Lake, 171
Avonlea Reservoir, 137

Baldy Lake, 179
bank fishing, 5, 43–45, 68–69,
    74, 81
Barrier Lake, 137
bass
    largemouth, 10
        catching, 49–51
        gear list, 223
        stocking, 23
    rock, 12
    smallmouth, 13–14
        stocking, 24–25
Batka Lake, 137
Battle Creek, 83–84
Bean Lake, 179
Bear Creek, 84, 137
Beaver, Al, 106
Beaver Lodge Lake, 191
Beet Lake, 191
Belanger Creek, 85, 137
belly boats, 82
Besant Creek, 137
Besnard Lake, 162
Big Sandy Lake, 162
Big Shell Lake, 137
Bigstone Lake, 162
Birch Lake, 137
Black Bear Island Lake, 166
Black Lake, 191
Blackstrap Reservoir, 138
bleeding a fish, 114
bluegill
    stocking, 21

boats, 65–66
    for fly fishing, 82
bobbers, slip, **61**, 61–62
Boiler Creek, 85
Bone Creek, 85, 138
bottom bouncers, 60
Boundary Dam Reservoir, 10,
    23, 138–39
bowfishing, 6
Bow River, 162
breeding, 18–19, **22**, 23, 24, 25,
    26
Brightsand Lake, 139
B-Say Tah Point, **151**, 152
Buffalo Pound Lake, 150
bullhead
    brown and black, 3–4
Burbidge Lake, 192
burbot, 4–5
    catching, 42–43
    gear list, 222
    ice fishing, 95–96
Burtlein Lake, 180

Calf Creek, 85–86, 139
cameras, underwater, 92, 94
Camp 10 Lake, 162
Candle Lake, 162
Canoe Lake, 163
Carey Special, 78
caring for fresh catch, 114–15
carp, 5–6
    catching, 43–45
    fly fishing, 71–75
    gear list, 222
    stocking, 73
catch-and-release
    as conservation method,
        206–10
    in the north, 189
    at tournaments, 107–9
catching and keeping fresh,
    114–15
catfish, 3
catfish, channel, 6
    catching, 45–46
Caton Creek, 86, 139
Chachukew Lake, 163
Charles, Tony, **129**
Chitek Lake, 139
chumming, 5, 43–45, 73

Churchill Lake, 165
Churchill River Watershed,
    163–68
ciscoe, 9
Clam Lake, 168
Clark Lake, 168
cleaning, 115–17
clubs, 216–17
Codette Reservoir, 139–40
Cold Lake, 177–78
Cole, Willie, 37–38
commercial fishing, 28–34
commercial fishing ponds, 158
competitive fishing. see tourna-
    ment fishing
Complex Lake, 168
Condie Reservoir, 140
Conglomerate Creek, 86, 140
conservation groups, 202–3. see
    also management
cooking, 118–22
Costigan Lake, **187**, 192
Cousteau, Jacques, 193
Cowan Lake, 140
cradles, 53
crankbaits
    basics, 65
    for largemouth bass, 50
    for trout, **47**
crappie
    stocking, 21
Crean Lake, 181
Cree Lake, 192–93
creels, 114
Crooked Lake, 153
Cub Hills, 86–89
    map, **87**
Cuelenaere Lake, 193
Cumberland Lake, 169
Cup Lake, 169
Cypress Hills, 82–86, 140
    map, **83**

Davin Lake, 193
Delaronde Lake, 169
depth finder/fish finder, 56, **57**,
    64, 66
Deschambault Lake, 171
Diamond Lake, 180
Dickens Lake, 169
Diefenbaker, Lake, 154–56

Dipper Lake, 166
Doc Spratley, 79
dogfish, 4
Dore Lake, 169
Douglas Provincial Park, 155
Downton Lake, 169
Drinking Lake, 167
Dygdala, Brian, 100–101

Eastend Reservoir, 140
East Trout Lake, 169–70
Echo Lake, 151–52
Egg Lake, 170
Elbow (town), 155
Elk Hair Caddis, 80
Emerald Pond, 170
endorsements, 205
equipment. *see* gear

Fairwell Creek, 140
Fairy Glen Lake, 180
Fedoruk, Sylvia, **187**
Feldspar Lake, 170
filleting, 115–17
First Nations
  commercial fishing, 29, 32, **33**
  and fishery management, 205
  as guides, 129–30
Fishing for Tomorrow, 110, 158,
  203
Fishing Lake, 141
flies, **69**, 78–80
  for lake trout, **75**
  for trout, 70
float tubes, 81–82
Florence Lake, 171
Flotten Lake, 178
fly fishing
  for carp, 71–74
  in Cub Hills, 86–89
  in Cypress Hills, 82–86
  gear, 76–82
  for grayling, 71
  Highway 102, 90
  for lake trout, 74–75
  for pike and walleye, 76
  Russell Creek, 89
  for trout, 68–70
Folk, Gary, 97–99, 100
footwear, 81, 93
Forestry Farm Pond, 158
Fort Qu'Appelle Hatchery, 19
Foster Lake, Lower, 193
Fox Lake, 180
Frenchman River, 141
Fresh Fish Marketing
  Corporation, 32, 34

Gardiner Dam, 155
gear
  basic, 64–66, 224
  for fly fishing, 76–80
  lists for specific fish, 221–24
  for northern fly-in trips,
    218–20
Generic Nymph, 79
George Lake, 170
Gillingham Lake, 171
Glacier Creek, 180
Global Positioning System unit
  (GPS), 56
gloves, 53
goldeye, 7–8
Good Spirit Lake, 141
Gordon Lake, 166
Gow Lake, 193
Granite Lake, 171
grayling, Arctic, 1
  catching, 39–41
  fly fishing, 71
  gear list, 221
  stocking, 19–20
Green Lake, 142
Greenwater Lake, 142
Greig Lake, 178
guided trips, 124–32
Guilloux Lake, 168

Hackett Lake, 173
Halkett Lake, 181
Hamell Lake, 171
handling, 207–10
Hanson Lake, 171
Hanson Lake Road (Highway
  106), 170–73
Hasbala Lake, 193
hatcheries. *see* breeding
Hatchet Lake, 194
Hawkrock River, 194
Hay Meadow Creek, 142
Heart Lake, 180
Heart Lakes, The, 182
Highway 102, 90, 173
Hobbs Lake, 171–72
Hollerbaum, Kevin, 112
Holt Lake, 173
hooks, 40
  barbless, 75
  removing, 208
Humpy, 80
hypothermia, 93–94

ice fishing
  burbot, 95–96
  clothing and safety, 93–94
  gear, 94–95

ice fishing (*continued*)
  lake trout, 96–97
  pike, 97–100
  rainbow trout, 100–101
  walleye, 101–3
  yellow perch, 104
Île-à-la-Crosse, Lac, 165
Iles, Lac des, 178
inner tubes, 81–82
Iskwatikan Lake, 167

jackfish, 10
Jackfish Creek, 142
Jackfish Lake, 142
Jade Lake, 180
Jan Lake, 172
jigs
  basics, 65
  for ice fishing, **98**
  for ice fishing trout, 97
  for largemouth bass, **51**
  for walleye, 56–59, **58**
Johnson Lake, 172
Johnson River, 194
Jumbo Lake, 142
Junction Lake, 173

Katepwa Lake, 152
Kazan Lake, 165
Keeley Lake, 173, 175
Keg Lake, 167
Kenosee Lake, 143
Kierstead, Jim, **99**
Kingsmere Lake, 182
Kipabiskau Lake, 143
Klopak, Andrew, 112
Knee Lake, 166
knives, filleting, 117

Lac La Plonge, 175
Lac La Ronge, 175–76, 209
lake fishing
  with flies, 71–72, 74–75, 76
  tips for, 38–39
Lake of the Prairies, 144
Lamont, Don, 106
landowners' permission, 83
Last Mountain Lake, 45, 144–46
  walleye in, 62–63
Lavilee Lake, 182
ledgering, 5, 43–45, 68–69, 74,
  81
Lenore Lakes, 146
limits, fishing, 201–2
lines, 48–49, 65
  for fly fishing, 76–77
ling cod, 4
Little Amyot Lake, 176

Little Bear Lake, 176–77
Little Jackfish Lake, 146
Lost Echo Creek, 88–89
Lost Echo Lake, 180
Lower Fishing Lake, 180
lures, **39**, 51. *see also specific names of lures*
Lussier Lake, 177

Madge Lake, 146
Maistre Lake, 177
Makwa Lake, 146–47
management of fishery, 29–31
    catch-and-release, 206–10
    conservation groups, 202–3
    modern approach, 203–6
    in Nipawin, 201–2
Manawan Lake, 177
maps
    central Saskatchewan, 160
    Cub Hills, 83
    Cypress Hills, 83
    northern Saskatchewan, 188
    southern Saskatchewan, 134
Marabou Leech, 79
Margo Lake, 147
Mawdsley Lake, 177
McBride Lake (central), 172
McBride Lake (south), 147
McDougal Creek, 87–88, 180
McIntosh Lake, 177
McLennan Lake, 177
Meadow Lake Provincial Park, 177–78
Meeting Lake, 147
Merean Lake, 147
mesh nets, 53
Meyomoot River, 178
Mid Lake, 172
Ministikwan Lake, 147
Mirond Lake, 172
Misaw Lake, 194
Mission Lake, 152
Mistohay Lake, 178
Montreal Lake, 178–79
Montreal River, 179
mooneye, 7
Moose Mountain Lake, 147
Mosher Lake, 172
Mossy River, 88
motors, electric trolling, 66
Mountain Lake, 167
Mustus Lakes, 178

Nagle Lake, 179
Namew Lake, 179
Narrow Hills Provincial Park, 179–80

national parks, 160, 181–82
Nemieben Lake, 180–81
nets, **31**, 53, 208
Nickle Lake, 147–48
Nipawin Lake, 180
Nipawin Pike Festival, 109
Nipawin (town), 200–202
Nipekamew Creek, 88
Nipikamew Lake, 181
Niska Lake, 165
Nistowiak Lake, 167
North Saskatchewan River, 148

Okipwatsikew Lake, 168
Oliver Lake, 194
Oneman Lake, 194
Otter Lake, 166–67
outfitted trips, 124–32
Oyama Reservoir, 148–49

Parkbeg Reservoir, 24
Parkinson, Colinda, **110**
Pasqua Lake, 150–51
Pasquia Hills, 149
pattern fishing, 38–39
    for walleye, 103
Paull River, 181
pay for play fisheries, 158
Peck Lake, 149
Pelican Lake, 172
Pelletier, Lac, 143
perch, yellow, 16
    catching, 63–64
    gear list, 221
    ice fishing, 104
    recipe, 119
    stocking, 24
Peter Pond Lake, 165
Phelps Lake, 194–95
pickerel, 55
Pierce Lake, 178
pike, northern, 10–11
    catching, 52–54
    filleting, 116–17
    fly fishing, 76
    gear list, 223–24
    ice fishing, 97–100
    stocking, 23
Pike Lake, 149
Pikoo Lake, 168
Pine Cree Creek, 86, 149
Pinehouse Lake, 166
Pink Lady, 48
Pipestone Lake, 195
Piprell Lake, 181
Pita Lake, 168
Pointer Lake, 181
Post, John, 207

Primeau Lake, 166
Prince Albert National Park, 181–82

Qu'Appelle Lakes, 200
Qu'Appelle River System, 6, 149–50
quotas, 29–31

Rafferty Reservoir, 153
recipes, 118–22
Reeds Lake, 168
Reid Lake, 153
Reindeer Lake, 195
Reindeer River, 168
rigs
    basics, 65
    for walleye, **59**, 59–60
river fishing
    with flies, 68–71, 76–77, 81–90
    for rainbow trout, 54–55
    for walleye, 57
Riverhurst, 155
Robinson, Jimmy, **123**, **127**
rod and reels, **36**, 64–65
    for fly fishing, 68, 76–77, **77**
    ice fishing, **95**
Round Lake, 153
Rowan's Ravine Provincial Park, 145
Russell Creek, 89, 153

safety equipment, 66, 81
safety tips, 82, 118
    for ice fishing, 93–94, 103
sales agents at trade shows, 130
Sandfly Lake, 166
Sands Lake, 154
Sandy Lake, 166
Sapphire Lake, 180
Saskatchewan Environment, 203
Saskatchewan Fly Fishers, 203
Saskatchewan River, 183, 200–201
Saskatchewan Walleye Trail, 107, 110–12
Saskatchewan Wildlife Federation, 203
Saskatoon Wildlife Federation, 158
sauger, 13
    catching, 55–63
saugeye, 13
Schlosser, Bob, 112
Schulz, Robert, 45, **105**
Scott Lake, 195
Seeley Lake, 180
selective harvest. *see* catch-and-release

Selwyn Lake, 195–96
Settee Lake, 183
Shadd Lake, 183
Shagwenaw Lake, 166
Shannon Lake, 180
sight-fishing, 53, 73
Silver Springs Trout Farm, 158
siscowet, 8
Sled Lake, 183
slip bobbers, **61**, 61–62
slipping, 57
Smith, Maurice, **123**
Smoothstone Lake, 183
Smoothstone River, 183
snells, 59–60
Sokatisewan Lake, 168
sonar units, 56, **57**, 64, 66
Souris River, 156
South Saskatchewan River,
    154–56
spawning. *see* breeding
spinnerbaits
    for bass, **50**
splake, 8–9, 14
    stocking, 25
spoons
    for ice fishing, **98**
    for trout, **47**
Stanley Mission, 167
Steepbank Lake, 183
Steephill Lake, 168
Steistol Lake, 157
stocking, fish, 18–26
Sturgeon, Lake, 8
Sturgeon-Weir River, 173
Sucker Creek, 86, 157
Summit Lake, 180
sunfish, 12
survival gear, 220
Swan River, 157
Swift Current Creek, 86, 157

tackle. *see also specific names of
    tackle*
    contents of basic tackle box,
        65
    list of shops, 225–26
    for northern fly-in trips,
        219–20
tailing, 74
Tazin Lake, 196
Theriau Lake, 196
Thompson Lake, 184
Tibiska Lake, 182

tippet, wire, 75
tip-up rigs, 99–100
Tobin Lake, 184–85
tolerance quotas, 30
Torch River, 185
tournament fishing, 106–12,
    184, 201
    and conservation, 205
    contacts, 216–17
Trade Lake, 167
trade shows, 130
travel contacts, 215
Triveet Lake, 185
trophy fish, 189
trout
    brook or speckled, 2
        catching, 41–42
        gear list, 221
        stocking, 21
    brown, 2–3
        catching, 42
        gear list, 221
        stocking, 21
    cutthroat, 7
    fly fishing, 68–70
    lake, 8–9
        catching, 46–49
        flyfishing, 74–75
        gear list, 222–23
        ice fishing, 96–97
        stocking, 21–23
    rainbow, 11–12
        catching, 54–55
        gear list, 222
        ice fishing, 100–101
        stocking, 24
    recipes, 119–22
    steelhead, 11
    tiger, 14–15
Trout Lake, 166
Tulabi Lake, 173
Tunnicliffe, Chris, **125**
Turtle Lake, 157
Tyroll Lake, 173
Ubiquity Lake, 196
Upper Fishing Lake, 180
Usinneskaw Lake, 157
Uskik Lake, 167

Vanity Cup, 107, 109–10

Wabeno Lake, 182
waders, 81
wading staffs, 81

Wakaw Lake, 157
walleye, 15–16
    catching, 38, 39, 55–63
    fly fishing, 76
    gear list, 223
    ice fishing, 101–3
    recipe, 118
    stocking, 25–26, 62
Wapata Lake, 196
Wapawekka Lake, 185
Wasawakasik Lake, 168
Waskesiu Lake, 182
Waskwei Lake, 185
Wassegam Lake, 182
Waterbury Lake, 196
Waterhen Lake, 178
weighing, 109
Weyakwin Lake, 185
Wheeler River, 197
whirling disease, 26
Whitebear Lake, 158
whitefish, lake, 9
    commercial, 28, 29
    stocking, 26
White Gull Creek, 88
Whitesand Lake, 158
Whiteswan Lakes, 186
Winnipeg Urban Fishing
    Partnership, 106
Winteringham Lake, 171
Wollaston Lake, 197–98
Wolverman Lakes, 198
Wood Lake, 186
Wooly Bugger, 79–80
Wulff, Lee, 206